AMERICA'S FIRST GREAT DEPRESSION

Also by Alasdair Roberts

Blacked Out: Government Secrecy in the Information Age

The Collapse of Fortress Bush: The Crisis of Authority in American Government

The Logic of Discipline: Global Capitalism and the Architecture of Government

AMERICA'S
FIRST GREAT
DEPRESSION

ECONOMIC CRISIS AND POLITICAL
DISORDER AFTER THE PANIC OF 1837

ALASDAIR ROBERTS

CORNELL UNIVERSITY PRESS
Ithaca and London

First published 2012 by Cornell University Press

Printed in the United States of America

Library of Congress Cataloging-in-Publication Data

Roberts, Alasdair (Alasdair Scott)

America's first Great Depression : economic crisis and
political disorder after the panic of 1837 / Alasdair
Roberts.

p. cm.

Includes bibliographical references and index.

ISBN 978-0-8014-5033-4 (cloth : alk. paper)

1. Depressions—1836–1837. 2. Depressions—
1847. 3. Financial crises—United States—
History—19th century. 4. United States—Economic
conditions—To 1865. 5. United States—Politics and
government—1815–1861. I. Title.

HB37171837 .R63 2012

330.973'057—dc23

The Americans make immense progress in productive industry, because they all devote themselves to it at once; and for this same reason they are exposed to very unexpected and formidable embarrassments. . . . Their commercial affairs are affected by such various and complex causes that it is impossible to foresee what difficulties may arise. . . . At the least shock given to business all private fortunes are put in jeopardy at the same time, and the State is shaken.

The return of these commercial panics is an endemic disease of the democratic nations of our age.

—Alexis de Tocqueville, 1835

☙ Contents

Introduction
Back to the Future

There was a time, not so long ago, when most Americans felt good about the economic prospects for themselves and their country. In 2006, according to polls, Americans thought that their personal circumstances and the economic condition of the nation as a whole were better than they had been in several years. Most regarded their personal finances as secure, and expected further improvement in the following year. Confidence was buoyed by rising home prices. Few Americans expected a significant decrease in housing values. A majority said it was a good time to buy real estate.

Confidence about economic conditions at home was matched by self-assurance about the United States' place in the world. In 2006 most people still viewed the nation as they always had: in the words of Paul Volcker, former chairman of the Federal Reserve, "as a huge and relatively self-sufficient country, in control of our own destiny." Many also regarded the United States as the keystone of the global order. In 2005, American political scientist Michael Mandelbaum argued that the world should be grateful to the United States for providing the prerequisites for global security and prosperity. The United States is like an elephant, Mandelbaum said, "which supports a wide variety of other creatures—smaller mammals, birds, and insects—by generating nourishment for them as it goes about the business of feeding itself." It takes hubris to tell the world that it should be happy to forage in a pile of elephant dung. But that was the temper of those times.

This air of assurance was shattered by 2009. In the preceding year, the economy went through something like a near-death experience. The financial system seized up. Major firms went bankrupt, and others were saved only after extraordinary governmental interventions. An economic meltdown was avoided, but the economy was still sliding into recession. "It was a humbling and humiliating moment for the United States," one observer said. The impression of U.S. wealth and power was dissipating quickly. So, too, was the country's credibility on matters of economic policy. All levels of American government, major businesses, and households now realized that they were living beyond their means. Some commentators thought that these bleak conditions would persist for a very long time. It seemed that we were entering a "new normal," just as we had a few years earlier, after the attacks of September 11, 2001. The United States, it appeared, would have to adjust to a more modest and vulnerable place in the global economy.

Fears about the decline of the United States were broadly aired. Economic historian Niall Ferguson warned that the country's status as a great power was at risk, and that the slightest external shock might cause dramatic shifts in the global order. Economist Jeffrey Sachs of Columbia University said that this shift had already happened and that the United States had ceased to be "the indispensable leader." Japanese Prime Minister Yukio Hatoyama agreed that "the era of U.S.-led globalism is coming to an end." (Hatoyama's end came more quickly: he resigned as prime minister after only ten months.) In September 2010, *The New York Times* observed that President Obama and his immediate predecessors

> have been forced to contend with the erosion of self-sufficiency. . . . [U]ntil the end of the Soviet Union, America's economic and national security were largely self-determined, thanks to its manufacturing might and its ability to negotiate treaties with other states. But the advent of truly global markets, along with threats from non-state forces like Al Qaeda, changed all that. Now we live in an integrated world where American jobs rely on the economic policies of governments in Asia or Latin America, while our security is subject to the whims of a cleric living in a cave.

One aspect of the predicament confronting the United States that troubled many observers was its relationship with China. Before 2007, it was not unusual for Americans to argue that they served an important role in the world economy as "consumers of last resort": that is, they could be counted on to provide the demand relied on by other export-oriented countries. Foremost among these was China, whose products clogged the west coast ports of the United States. The other side of this relationship gained little attention until after 2007. China used its massive earnings to finance American consumption. In 2008, China passed Japan to become the U.S. government's largest foreign creditor.

This appeared to put the United States in the uncomfortable position of dependence to a foreign power. During the early phase of the crisis, U.S. Treasury Secretary Henry Paulson phoned senior Chinese officials to reassure them that the U.S. government would "live up to our obligations." This is not the sort of call usually made by a superpower to a developing nation. But decision makers in Washington became very sensitive to Chinese preoccupations after 2007; they paid attention when China criticized its monetary policy and worried about the United States' ability to deal with chronic budget deficits. Pete Peterson, former chairman of the Blackstone investment firm, saw a risk that U.S. foreign policy would become hostage to Chinese debt. As Gao Xiqing, president of the state-owned China Investment Corporation, explained in 2008, it is important to "be nice to the countries that lend you money."

Concerns about the rising influence of China were sometimes discounted. After all, similar apprehensions were voiced about Japan several decades ago. In 1970, the futurist Herman Kahn called Japan "the emerging superstate" and predicted that its gross domestic product (GDP) would exceed that of the United States by the year 2000. Japan, it was said, had accumulated resources "on a hegemonic scale" and seemed bent on "doing with money what it did with guns fifty years ago." But this turned out to be exaggeration. The Japanese economy imploded in the mid-1990s and never fully recovered. Today, its GDP is only a third that of the United States.

If we were wrong about the rise of Japan four decades ago, could we be wrong about the rise of China today? Perhaps. Assessments about the global role of the United States tend to have their own euphoria-and-depression cycle, and we are very definitely in the depressive phase at the moment. Despite the current crisis, the United States is a rich and militarily powerful country, and it will remain this way for many years to come. Having stated this, however, it is undoubtedly true that the *relative* importance of the United States in the global economy will decline over the long run.

The American predicament is illustrated by Figure 1. Based on data produced by economist Angus Maddison, it shows the shares of global GDP produced by the United States and two regions—western Europe and east Asia—between 1820 and 2008. The chart vividly illustrates the effect of

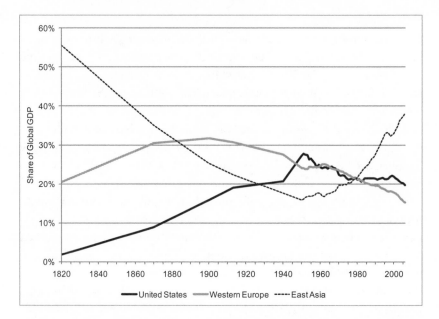

FIGURE 1. Share of World Gross Domestic Product Accounted for by the United States, Twelve Major Western European Countries and Sixteen Major East Asian Countries. Source: Estimates by Professor Angus Maddison, University of Groningen, Groningen, the Netherlands.

industrialization in giving an economic lead to Europe and the United States up to the start of the Second World War. It also provides a graphic reminder that, in the aftermath of the war, the United States was very much the anchor of the global economy. But there is also a third truth that is evident in the chart. The relative significance of the United States (and also Europe) has been declining for the last sixty years. The benefits of economic modernization have come to east Asia, and as a consequence the region is recovering its place in the world economy which it held before the advent of the industrial revolution.

In the very short run, American economic clout might ebb and flow. We can see this in the chart—for example, look at the uptick in the U.S. share of global GDP following the Asian crisis of 1997–1998. But the broad trend is unmistakable and, barring some immense cataclysm, irreversible. The relative importance of the United States within the global economic order is indeed declining.

Shaken by the financial crisis of 2007–2008, many Americans have been drawn to a more sober view of the nation's future. In this "new normal," the United States will not have all the advantages of an economic hegemon and the comfort of a large degree of self-sufficiency. It will no longer be the sole master of its own destiny. The country's well-being will hinge increasingly on decisions taken by major trading partners, foreign investors, and speculators, and its borders will no longer protect it so well from shocks or crises overseas. These economic changes will undoubtedly have important implications for domestic politics. This seems like new and potentially treacherous terrain.

But is it really unfamiliar territory? Not exactly. Certainly, there are few living Americans who can remember a time when the United States was not the economic hegemon. But their experience is unusual. Indeed, Figure 1 reminds us that the period of American dominance—roughly 1945 to 2000—was an historical anomaly. Before the First World War, no one would have thought to call the United States an economic hegemon. This may seem a very long time ago. But think of it this way: a much larger part of American history has been characterized by vulnerability, rather than hegemony, within the global economic order.

We can illustrate this point in other ways. Figure 2 illustrates the value of American exports and imports as a share of the country's GDP. It also reminds us that the relatively closed character of the American economy in the decades following the Second World War was unusual. In the last

FIGURE 2. Sum of Exports and Imports as Share of Gross Domestic Product, United States, 1800–1998. Source: *Historical Statistics of the United States, Millennial Edition Online,* hsus.cambridge.org/.

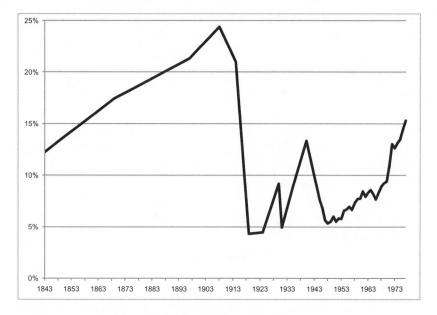

FIGURE 3. Foreign Investment in the United States as a Share of Gross Domestic Product, 1800–1998. Source: *Historical Statistics of the United States, Millennial Edition Online,* hsus.cambridge.org/.

quarter-century we have been returning to a situation that would have been familiar throughout the first 130 years of American history. Figure 3 shows foreign investment in the United States as a share of GDP; while the figure is based on limited data, it demonstrates that dependence on overseas investors is hardly a new phenomenon. In key respects, then, the country's economic future is not unknown territory. Its future will be something like its past. This raises an intriguing question: Is it possible to anticipate something about the nature of American politics in the years ahead by learning more about American politics in the long years before the country became an economic hegemon?

Of course, there have been substantial changes since the nineteenth century: in size and population, the structure of the economy, information and communication technologies, and, of course, the stock of our collective experience. But there are also strong commonalities. Then, as now, the United States was a federation, in which there was no consensus about the proper division of responsibilities between federal and state authorities. Nineteenth-century Americans also shared a strong commitment to the ideals of popular sovereignty and individual freedom, although they had divergent ideas of what these ideals implied in practice. And Americans of the nineteenth century, like Americans today, often believed that the nation had a special role in propagating the doctrines of political and economic liberty around the world.

How does a system of government with these features, which is in many ways hostile to the idea of forceful or coordinated government action, respond to external shocks, the bolts from the blue that threaten to destabilize the nation's economy? How does it reconcile its ambition for global influence with the reality of dependence on major trading partners and often fickle investors? How does it square its beliefs about the inviolability of national sovereignty and personal liberty with the global market's demand for discipline and consistency? These are the questions that will likely absorb the country's attention in the years ahead. And they were also the questions that absorbed its attention in the long period between 1789 and the early twentieth century.

I have chosen to explore this topic by looking at one critical period in the economic history of the nineteenth century—the years 1836–1848. This period began with the collapse of a speculative boom and panic that caused (in the words of one financier writing in 1837) a "paralysis of credit" among U.S. financial institutions. My aim is to show how the boom and panic were both closely related to economic developments abroad. The panic was eventually followed by a dramatic decline in economic activity and defaults by eight of the country's twenty-six state governments. By 1843, the United States was frozen out of international financial markets. The nation was thrown into political turmoil so deep that some observers wondered whether it could survive intact. Economic decline unleashed civil and political disorder and caused an unraveling of the unwritten compact that held the federal system together.

This might seem to be an obscure topic. The crisis of 1836–1848 does not loom large in public consciousness—certainly not like the Great Depression of the 1930s, about which anyone can provide a pocket history at the drop of the hat. But the crisis was, indeed, profound. Early in the crisis the British ambassador to the United States, Henry Stephen Fox, told London that "it would be difficult to describe, or render intelligible in Europe, the stunning effect which this sudden overthrow of commercial credit and honor of the nation has caused. . . . The conquest of the land by a foreign power could hardly have produced a more general sense of humiliation and grief." Six years later, the American ambassador to the United Kingdom, Edward Everett, said: "I doubt if, in the history of the world, in so short a period, such a transition has been made from a state of high prosperity to one of general distress, as in the United States within the last six years." Reginald

McGrane, an economic historian, said in 1924 that the Panic of 1837 "was one of the most disastrous crises this nation has ever experienced." Writing after the 1930s, Douglass North (a Nobel Laureate for his work in economic history) still counted the earlier depression as "one of the most severe in our history."

Caveats are necessary, however. In 1837, the measures that we use today to describe the state of economy—GDP growth, the unemployment rate, the inflation rate, and so on—had not yet been invented. Indeed, the very concept of a national economy, an abstraction that is second nature to us today, was not widely understood at the time. Americans often used meteorological or medical terms—pressure, panic, tempest, convulsion—to describe what was happening to the world about them. Very often the slump was described simply as "hard times." It may be that our difficulty in understanding how much the country suffered in the years following 1837 is constrained by the inability of Americans living at the time to tell their story with the technical vocabulary we would use today.

Economists have made retrospective estimates of the dimensions of the crisis using modern concepts and measures. These estimates suggest that the economic downturn was less severe than during the Great Depression of the 1930s, and also that the worst of the earlier crisis was over by 1843–1844. McGrane and North concur that the crisis lasted six or seven years at most. After 1844, McGrane says, economic conditions had stabilized and the country's attention had been diverted to unrelated issues, such as the annexation of Texas and the advent of the Mexican-American War.

However, we cannot gauge the significance of a crisis by looking only at aggregate economic data. This is one of the three major themes of this book. The 1836–1848 economic crisis was a political and cultural phenomenon as well. Economic uncertainty and stagnation produced unprecedented political and social instability. Voter turnout reached levels never seen before, and rarely seen since. Incumbent politicians were enthusiastically hoisted from office, and so were their unlucky successors. Anti-government violence—sometimes planned, sometimes not—broke out across the country. There was a widely shared feeling that the country had lost its way. The descent from the boom times of the mid-1830s was often taken as evidence of a moral failure. In sum, if we measure a crisis by the degree of political and cultural shock which it produces as well as by the degree of economic dislocation, then the crisis of 1836–1848 is clearly a rival to the depression of the 1930s.

A second major theme of this book has to do with the way in which the country pulled itself back together. These words are chosen deliberately. In this new democracy, economic crisis had the effect of destabilizing the existing order and causing its constituent elements to fly apart. This could be seen at many levels. Across the nation there was confusion about precisely how the country had plunged so quickly from prosperity to hard times. As a matter of grand national policy, the crisis caused the unraveling of the delicate compact that united North and South. In states which defaulted or repudiated their debt, the central question—one with moral and pragmatic aspects—was whether democratically elected governments could achieve the self-discipline necessary to honor commitments to overseas investors and thus remain integrated within the global economy. More locally, riots and rebellions posed an obvious challenge to the social order. There was a fear of moral as well as political dissolution. Something essential about the country's character appeared to be unraveling.

Recovery from crisis required the restoration of order, an uncomfortable task for a country committed to popular sovereignty and individual liberty. Voters, many newly enfranchised, were asked to accept new constraints on governmental action, such as the restrictions on spending and borrowing adopted by many states in this period. Often they were compelled to accept distasteful compromises for the greater good, such as compromises within the Union, undertaken so that it could be preserved; or compromises with the United Kingdom, a rival for territory and markets but also the undisputed military and economic hegemon. And sometimes popular dissent had to be constrained more brutally. It is no coincidence that all of the major cities of the Northeast established police forces in this era.

The careful use of military force also played a role in resolving the crisis that began in 1836. The Mexican-American War was not an unrelated matter, as the historian Reginald McGrane suggests. In many ways, and often inadvertently, it played a critical role in consolidating the nation's recovery. The war guaranteed American control over newly discovered gold fields in California. By recruiting soldiers, the federal government relieved tensions in the slums of northern cities. And the country's success in war encouraged patriotic sentiment and momentarily encouraged national unity. The United States was careful in its choice of antagonisms. Throughout the crisis, and despite popular antipathy toward the British, its leaders avoided open conflict with the United Kingdom. But war with Mexico—militarily weaker and economically less consequential—had a tonic effect on the country as a whole.

Readers will be struck by the extent to which domestic and international politics are entangled in this story. We are accustomed to thinking about U.S. domestic politics as a self-contained sphere, in which the great issues of the day are defined and resolved by Americans alone. International affairs *might* inform domestic politics, and in unusual circumstances—a major war, perhaps—guide it in some ways; but typically international affairs are a separate and subordinate concern. Domestic and foreign policy are labels for separate boxes, and the first is larger and more important than the second.

This might be a reasonable way to think about politics in a country that is a global hegemon, and in which international trade and finance are relatively unimportant. However, it is the wrong way to think about politics in a country that is heavily dependent on international trade and finance and which occupies a subordinate position in the international order. This is the third major theme of the book. As we shall see, domestic and international affairs were deeply entangled during the First Great Depression. Politics in the United States was constantly undertaken with an eye to what the British appeared to say or want. Some U.S. citizens were allied with the British—indeed, some were paid agents—and some were opposed. Sometimes factions in the United States were defined precisely by the character of each side's relationship with the British. At the same time, the British were deeply engaged in U.S. political debate. In some ways political discourse could be regarded as an ongoing call-and-response between the two countries, whose rhythm was determined by the two-week passage of steamships across the north Atlantic.

The interconnection of domestic and international politics—indeed, the impossibility of separating the two—is understandable once we appreciate the structure of the U.S. economy at the time of the crisis. Indeed, it might be equally misleading to talk about an "American" economy, given the extent of its integration into the British economy. Britain was the main market for U.S. cotton, and a main supplier of capital and finished goods. It is easier to comprehend the crisis if we view the U.S. economy as an important component of a tightly integrated north Atlantic economy. The structure of politics followed naturally from the structure of the economy. Other considerations such as the heavy flow of immigration from Britain and Ireland and the fact of a shared language and culture also contributed to the fusion of domestic and international politics.

This is an unconventional way of thinking about the crisis of 1836–1848. There are three reasons why it is not more commonly applied. The first is the habit, common among many countries in the modern era, of assuming that the nation-state is the natural unit of analysis in historical inquiry. (This is connected to the normative project of using history to legitimize newly created nation-states, including the United States.) The second is that a significant amount of American history has been written during the period of American hegemony, and there is a tendency to assume that the structure of politics in the past is comparable to what it has been recently; that is, a sphere in which domestic affairs are separate and dominant.

The third reason is more complicated. I will argue that the democratic process operating at the time had a tendency to diminish the significance of international factors in domestic affairs. This was a natural result of the two activities that are central to democratic politics: blaming and credit-taking. Opposition politicians say that incumbents are responsible for bad times, and must be removed; incumbents say that they are responsible for good times, and must be retained. The inevitable consequence is that everyone within the system acquires an outsized view of the politicians' significance in determining the country's well-being. When the system being governed is highly complex, and there is no easy way to discern precisely how it actually works, then conditions are ripe for the erroneous attribution of responsibility. Leaders are thought to control events over which they have little actual influence.

The predicament of American statesmen during the First Great Depression was unenviable. Confronted at home by a frustrated and sometimes violent electorate, and abroad by enraged investors; uncertain about the true causes of the hard times surrounding them, and about the path to recovery; denied the advantages of a full treasury, and often limited in their formal powers—leaders who survived in office under such conditions, and preserved the rudiments of political and social order, must have regarded themselves as lucky. This was the character of politics in a period of economic crisis, in a nation that was tightly integrated within the global economy, but not powerful enough to dominate it.

CHAPTER 1

Boom and Bust

The First Great Depression might be regarded purely as an economic crisis, and in its early phases the economic aspects—the see-sawing of trade, employment, and investment—were certainly the most easily observed. But a great trauma such as this should not be regarded only as an economic phenomenon. Economic woes soon spawned other troubles, and in its later phases the Depression could as easily be viewed as a political, and a cultural, and a diplomatic crisis. Regardless of how the Depression is perceived, though, there is a common theme: the pervasive influence in American affairs by the superpower, Great Britain. For this reason it is probably fitting that one of the most eloquent observers of American woes was an Englishman, Charles Dickens. The nation which he described during his 1842 visit was one whose economy was deeply integrated with, and heavily dependent on, that of Britain.

While many Americans believed that the spectacular boom of 1835–1836 and the extraordinary collapse of 1837–1839 were primarily the result of decisions taken by businessmen and politicians in the commercial and political centers of the United States—and indeed, were encouraged to believe this by many in the country's political class—the truth was more complicated. In reality, national prosperity hinged heavily on the actions of institutions and businessmen on the other side of the Atlantic, who were far removed from the tempest of American politics.

❧ Hard Times

> Let's all be unhappy together.
>
> —Motto of the World's Convention of Reformers,
> New York City, October 1845

In January 1842, Charles Dickens arrived in Boston. He was only thirty years old, but already famous in America as the author of *Oliver Twist, Nicholas Nickleby*, and other works. He was in the United States to give lectures, and besieged by admirers from the moment Cunard's steamship *Britannia* docked in Boston harbor. But the mood of the country was not good. "They certainly are not a humorous people, and their temperament always impressed me as being of a dull and gloomy character," Dickens wrote. "In travelling about out of the large cities, I was quite oppressed by the prevailing seriousness and melancholy air of business."

Dickens visited Philadelphia, a rival to New York as the nation's financial center, in early March. He arrived late at night, and while looking out his hotel room window he saw across the street

> a handsome building of white marble, which had a mournful, ghost-like aspect, dreary to behold. I attributed this to the sombre influence of the night, and on rising in the morning looked out again, expecting to see its steps and portico thronged with groups of people passing in and out. The door was still tight shut, however; the same cold, cheerless air prevailed . . . I hastened to inquire its name and purpose, and then my surprise vanished. It was the tomb of many fortunes; the Great Catacomb of investment; the memorable United States Bank.

The vast headquarters of the Second Bank of the United States, modeled on the Parthenon and completed in 1824, was built as a temple of finance. President Andrew Jackson tried to kill the bank just eight years later, when he vetoed the renewal of its federal charter, but the Bank refused to die. Its president, Nicholas Biddle, persuaded the legislature of Pennsylvania to give him a state charter, and the bank carried on as the most powerful financial institution in America. It was financial crisis that finished Jackson's work, when the bank finally collapsed in February 1841.

"The stoppage of this bank, with all its ruinous consequences," Dickens wrote, "had cast (as I was told on every ride) a gloom on Philadelphia, under the depressing effect of which it yet labored." On the edge of the city, Dickens saw the unfinished marble structure of Girard College. "The work has stopped," he said, "like many other great undertakings in America." The gift that supported the new college had been heavily invested in Bank of the United States stock. (Much of the rest of Girard's gift was invested in Pennsylvania state bonds, an apparently conservative decision until Pennsylvania itself defaulted in August 1842.) The Girard Bank, also founded by the college's benefactor and coincidentally based in the old offices of the First Bank of the United States, collapsed after a run by depositors five weeks before Dickens's arrival.

And yet, there were parts of the country in even worse condition. In April, Dickens found himself on a mail boat steaming from Louisville to St. Louis. As the ship steamed from the Ohio into the Mississippi River, Dickens saw on the starboard shore

> a spot so much more desolate than any we had yet beheld. . . . At the junction of the two rivers, on ground so flat and low, and marshy, that at certain seasons of the year it is inundated to the house-tops, lies a breeding-place for fever, ague, and death. . . . A dismal swamp, on which the half-built houses rot away; cleared here and there for the space of a few yards; and teeming, then, with rank, unwholesome vegetation, in whose baleful shade the wretched wanderers who are tempted hither droop, and die, and lay their bones; the hateful Mississippi circling and eddying before it, and turning off upon its southern course, a slimy monster hideous to behold; a hotbed of disease, an ugly sepulchre, a grave uncheered by any gleam of promise; a place without one quality, in earth or air or water, to commend it.

This was Cairo, Illinois. Only seven years earlier, there had been little here at all. Then an entrepreneur named Darius Holbrook launched a grand plan to build a city, "a great commercial and manufacturing mart and emporium," at the confluence of the two rivers. In 1836 Holbrook went to London and retained a prominent investment bank, Wright & Company, to borrow large sums for his scheme. British investors, lured by color lithographs showing the factories, churches, domed municipal buildings, and crowded streets of the new metropolis, bought million of dollars in Cairo bonds. Wright & Company went bankrupt in November 1840. Holbrook defaulted too, and so did the state of Illinois itself, just as Dickens was arriving in Boston. Many Britons vowed never to do business in America again. "A mine of Golden Hope," Dickens called Cairo, "speculated in, on the faith of monstrous representations, to many people's ruin."

Americans loved "smart dealing," Dickens said. But they did not understand how much it had damaged the country's reputation and prospects, "generating a want of confidence abroad, and discouraging foreign investment."

FIGURE 4. Two Views of Cairo, Illinois. Top: *Prospective View of the City of Cairo, 1838.* Source: Chicago History Museum. Bottom: *View of Cairo, Illinois in 1841.* Source: Library of Congress.

Nor did he have confidence in the capacity of the country's leaders to repair the damage. President John Tyler, whom he met in Washington in March, "looked worn and anxious" after only a year in office. "And well he might," Dickens added, "being at war with everybody." In the House of Representatives, meanwhile, Dickens saw "the meanest perversion of virtuous Political Machinery that the worst tools ever wrought . . . in a word, Dishonest Faction in its most depraved and most unblushing form, stared out from every corner of the crowded hall."

Dickens left the United States in May 1842. When he had arrived, four months earlier, he was burning to learn more about America. His departure was more subdued. "I don't like the country," he confided to his friend John Forster. "I would not live here, on any consideration. I think it impossible, utterly impossible, for any Englishman to live here, and be happy."

It was not the best of times. The United States enjoyed extraordinary growth until the fall of 1836, but then it was convulsed by a panic in the financial sector in the spring of 1837. It seemed to be on its way to recovery in 1838, but by the end of 1839 the country was sliding into a deep, apparently irreversible depression. Dickens's view of the United States a little more than two years later was bleak but not unusual.

In Philadelphia, the diarist Sidney George Fisher had at first dismissed fears about an economic collapse. "The Capitalist is the most easily frightened of beings," Fisher wrote in 1837. "A few speculators & imprudent merchants may fail, but the thunderstorm will soon be over & the atmosphere will be clearer than before." Fisher himself was a capitalist, the head of one of Philadelphia's leading merchant families, but he completely misjudged the oncoming storm. In July 1842, Fisher confirmed the dismal prospect of the city that Dickens had offered five months earlier:

> No society, no life or movement, no topics or interest of any kind. Everybody has become poor & the calamities of the times have not only broken up the gay establishments & put an end to social intercourse, but seem to have covered the place with a settled gloom. The streets seem deserted, the largest houses are shut up and to rent, there is no business, there is no money, no confidence & little hope, property is sold off every day by the sheriff at a 4th of the estimated value of a few years ago, nobody can pay debts, the miseries of poverty are felt both by rich & poor, everyone you see looks careworn and haggard, and the whole community seems watching with trembling anxieties the movements of a set of selfish and corrupt politicians at Washington & Harrisburg.

New York City was also desolate. On Wall Street, business was "next to nothing," the *United States Democratic Review* reported. "Prices have been steadily falling for many months. The transactions, which once were sufficient in New York to give employment to a board of eighty brokers and upward, are now dwindled to very unimportant amounts." The harbor was quiet as well. "The past season has been one of unusual prostration of business," reported the *Sailor's Magazine*. "The large number of ships lying at our wharves for months unemployed, have borne melancholy testimony of the complete stagnation of trade. Thousands of seamen have been cast on shore with but a few dollars in their pockets, scarce enough to pay a fort-night's board."

The novelist Charles F. Briggs, an aspiring Dickens, published his first novel, *The Adventures of Harry Franco*, in 1839. It was set in New York City in the early months of the crisis, when "a panic seized upon the whole people, such as had never been known before, except when sudden fear has struck upon the hearts of a city, from a convulsion of nature, or the approach to the gates of a hostile army." His next novel, *The Haunted Merchant,* was published in 1843. It described the anguish of a New York businessman bankrupted in "those unlucky years when everybody loses money, and a poverty-struck feeling, for some unaccountable cause, pervades the community." Briggs's fiction reflected the hard reality. Philip Hone, a former mayor of New York, wrote in his diary in July 1842 about the city's newly completed federal cus-toms house, another marbled Parthenon whose construction had begun dur-ing the boom years eight years before:

> It is intended to collect the import revenue upon the commerce of the nation; but how if it should prove that, the commerce being an-nihilated, there will be no revenue to collect? A splendid reservoir has been prepared, with fountains whose streams are to irrigate the lands in all quarters; but how melancholy would it be to discover that, after all of these preparations, the springs are to be dried up and the waters have ceased to flow. It looks awfully like it just now. . . . The cage is splendid, but the bird has fled. . . . There must be a recu-perative principle in this great country to restore things some time or another, but I shall not live to see it.

The great pride of New York State was the Erie Canal, a 360-mile-long waterway that connected the Hudson River to the Great Lakes and radically reduced the cost of shipping from the Atlantic seaboard to the western states. Completed in 1825, the canal was a technological and economic marvel which encouraged a massive expansion of canal systems across the whole country. In 1836, the New York legislature authorized a debt-financed ex-pansion of the canal that it projected would be entirely repaid by burgeoning toll revenue. Six years later, freight going to western states was down by 40 percent, while eastward traffic was stagnating. The legislature halted canal improvements in March 1842.

The West, as Dickens had seen, was in trouble too. In 1837, Horace Gree-ley called it the "Great West . . . the true destination" for newly landed im-migrants. But the West was great no longer. In the wake of financial crisis, historian Roy Robbins wrote in 1942, came "desolation, chaos, and ruin." In Cincinnati, a newspaper reported: "Working men are becoming almost desperate for want of work. There is nothing for them to do—they are actually offering to work for their board along the river streets. This is not exaggeration, it is a melancholy fact. It is rumored that the two steamboats burnt a day or two since, just above the city, were set on fire by men out of employ, so as to get the work to rebuild them."

James Kirk Paulding, Secretary of the Navy in the cabinet of former President Martin Van Buren, gave a firsthand account of the devastation in the West. Soon after his defeat in the 1840 election, Van Buren decided to rebuild his political fortunes by making a tour of the West. Paulding travelled with him. In June 1842, Van Buren and Paulding parted company in Cincinnati, with Paulding taking the steamboat down the Ohio to the Mississippi and then north to St. Louis. He was following the path Charles Dickens had taken only two months earlier. But Paulding continued north to the mouth of the Illinois River, and then up the Illinois itself toward Chicago. All along the shores, Paulding found people "almost without exception, complaining of hard times." The market for crops and livestock had collapsed. "All wish to sell and nobody cares to buy," Paulding wrote.

Signs of decay multiplied as Paulding headed northward. In 1835, the Illinois legislature had approved a plan to connect the head of the Illinois River to Lake Michigan by building a one-hundred-mile canal from Peru to Chicago. The project was financed by state-guaranteed bonds, many sold to British investors. The prospect of a navigable route from Lake Michigan to the Mississippi triggered rampant speculation in land along the route. By 1840, however, the state's financial condition was so bad that the legislature stopped work on the canal with the last thirty miles to Chicago unfinished. The state's default in January 1842 made immediate resumption of construction unlikely. The result was a series of ghost towns on the banks of the Illinois. They were "a mere spasmodic effort of speculation," Pauling said, some marked by a few lonely houses, and others with "nothing but a name and a lithographic map to demonstrate their existence." Paulding concluded that the people of Illinois "had been precipitated from the summit of hope to the lowest abyss of debt and depression. It was the feverish anxiety, the headlong haste, the insatiable passion for growing rich in a hurry, that brought them and other states where they are now standing shivering on the verge of bankruptcy."

In Chicago itself, by another account, "the hotels were emptied of guests and the streets deserted. Business had vanished like smoke, leaving 4,000 ambitious resourceful people stranded amid the wreck of their fortunes without any outlet for their energies."

Eighty miles north of Chicago, the residents of Milwaukee were suffering as well. James Buck had been there for only six years in 1842, but was already one of the longest residents in this infant city. Once a sailor, Buck had just returned to Boston from Calcutta in 1836 when he met an old schoolmate who was striking out for the frontier. The stream of emigration to the western states was "like a tidal wave," Buck said. Building lots in Milwaukee were already selling "for prices that made those who bought or sold them, feel like a Vanderbilt. Everyone was sure his fortune was made. . . . Nothing like it was ever seen before; no western city ever had such a birth." Then came the crash. Buck recalled:

> The emigrants were few and far between. A wave of disappointment rolled over the little hamlet, filling the hearts of the people with sadness, blasting all their hopes, and leaving them to live, as best they could, upon their own resources, and to prey upon each other. The wealth that many of them supposed they possessed, took to itself wings and flew away. Lots and lands for which fabulous prices had been paid in '36, were now of no commercial value whatever. The desideratum was bread and clothing, and the man who could procure these, was lucky.

In 1836, the engine of the American economy had been the cotton plantations of the South. But now "the sad, monotonous complaint of hard, hard times"—as Augusta, Georgia's *Southern Cultivator* called it—could be heard across the South as well. A state legislator in Richmond in March 1842 said that

> the pecuniary embarrassment that now pervades every portion of the Commonwealth, threatening ruin and disaster to all classes of society, is a fact as notorious as it is deplored. . . . [I]t presses with accumulated violence and intensity on the south-western portion of Virginia. The intelligence received from every part of that country by every mail that reaches this city, discloses a scene of suffering, of anguish, and distress, that can scarcely be imagined.

The mail arriving overseas from Liverpool brought news of a horrifying murder and attempted suicide by William Jenner, a cotton broker from Georgia. Police broke into Jenner's home and found his wife dead on the kitchen floor, shot several times in the head, while his child lay lifeless in the bedroom upstairs. Jenner told the officers "that he thought it better to see his wife and children dead, than to see them in poverty and distress. . . . [H]e lost the whole, or nearly the whole, of his property in cotton speculation, and has since struggled hard against difficulties."

A British diplomat traveling through New Orleans in January 1842 said that the country "presents a lamentable appearance of exhaustion and demoralization." "All that is talked of nowadays here is the hard times, hard times," wrote a plantation owner in St. Mary, Louisiana. "The planters nearly all made bad crops and cannot get much for them—the latest news from New Orleans is that the Sheriff has shut up six banks." "I am distressed in mind," wrote Rachel O'Connor, the mistress of another Louisiana plantation, in June 1842. "I am in great trouble about getting the taxes paid and getting provisions for the Negroes." Plantation owners were compelled to sell slaves to satisfy their debts, and some fled west to evade creditors. Sheriffs who attempted to collect judgments against defaulting debtors returned their writs with the notation "G.T."—Gone to Texas. One newspaper reported "a good deal of emigration" from the state of Mississippi, "in different directions, but principally to Texas." But not all debtors fled; some stayed and fought their creditors. James Buckingham, a British traveller in the South, reported in 1842 that "all law, civil and criminal, seemed to be at a stand" in Mississippi because of mob resistance to the collection of debts.

"Never, we imagine, has the future been shrouded in a deeper and more portentous gloom than at this time," wrote the editor of the Vicksburg, Mississippi, *Whig*.

> The darkest days of 1837 presented but a faint picture to what is now exhibited, and from every town and county in the State we have the same melancholy prospect. The whole community is literally upon the rack, and the best men in the country find it impossible to raise any amount of money, except at the most ruinous sacrifices. . . . Men give up all they possess to satisfy their creditors, see their property knocked down under the hammer of the sheriff or the marshal, at one-fourth at least of its value, and find themselves beggars. . . . We are informed that land and negroes are selling under execution for a fifth of their real value.

> When or where this will stop, God only knows. When, or from whence relief is to come, we know not; but unless relief does come, and come speedily, this country will present a scene of widespread ruin and desolation, such as has never been witnessed before. The prospect is frightful to contemplate.

Gauging the Losses

> Our alms house is overrun. The city hospitals are full.
> There is a great deal of sickness abroad, caused by
> want of proper food. . . . Of business we have none.
> There is nothing doing. . . . Masons, mechanics, &c.
> suffer much. There has not been a time, probably,
> since the war, when there was such a stagnation of
> all employ.
>
> —New York correspondent to *National Intelligencer*,
>   January 1840

Sorting out the exact scale of the crisis became a popular pastime. An 1841 estimate concluded that the initial phase of the crisis had produced thirty-three thousand business failures causing a half billion dollars in losses. The *United States Almanac* calculated that the losses on real estate, stocks, and deposits between 1837 and 1841 approached one billion dollars. Another anonymous author attempted to tally the amount of depreciation on assets, and lost value of production, and concluded that total losses for the period of 1837–1840 were over six billion dollars. Of course, the method behind all these estimates were suspect, and it was difficult to know precisely what to make of the final tabulations. Six billion dollars is not a large amount today; presumably it was a bogglingly large amount in 1841, but Americans of that era still had no way of assessing that figure in the context of the country's total economic potential. Perhaps the most significant fact about these estimates is that they were made at all. That Americans were attempting "to gauge the terrible havoc" is evidence of how massive and bewildering the crisis must have been.

The attempt to impose order out of economic and social convulsion is a theme that recurs throughout the story of the 1836–1848 crisis. One of the ways in which this drive to restore order was manifested was through more systematic collection of data about commercial activity. Accurate and timely economic data was difficult to obtain in antebellum America, but this began to change because of the crisis. In good times, entrepreneurs could be casual about measuring the ebb and flow of business; in hard times, carelessness could be fatal. One entrepreneur who exploited the hunger for information was Freeman Hunt, who launched his *Merchants' Magazine* in 1839. In Hunt's journal, reams of commercial statistics were accompanied by calls for a new "science of business" combining "vast comprehensiveness with a most minute grasp of details."

Hunt's magazine thrived, but the figures jumbled within its pages revealed the surrounding troubles. In the first six years of the crisis, the yardage of imported dyed cotton goods plunged by 85 percent. Imported iron and steel manufactures dropped by half, and imported wine by 60 percent. The average price of cotton in New Orleans was cut in half. In Boston, the wholesale price of pork declined by 60 percent, the price of beef dropped by half, and the price of codfish and flour dipped 40 percent. The tonnage of ships engaged in the cod fishery was down by one quarter between 1839 and 1842, in the mackerel fishery it was down by half, and in whaling it was down by 15 percent. The Delaware and Hudson canal and railroad reported that its revenues were down by 30 percent between 1836 and 1843. The total capital of American banks dropped by over 40 percent between 1839 and 1843. Loans extended by New York banks in 1842 were down one-third from five years earlier.

A century later, the Great Depression of the 1930s spurred a similar movement for the improvement of statistics that measured the state of the national economy. That crisis gave us the term *macroeconomics*, referring to the study of the economy as a whole. It also entrenched a number of concepts that were necessary for macroeconomic planning—such as the notion of national income, aggregate consumption and investment, and the rates of inflation and unemployment—and pushed governments to create statistical offices that could measure all of these concepts on a regular basis. It is this theoretical and administrative accomplishment of the mid-twentieth century that makes it so easy to have a conversation about the state of the economy today. In January 2009, we already knew (because the federal government told us) that the total production of goods and services in the United States in the last three months of 2008 decreased at an annualized rate of 3.8 percent, that household consumption had decreased by 3.5 percent, that business investment had plunged by 19 percent, that prices had declined by 4.6 percent, and the unemployment rate was over 7 percent. It was this ready access to data that allowed economists to conclude so quickly that the 2008 recession was the longest and deepest since World War II.

Obviously none of this type of data was available in the mid-nineteenth century. However economic historians have attempted to apply today's concepts to make retrospective estimates of the state of the economy throughout the earlier part of American history. Estimation becomes increasingly difficult as we move further back in time. Nonetheless, it is possible to view the crisis of 1836–1848 in a longer-term perspective. We can concede that it was not the first significant economic collapse in American history. An earlier financial panic in 1819 also triggered three years of depression, but the consequences of the 1836–1848 crisis were likely much more severe (one historian suggested that the Panic of 1837 produced "an economic crisis so extreme as to erase all memories of previous financial disorders"). Nor was it the country's worst depression, if judged purely by its effect on national income. In this respect it was exceeded in severity by the Great Depression of the 1930s and, perhaps, by the Long Depression of 1873–1879.

However, the significance of an economic crisis should not be judged by looking at a handful of economic indicators alone. Well before the term was used to describe severe slumps in economic activity, *depression* conveyed a mental state: a condition of deep dejection and hopelessness. We can see, in the contemporaneous descriptions of the 1836–1848 crisis, how tightly the economic and psychological conceptions of depression were intertwined. Many Americans were confused about why the good times of the 1830s had vanished so suddenly. Some took the fall from prosperity as a just punishment for selfishness and greed. There was broad confusion about what should be done to revive commerce. For many, shattered by five long years of turmoil and decline, there were also doubts about whether anything could be done to relieve the country's distress—and fears, too, about what would happen if the country's course could not be corrected.

The 1836–1848 crisis did more than demoralize the American people; it was also recognized as a test of the country's nascent democratic institutions. A British envoy to the United States, Lord Ashburton, shared Dickens' dismal view of the American political scene. In May 1842 he confided to the British Foreign Secretary, Lord Aberdeen, that he viewed the United States as a "mass of ungovernable and unmanageable anarchy." The *Times of London*, reflecting the mood of angry British investors, wrote in the same month: "It remains to be seen with what patience and judgment the democracy of America will endure and remedy these self-inflicted evils: but institutions like those which the American people have adopted are especially ill-fitted for a country where the plainest truths of public economy are disdainfully denied by the Legislature, and where the most obvious interests of the community are sacrificed to the passions or prejudices of the people." Britons were not alone in wondering about the durability of democratic institutions in the United States. "The times are out of joint," Philip Hone wrote in his diary in December 1838, after the militia was called out to suppress rioting at the state capitol in Harrisburg, Pennsylvania. "Now is the critical moment of our country's fate. . . . The United States are surrounded by difficulties and dangers requiring a strong arm and a better head and purer political morality than are ever to be found in a mere party manager and popular demagogue."

By March 1842, national politics had become so unsettled that Navy Secretary Abel Upshur said he "should not be surprised to hear of popular outbreaks in all the large cities, and of desperate measures calculated to overthrow all law and all order." Opponents of President John Tyler seemed to be set on pursuing their aims "even at the hazard of revolution," Upshur wrote. "If the moral sense of the country does not rise against it in disgust, the proof will be complete, that they are without the virtue that is necessary to the preservation of free institutions."

The crisis of 1836–1848 had significance not only because of the massive economic costs that it imposed on the nation, but also because it threatened to undermine social order and the integrity of the nation's major public institutions. It is for this reason we can call it the country's First Great Depression. The crisis was a test of the maturity of the American polity. From the moment of its founding, the country had professed its commitment to a decentralized system of government and broad political enfranchisement. Those principles were more deeply entrenched in the two decades before 1837. But the United States was also an open economy, vulnerable to unexpected shocks from abroad, and dependent on the goodwill of foreign merchants and lenders. The question was whether the country's political culture and institutions could accommodate the pressures that followed from its place in the international economy. In essence, an expansive and increasingly fractious polity would have to negotiate its response to economic problems that were poorly understood.

❧ The Bubble

> Everyone with whom I converse, talks of 100 percent as the lowest return on an investment. No one is known ever to have lost anything by a purchase and sale of real estate.
>
> —John M. Gordon, an investor from Baltimore, reporting on land sales in southern Michigan, 1836

The historian Frederick Jackson Turner became famous for an argument about why the United States was different than Europe. In 1893, at a scholarly conference at the Chicago World's Fair, Turner argued that the whole of American history to that point had been concerned with taming, and then extending, the nation's frontier. The national character, its democratic temperament, its restlessness—all of this came from the fact that the nation underwent a "perennial rebirth" on its western edge, until the idea of a frontier line was finally abandoned in 1890.

FIGURE 5. The United States in 1840. Source: From S. E. Forman, *Advanced American History* (New York: The Century Company, 1919).

By the early 1930s, though, Turner was in a different mood. "We are more like Europe," Turner said in 1932. "We have become a nation comparable to all Europe in area, with settled geographic provinces which equal great European nations. We are in this sense an empire, a federation of sections, a union of potential nations." The American provinces were distinct in culture, in politics, and, above all, in material interests. In the United States, as in Europe, the great task of statesmanship was to conciliate among the sections, to compromise and bargain, and often to "straddle upon vital problems."

This way of thinking about the economic and political structure of the United States was hardly new. In a sense, the United States had always been like Europe. Even in the 1830s, Americans could be divided into at least three sections. The material interests of the northeastern states—from Maine to Delaware—were increasingly rooted in manufacturing, finance, and ocean trade, although small-scale farming remained important. The southern states—especially the new states in the Gulf Plains—were dedicated to the production of cotton, rice, sugar, and tobacco on large plantations, using slave labor. The West—those new states of the upper Mississippi and Ohio River Valleys—grew wheat, corn, and livestock, and produced derivative goods of flour, corn meal, whiskey, beef, and bacon. Some people saw an unintended harmony in the organization of the American economy; the three sections were distinct but dependent upon one another. Southern plantations consumed the produce of western farms; northern factories relied on the produce of southern plantations; westerners and southerners alike depended on northern manufacturers and financiers. The country was "connected . . . by the interchange of the products of our industry. . . . Among ourselves, in the differences of our climate, our soil, and our employments, our interests are in unison."

This was a simple, happy, and misleading picture of the American economy. It missed a fourth section, arguably more dynamic than any of the other three, and most easily regarded as the real engine of American economic development. With the addition of this section, the United States was not only *like* Europe, as Turner claimed, it was also *of* Europe. This fourth section was Great Britain.

In the first half of the nineteenth century, Britain was undergoing an extraordinary economic transformation, as capitalists and inventors collaborated to revolutionize the production of basic goods. Nowhere was this more obvious than in cotton manufacturing, "the wonder industry" of the British industrial revolution. A series of technical breakthroughs—principally the spinning mule, the power loom, the improved steam engine, and cylinder printing—allowed for a dramatic reduction of the labor required to produce plain and fancy cotton goods. At the same time, British entrepreneurs learned how to combine many of these innovations within a single building, the integrated cotton mill. The factory itself was a marvel: "the most striking example of the dominion obtained by human science itself over the powers of nature, of which modern times can boast," as a British journalist said in 1835. The model mill was built of fire-resistant brick or stone, four or five stories high, about two hundred feet long, and fifty feet in width. By 1835, Britain had over twelve hundred factories like this, employing at least one-third of a million people.

The rate of expansion in the cotton industry was dizzying. In 1820, it was estimated that British factories employed fourteen thousand power looms; by 1833, the number of power looms had increased to one hundred thousand; and by 1850, the country had a quarter million. No other country could match the scale and sophistication of British cotton production. "We see no ground for apprehending that England will lose her present manufacturing pre-eminence," a British political economist boasted in 1835. "English cotton manufacture is in little danger from that of the United

States." By the late 1830s, British mills were producing three hundred million pounds of cotton goods a year. Britain itself was still the most important single market for its own cotton manufactures, and one that was growing rapidly: the British population increased by almost 80 percent between 1801 and 1841. The half of production that was sent overseas was divided among many nations. The United States took only 15 percent of British exports in 1835; Central and South America took 30 percent; continental Europe, 30 percent; and south and east Asia, 15 percent.

Much of the cotton industry was concentrated in the county of Lancashire in northwest England. "It has thoroughly revolutionized this county," a young Fredrich Engels wrote in 1844, "converting it from an obscure, ill-cultivated swamp into a busy, lively region, multiplying its population tenfold in eighty years, and causing giant cities such as Liverpool and Manchester . . . to spring up as if by a magic touch." Manchester, home to one hundred mills, was called the Cottonopolis of the Universe. Liverpool, thirty miles to the west, was (after London) the "greatest emporium of the British empire, and in fact, of the world." It was the seaport through which passed almost all Anglo-American trade.

This included, in 1836, almost one-third of a billion pounds of American cotton. British cotton manufacturers and American cotton growers had grown thoroughly dependent on one another. In the mid-1830s, almost 90 percent of the cotton used in British factories was imported from the United States, and 60 percent of total American cotton production was shipped to Liverpool. Almost half the total value of *all* U.S. exports in 1836—about fifty million dollars—was accounted for by the sale of cotton to Liverpool brokers. The next most important American exports were tobacco (ten million dollars in 1836), then manufactures (six million), lumber and wood products (four million), flour (four million), and rice (three million). The cotton trade with Liverpool dominated them all.

Many Americans credited the cotton revolution in the American South to a Massachusetts inventor, Eli Whitney. Upland cotton grew well in the South, but the task of picking seeds from its fiber was painfully slow. So much labor was needed to clean the cotton that it was difficult to see how the crop could be grown economically, even with slave labor. While visiting a Georgia plantation in 1793, Whitney devised a simple machine, the cotton gin, which radically reduced the effort required to clean cotton. "One person is able to perform with it, in a day, the work of one thousand without it," Treasury Secretary Levi Woodbury said in 1836.

Whitney, a nineteenth-century Georgia historian said, "made the raising of cotton the great industry of the people of the South." But this was not

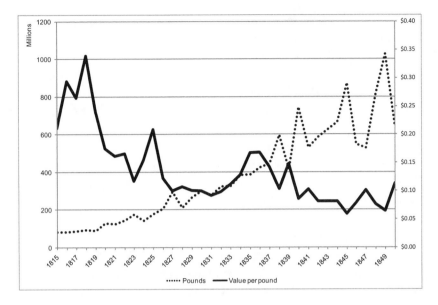

FIGURE 6. Cotton Exports, 1815–1850. Total Volume of Cotton Exports, in Pounds, and Average Value per Pound. Source: House of Representatives, Miscellaneous Document No. 49, 48th Cong., 1st Sess., 1884, Part 2, Table 2.

quite right. A whole series of technical and organizational innovations were required to make large-scale cotton manufacturing feasible, and thus to create demand for massive amounts of cotton. Whitney's invention was a necessary but hardly sufficient condition for the expansion of cotton production in the South. Whatever the cause, though, American cotton production grew at an extraordinary pace in the early nineteenth century. In 1790, it had been inconsequential. By 1800, one-third of a million acres of Southern soil were dedicated to cotton production; by 1830, well over two million acres were under cultivation; and by 1840, almost five million. By this time the United States was growing more cotton than all other nations combined. Entrepreneurs were flooding into the new southern states of Alabama, Mississippi, Louisiana, and Tennessee, buying cheap public land, and converting it to cotton cultivation. By the mid-1830s, these new states on the Gulf of Mexico were producing the larger share of American cotton. They were also an added force for the preservation of slavery, on which the plantation economy depended. The slave population of the United States grew by almost one million between 1820 and 1840, mainly in the new states, while the price of slave field hands nearly doubled between 1825 and 1835.

Other sectors also benefited from the expansion of the cotton economy. "Every interest throughout the land . . . receives from it active and material aid," a Treasury Department study said. "Like the light and heat of the sun, the genial effects of this inestimable blessing which Providence hath bestowed upon this favored people, reach every portion of the land." As plantations expanded, so did the demand for tools, rough cloth, and other Northern manufactures, as well as the need for Northern shipping. The burgeoning population of the Gulf states also had to be fed. The price in New Orleans for pork, lard, flour, and corn rose steadily, and this encouraged a subsidiary boom in the new western states that traded down the Ohio and Mississippi. The amount of pork and bacon delivered to New Orleans annually from the interior rose from one million pounds in 1826–1830 to five million pounds in 1831–1835.

The architecture of the transatlantic cotton economy was complex and delicate. To build their mills, British cotton manufacturers were amassing capital on an unprecedented scale, and wagering on supply and demand for cotton goods a year or more in the future. Mill owners rarely had a good sense of the investment decisions being taken by their competitors. As a result, there were recurrent problems of over-investment in addition to other factors that could cause a weakening of prices, such as an unexpected slump in consumer income. American plantation farming was also capital-intensive and speculative. Plantation owners borrowed against their land, their slaves, and even against future crops, all on the expectation of good cotton prices and without a clear sense of how many other farmers were making similar investments in new production capacity. "Buying a plantation," one grower later told Frederick Law Olmsted, "is essentially a gambling operation."

Business transactions were made difficult by vast distances and slow communications. A fast steamboat could cover the fifteen hundred mile stretch from Louisville down the Ohio and Mississippi Rivers to New Orleans in eight days in good weather, but steamships were not yet established on sea routes in 1836. A vessel might need three weeks to sail the seventeen hundred miles from New Orleans to New York City. (Urgent messages could be sent overland from New Orleans to New York in seven days, but this was very expensive.) It took another three weeks to send letters and cargo from New York to Liverpool if winds were favorable, which they often were not. Even after steamships were introduced on the North Atlantic in 1838, the transit from New York to Liverpool required two weeks.

The span of the market complicated commerce in several ways. No businessman—manufacturer, planter, farmer, financier—made decisions with an understanding of what prices actually prevailed in a distant market at that moment. He knew only what prices had been days or weeks before.

Often, businessmen would hire agents to work on their behalf in distant markets; for example, buying cotton in New Orleans to resell in Liverpool, or buying manufactures in Liverpool to resell in New York. But the agents themselves might be asked to pay for goods long before they were delivered to their final destination and available for resale. This tied up working capital. And if sellers demanded payment in gold or silver, buyers had to bear the hazard of shipping it securely.

In practice, such problems were avoided by settling transactions with written promises that payment would be made at the buyer's bank, usually two or three months ahead. These promises were known as bills of exchange. A seller rarely held on to a bill and attempted himself to collect on it. Bills were assets: they could be sold, or used to settle debts, or pledged as security for loans. A bill might be transferred several times before it eventually arrived in the hands of a businessman who could redeem it at the buyer's bank.

In 1836 bill brokerage—the business of buying and selling bills—was a massive transatlantic enterprise in its own right, much larger than it had been a decade or two earlier. It was a trade that involved delicate calculations about the odds that a promise to pay would eventually be honored. Ultimately, the health of the market depended on the willingness of the Bank of England to buy good bills from brokers. ("London is the centre of the credit system of the whole commercial world," an American writer said in 1838, "and the Bank of England is the sun of that system.") The amount by which the Bank of England discounted those bills—that is, the difference between what it was prepared to pay for a bill and its face value—was the main mechanism by which it influenced prevailing interest rates.

Bill brokerage was not the only aspect of the financial system that was mutating rapidly. In the United States, the demand for credit, and the perception that there could be easy profits in lending, caused a surge in the number of banks chartered under state law. There were 329 state banks in 1830 and 713 in 1836. Each could issue its own banknotes which their bearer could redeem for specie (that is, gold or silver coin, the most dependable form of money) at will. When banks advanced credit, either by discounting bills or lending against property, they often did so by giving banknotes to the lender. The volume of bank notes circulating per capita in the United States increased by 40 percent between 1834 and 1836.

Few Americans really understood how the financial system worked. Only one in ten Americans lived in cities. Most lived on the land, where they grasped the hard realities of agrarian life and traveled little. From that perspective, there was something unnatural and arbitrary about the whole scheme by which finance was conducted. Financiers produced no tangible goods and rarely handled coin. They made complicated trades in nothing but paper promises. The far-away institutions with which local financiers corresponded, and upon whose favor they depended, were nothing more than abstractions to the ordinary mind.

In bad times, finance could seem like the weather: incomprehensible, fickle, and dangerous. In good times, when everyone was making money, this analogy was easily forgotten, and in 1836 the weather still seemed good to many people. "On whatever side we turn our eyes," the New York editor Horace Greeley said, "we are greeted by the gratifying evidences of universal prosperity. . . . [E]ach successive year adds many millions to the aggregate of the National wealth."

And yet, there were signs of trouble on the horizon. Across the country, prices were beginning to skyrocket. According to one index, wholesale prices for key commodities in New Orleans increased by over 30 percent between January 1835 and April 1836. In Cincinnati, commodity prices were up by 60 percent in those fifteen months. Inflation in the eastern cities was only slightly less severe—roughly 25 percent in the same period in New York and Philadelphia. Urban workers were becoming better organized, and strikes were more frequent and increasingly violent. "These extremely high prices are bad indeed for the poor," said the *New York Journal of Commerce*. "Their wants call for a liberal relief from the overflowing abundance of the wealthy."

The increase in commodity prices, although startling, was nothing when compared to the rise of land values. Most of the land that was required for agricultural expansion in the South and West was owned by the federal government, and in the 1830s it was engaged in one of the most massive privatizations of public assets in history. Between 1830 and 1836, the federal government disposed of 72,000 square miles of land. Most of this—50,000 square miles, an expanse equal to the whole of England—was sold in the twenty-four months between January 1835 and December 1836. Land offices on the frontier were besieged by settlers and speculators determined to turn an easy profit. "The mania for obtaining land . . . is astonishing," an Ohio correspondent wrote in June 1836. "The speculators sweep as they go, seemingly having little or no regard for situation or quality." On the days on which auctions were held, land office towns were flooded with prospective buyers. Bars and dining halls were converted to barracks, and tents were thrown up around the town like a military camp. Speculators often connived with corrupt land officers to corner the best property, which they quickly resold for immense profits. Near New Orleans, a town site that had been purchased from the federal government for thirty-five thousand dollars was resold for six hundred thousand dollars nine months later. In Manitowoc, Wisconsin, prices rose twenty-fold within a week. "Speculators went to bed at night hugging themselves with delight over the prospect that the succeeding morning would double their wealth."

Delusions of imminent grandeur hung over the whole of the West and South. In northern Illinois, promoter A. C. Ransom offered far-away investors the chance to purchase tracts in Ransomberg, a town which boasted (in lithographs) "streets and avenues in beautiful and regular arrangement . . . [and] parks, made attractive by shrubbery, fountains and statuary." Of course none of this actually existed. Neither did the great mills and warehouses shown in the prospectus for the city of High Bluffs, Illinois; nor the proud lighthouse of Port Sheldon, Michigan; nor the handsome theater of Marion City, Missouri—a miserable plot of land that was, in the spring of 1836, several feet under the Mississippi River. "Yet nobody perceived the illusion," said Francis Wayland, a leading nineteenth-century political economist. "The dream seemed reality for the time."

Nor were the eastern states immune from land fever. "A speculating mania is spreading like a contagion across the country," the Gettysburg *Compiler* said in May 1836. The Baltimore *American* reported on the resale of land near the city for twice the price fetched only two years earlier. "It is nevertheless a cheap purchase," the newspaper said. In 1836 a correspondent from Buffalo reported that everyone was making money on real estate: "We have heard of a good number of sales, and uniformly at an advance." One property purchased in 1834 for twelve hundred dollars had been resold for twelve thousand. In Maine, there was a rush for timberland. "The speculators here . . . have a kind of *dare devil* feeling," a correspondent to *Niles' Register* said. "A man who is not the owner of one hundred dollars, will buy a township and sell it again within an hour, at a small advance, and pocket the profit. . . . This is the grand secret of 'trade and commerce' in this hot bed of speculation and enterprise. . . . Ten lots of land which were sold yesterday at 1200 dollars per lot, were purchased for the sum of 2500 dollars [today]. . . . [T]his is an every day story in Bangor."

This was a real estate bubble, and eventually it would burst. When it did, many Americans attempted to understand how it had inflated in the first place. Some citizens blamed state governments for granting charters for the establishment of so many new banks. The banks were poorly regulated and often indiscriminate in lending. (Many were lending to their own officers or shareholders.) State banks were supposed to maintain a reserve of specie to anticipate sudden demands from depositors or holders of banknotes, and the reserve requirement was regarded as a check on the extension of credit. But as the boom accelerated, banks became careless about reserves. In the Gulf coast and western states, banks had specie reserves equal to 21 percent of their liabilities in 1835. The reserve ratio dropped to 15 percent by 1836.

Other Americans blamed President Andrew Jackson for the bubble. In 1832, Jackson vetoed a bill to renew the charter of the Second Bank of the United States, which was set to expire in April 1836. The bank was a powerful institution. It was the only national bank, with twenty-eight branches across the country. Because its banknotes were more easily redeemed, and implicitly backed by the federal government, they were generally preferred to those of state banks. The bank also collected revenue and made disbursements for the federal government. But the bank was also deeply flawed in its design. Although it wielded great power, it was barely subject to federal control. Only five of the bank's twenty-five directors were federal appointees, and these five had scarcely any influence over bank activities. The bank's president, Nicholas Biddle, bristled at the notion of accountability to federal authorities. Meanwhile, the bank became an easy target for a populist president and Democratic voters in the South and West who believed that it was a tool of an Eastern moneyed oligarchy.

In 1833, Jackson struck another blow against the bank by withdrawing federal deposits and placing them with about thirty state banks. By 1835, then, the bank was a weakened institution. Its deposits had fallen by half in just three years, and it was preoccupied with the task of winding up its business. In April 1836 only five of its branches remained in operation.

The decline of the Second Bank of the United States contributed to the economic bubble in two ways. In its heyday, the bank received a large volume of banknotes issued by state banks, and it maintained a policy of promptly returning these notes to issuing banks for redemption in specie. State banks responded by being more cautious in the issuance of notes—or, in other words, by maintaining a larger specie reserve in relation to outstanding notes. The collapse of the national bank also destroyed its capacity to police the state banks. It had ceased to be an effective "regulator of the currency," and thus a check on the expansion of credit was removed. At the same time, a positive stimulus to the expansion of credit by state banks was added. By April 1836, the federal treasury had deposited over thirty million dollars in state banks, most of which were located in southern and western states. (At the time, total private deposits in state banks were only about eighty million dollars.) Because the federal government was running a substantial surplus, the probability that there would be an immediate call on these deposits seemed low. The state banks that were favored with federal deposits used them to extend their lending, principally for the purchase of real estate, again without maintaining the necessary reserves.

The blame for the bubble was put on Jackson early and remained there for a very long time. "All the evils . . . that afflicted the people, were attributed to the experiments of General Jackson," said George Boutwell, a Massachusetts Democrat. "As these evils were coincident in time with the measures, the measures were treated as the guilty cause." In 1924, historian Reginald McGrane still insisted that it was the "contest between the cohorts of Andrew Jackson and Nicholas Biddle [that] prepared the ground for the hard times of 1837." Twenty years later, the landmark biography of Jackson by historian Arthur Schlesinger Jr. also conceded that Jackson's policy toward the bank "removed a valuable brake on credit expansion . . . [and] accelerated the tendencies toward inflation." The domestic crisis was presumed to have primarily domestic causes.

But we forget, in looking only at errors in American policy, that its economy did not stand alone. The United States was only one component of a tightly integrated trans-Atlantic system of commerce and finance. The American economy was booming in large part because the much larger British economy, to which it was closely attached, was also booming. Investment in British cotton manufacturing was surging ahead. (So, too, was investment in other new technologies, such as railroads.) This meant higher demand for cotton and favorable prices for American producers. The American boom would never have started, and the bubble never inflated, if it had not been for the fact that there was a heavy call for American cotton.

At the time, the British boom was explained as the happy result of the nation's genius for invention and entrepreneurship. But credit also has to be given to meteorological luck. Britain enjoyed four extraordinary harvests between 1832 and 1835. As a result, the price of wheat fell by 40 percent from 1830 to 1835; wheat was cheaper than it had been for half a century. This was a boon for Britain's working-class households, who spent two-thirds of their income on food, and almost one-third on bread and flour alone. Money not needed for food could be spent on clothing and other manufactures. This helped to maintain the price of cotton goods despite the rapid expansion of manufacturing capacity. And this, in turn, sustained the demand for American cotton.

The American economy was also inadvertently supercharged because of a lax policy on the part of the Bank of England, the so-called sun of the global credit system. One of the bank's primary concerns was the protection of its reserve of bullion and coin, kept in the vaults of its London headquarters. When the harvest was poor, and food had to be imported, the reserve tended to decline, because gold was needed to settle accounts with foreign sellers of wheat and flour. In such circumstances, the bank became protective of its reserve, mainly by purchasing bills of exchange at less favorable discounts. This pushed up the market rate of interest.

Of course, this was not the situation in the mid-1830s. Harvests were good, and the volume of wheat imported in 1835 was only one-third of what it had been four years earlier. Until the summer of 1836 there was little pressure on the bank's reserve. As a result, credit was easy. In retrospect it would become clear that the bank had underestimated the speed with which circumstances could change and its reserve could be drained. It kept rates too low for too long. While low rates in London encouraged investment in British manufacturing and railroads, it also drove British investors to look for better returns overseas. The American economy was an appealing prospect: growing rapidly, similar in language and culture, closely connected to British manufacture and commerce, and more stable (or so it appeared) than some of the alternatives, such as Latin America or India. A high-grade American bond yielded a return of 5 or 6 percent per annum, while long-term British government bonds paid little more than 3 percent.

"In the choice of investments by moneyed men," a British newspaper reported in 1836, "there has been . . . a very decided bias in favor of American securities, on account of the superior interest they yield compared with Government stocks and other modes for the employment of capital in Europe." British lending to the United States surged in 1834–1836. In 1833, total American foreign indebtedness was one hundred ten million dollars—not far from the average for the preceding two decades. By 1836, it had doubled to two hundred twenty million dollars. This was an immense stimulus to the American economy, and an important cause of the speculative fever in southern and western states. The amount of British capital flooding into the United States greatly exceeded the sums that the federal government was transferring to state banks.

Why did Americans tend to dwell so heavily on the domestic factors that contributed to the boom and bubble? There are several potential explanations. The first is that the actions of the country's own political leaders, publicized and debated in the nation's newspapers, were more easily observed than those of overseas investors and financial institutions. Simply because these actions were more likely to be monitored, they were also more likely to be identified as the immediate explanation for the state of the economy.

Of course, political struggle aggravated this tendency to emphasize the significance of domestic policy decisions. Before the economy went sour, Jackson and his supporters had strong incentives to credit the nation's well-being to his own stewardship. (The "prosperous condition of our beloved country," Jackson said in December 1834, could be explained by his decisive action against the bank. Many people "began to believe that the sudden prosperity that they saw around them was really caused by the determined conduct of the President.") And after the economy went sour, Jackson's enemies had equally strong incentives to put the blame on Jackson himself. The tendency of practical politics to overstate the significance of domestic policy decisions was noted at the time. "The direct and immediate effects [of Jackson's decisions] cannot be correctly ascertained," Albert Gallatin said in 1841, "but they have been greatly exaggerated by party spirit."

National pride also shaped understandings of complex events. In 1836 the United States was a new nation that was proud of its independence, won through two hard struggles with a great power. It would be difficult for any American politician to acknowledge the nation's dependence in matters of trade and finance on the same power from which it had won its political autonomy. Some Democrats tried to do it. In September 1837 Jackson's successor, Martin Van Buren, attempted to argue that the unfolding American crisis was the incidental result of British commercial troubles. But there was something unseemly about an American president making such a direct admission of impotence in the face of larger economic forces. The principle of political sovereignty demanded that domestic problems should have domestic causes.

The very complexity of the financial system made it easier for Americans to craft an interpretation of events that emphasized domestic factors. As one economist wrote in 1840, the facts about the boom and collapse presented themselves "in a confused heap, from which reasoners, on one side or another, feel themselves at liberty to select such as suit their purpose." In the earliest phases of the crisis, this complexity also made it possible for Americans to draw very different conclusions about the true state of the economy. In the spring of 1836, many still thought that everything was going well. But there were some who believed that it must all come to a bad end.

"There is a limit to speculating in land," warned the *Milwaukee Advertiser*. "Before three years pass, numbers of speculators will be as anxious to sell out their lands as they have been this year to buy them."

"Unless this mania is corrected in season, it *must* operate against the best interests of the community," proclaimed the Alton, Illinois *Observer*. "The minds of the young . . . are perverted by this sudden, though hazardous means of obtaining wealth, from the more sure and steady pursuits of industry and economy."

"When will the bubble burst?" asked the New York editor William Cullen Bryant in the *Evening Post* of April 7, 1836. "When will the great catastrophe which the banks have been preparing for us actually come about?"

☙ The Collapse

> It is evident that we are approaching a momentous crisis.
>
> —*Niles' Weekly Register*, April 23, 1836

By late fall of 1836 the land bubble was collapsing. In the fourth quarter of that year, federal land sales were down 30 percent from the average for the previous four quarters. Sales for the whole of 1837 would be less than they had been in the boisterous second quarter of 1836. "Speculations in public lands . . . have been entirely suspended," the *New York Herald* reported in early 1837. "Even the holders of these lands begin to find that they have more on hand than they know what to do with. Government lands in speculators' hands are now selling at nearly the original price. . . . Lands in Illinois and Indiana that were cracked up to $10 an acre last year, are now to be got at $3, and even less. The reaction has begun, and nothing can stop it."

The American financial system was also teetering on the precipice. In New York City, interest rates for short-term commercial loans were nearly 30 percent by the end of October 1836. "The money pressure is . . . exceedingly severe," the *Journal of Commerce* reported on October 22. "[It has] given monied men the power of extorting enormous rates of usance, and put active business men upon the rack. . . . We are visited with a paralyzing scarcity of money." On November 3, the *New York Spectator* reported that many businesses were on the verge of bankruptcy: "Our citizens are in a perilous situation. . . . Money is not to be had for any consideration. . . . Is there any explanation of this singular crisis?"

Many put blame for the crash on Andrew Jackson, just as they had for the bubble. By the spring of 1836, Jackson and his advisors were also alarmed by the "raging mania for wild speculations" that had seized the South and West. Jackson had been hostile to the Bank of the United States because of the power which it seemed to wield through the manipulation of paper credit; but the financial structure that was emerging as the bank declined seemed hardly less odious to any proponent of hard currency. It, too, was a "system of fictitious credit—a raising of the wind—a system of bubbles." And its hazards appeared increasingly clear. In July 1836, the Treasury Department issued an order that was designed to ease the land mania. After August 15, federal land offices would refuse to take paper currency for purchase of public lands. Gold and silver coin would be the only acceptable form of payment. The Specie Circular, as the order was known, created an immediate demand for gold and silver coin in the South and West. This appeared to create a significant drain on the specie reserve of eastern banks. Large sums were drawn from New York and Philadelphia "to be locked up in the coffers of land offices and deposit banks in the states bordering on the great western wilderness." As reserves were reduced in the east, so too was credit. At the same time, holders of bank notes and deposits had more reason to doubt whether eastern banks could honor promises to redeem their calls for specie.

The effect of the Specie Circular was aggravated by a second policy approved by Congress in June 1836. The federal government was receiving windfall revenues from the sale of public lands, and Congress decided that this money should be distributed to states, according to their population. The first part of the distribution was to be executed in January 1837. Congress also mandated an increase in the number of federal deposit banks and a more equal allocation of funds among them. All of this required a complex series of transfers among state banks that held federal funds, and also between those banks and others selected by state governments to hold their share of the distribution. Consequently, there would be pressure on banks that were about to lose federal deposits, particularly in New York, and uncertainty as the tangle of transactions was sorted out.

That these federal actions contributed significantly to the puncturing of the bubble cannot be denied. "The whole trading and commercial interest has been put into confusion and dismay by a well-meant, but *extremely mistaken* system of operations set in motion by the Secretary of the Treasury," the *Portsmouth Journal* complained in December 1836. "The monetary affairs of the whole country were convulsed," said an anonymous 1839 writer, believed by many to be Nicholas Biddle:

> Millions upon millions of coin were *in transitu* in every direction, and consequently withdrawn from useful employment. Specie was going up and down the same river, to and from the South and North and the East and West at the same time; millions were withdrawn from their usual and natural channels, and forced against the current of trade, in literal fulfillment of the distribution law, to points where public money

had previously never been either collected or expended, except to a very limited degree.

In New York City, the main point at which federal revenue was collected in 1836, the drain on reserves was especially severe. Specie held by New York banks dropped from six million dollars in August 1836 to less than four million in December. Money in the main eastern centers became scarcer.

During the presidential election year of 1836 there were strong incentives for opposition Whigs to stick blame for the economic troubles on the Democratic nominee, Vice President Martin Van Buren. It did not work: the crisis was still incipient, and Van Buren won cleanly. But a tradition was begun of assigning the primary responsibility for the collapse of the boom on the Jackson's signing of the Distribution Act in June 1836, and his adoption of the Specie Circular in the following month. (The circular, said one nineteenth-century economist, was "the pin that pricked the bubble.") This, again, was not the whole story. Thousands of miles away, the Bank of England was making decisions that also contributed to the financial implosion in New York.

"The pressure of 1836," a British economist wrote at the time, "may be said to have commenced from the month of May in that year"; that is, before adoption of the Distribution Act or the Specie Circular. In early May 1836, the Bank of England's bullion reserve stood at almost eight million pounds. But it was beginning to decline at the rate of about a half million pounds per month, which implied that it would be exhausted sometime in 1837. A former governor of the bank, Horsley Palmer, believed that the drain was largely due to the rush of investment to the United States. There was, he said, "an inordinate amount of American paper upon our markets."

The Bank of England was often criticized for the roughness of its policy changes. Many of its directors were rich merchants, not trained bankers, and they lacked a good understanding of the system they sought to regulate. They also tended to keep inadequate reserves. The discount rate had been left too low, and the bank did not respond immediately when it became clear that the reserve was declining in the spring of 1836. Finally, in the summer, the directors put the brakes on hard, raising the bank's discount rate to the unusually high level of 5 percent by early September.

There is no doubt that the bank's decisions were partly founded on fears about the stability of American markets, the disruptions that might be caused by the policies introduced in the United States in June-July 1836, and the implications that all of this might have for the capacity of American borrowers to honor British debts. In this sense, American problems in the fall of 1836 did have American causes, with the important caveat that causality ran from Washington, through London, and back to New York. It was not simply what federal authorities had done; what also mattered was the Bank of England's *perception* about what federal authorities had done.

The bank's anxieties about conditions in the United States were illustrated by its abortive attempt to restrict credit to firms that specialized in financing Anglo-American commerce. The most prominent of these were the "Three Ws"—the firms of Wildes, Wiggins, and Wilson. The bank suspected that American businessmen, with the connivance of these firms, were simply rolling over debts that they could not honor, and it wanted to put a stop to the practice. On August 26, the bank instructed its Liverpool branch to stop discounting bills that were related to American commerce. This was a clumsy intervention that provoked howls of outrage among businessmen in Liverpool and Manchester, and four days later the bank reversed itself. Still, British lenders became more cautious about extending credit to the Three Ws.

However, the Bank of England's policy was not wholly driven by concerns about developments in the United States. There were also domestic considerations that influenced its decision making. The British banking industry had expanded, although not so wildly as in the United States, and the bank's directors worried that this was encouraging speculative bubbles at home. By fall of 1836 there were clearly other pressures on the Bank's reserve. Its sudden hike of the discount rate caused "disarrangement" closer to home. In October 1836 there was a run on Irish banks, which resulted in a heavy call for support from the Bank of England. By November, some English banks were also troubled and in need of aid. By the end of 1836, the bank's reserve had been slashed to four million pounds.

News about the Bank of England's actions reached the United States in late September. By the late fall, then, American bankers and merchants were being squeezed "from two sides at once." Federal policy had introduced confusion and put a strain on the reserves of important eastern banks. At the same time, Bank of England policy made credit less accessible in London, especially for American borrowers. Worried British creditors were calling on the Anglo-American firms to settle their debts with specie, and these firms were in turn calling on their American clients to do the same. Indeed, some contemporary writers thought that it was British, not American, policy that was the "effectual check" against speculation on lands in the

West and South. Even if Jackson had withdrawn the Specie Circular, they argued, speculation would have ended because the Bank of England had constricted the flow of credit that made it possible.

March 4, 1837, was inauguration day in Washington. President Jackson and Martin Van Buren rode to the Capitol in a carriage made of wood taken from the U.S.S. *Constitution*, one of the Navy's most venerable fighting ships. Shortly after noon on the east portico, Chief Justice Roger Taney administered the oath of office, and Van Buren delivered his first address as president. "In all the attributes of a great, happy, and flourishing people we stand without a parallel in the world," said the new chief executive. "We present an aggregate of human prosperity surely not elsewhere to be found."

The directors of the Bank of England took a different view. Only a few hours before the inauguration, and thousands of miles away, they met at the bank's headquarters on London's Threadneedle Street. The main financiers of Anglo-American trade—the three Ws—had been struggling for months, and at the start of March were at the brink of total collapse. On March 4, after two days of argument and private consultation with the British Cabinet, the bank's directors agreed that it would provide emergency aid to one of the Three Ws, Wildes & Company, on the condition that it would undertake no new business until the assistance was repaid. By the end of April, all three firms were being supported by the bank on the same terms.

The Three Ws' predicament had been aggravated by an unexpected drop in the price of cotton. Weakening British demand resulted in a 30 percent price decline in the first twelve weeks of the new year. The hope that Americans might earn enough from their principal export to settle accounts with British creditors was now dashed.

News about the sudden drop in Liverpool cotton prices reached New Orleans, the main cotton port, in early March. "Those who have been speculating in cotton," the *Times Picayune* announced, "find it very inconvenient, we could almost say impracticable, to meet their demands." One of the city's largest and most prestigious cotton brokers, the firm of Hermann, Briggs—starved of income and unable to borrow—announced its failure only hours before Van Buren's inauguration. The city quickly fell into a state of paralysis. "Failures are taking place daily," the *Times Picayune* reported on April 13. "Many who have not already failed are failing very fast." By the end of the month, the city was the "scene of melancholy transactions." On May 2 a well-established merchant, Theodore Nicolet, "unwilling to survive the ruin of his fortune . . . repaired to the house of Mr. Lesseps, where, about noon . . . he blew out his brains."

Reports about the Hermann, Briggs collapse reached New York City on March 17. The New Orleans firm owed a large amount of money to Joseph & Co., one of New York's most substantial bill brokers, and when the news arrived from New Orleans, Joseph & Co. immediately announced its failure. A sense of dread settled over the city. Within days, New Yorkers also learned that the Three Ws were surviving only with the support of the Bank of England. The Bank of the United States—a shadow of its former self, now carrying on business under a new charter granted by the state of Pennsylvania—tried to help American merchants and bankers by drawing on its own remaining credit in London, but this had little effect. The federal government offered no relief.

On May 4, a rumor spread through New York that the president of Mechanics' Bank had committed suicide. It was not true—he had died of a heart attack "occasioned by strong mental excitement"—but it was enough to start a run on the bank. On May 8, there was a run on Dry Dock Bank, one of the select few in New York that was trusted with federal deposits. The next day, the panic spread to the rest of the New York banks. By the close of business on May 10, all had suspended the redemption of their bank notes for specie. City leaders called out "a large body of troops under arms . . . ready to act a moment's notice," but there was no violence. As news of the developments in New York spread across the country, other banks also stopped honoring demands for specie.

The moment of absolute panic was over. "A dead calm has succeeded the stormy weather of Wall Street," Philip Hone, the former mayor of New York, wrote in his diary on May 11. "All is still as death; no business is transacted; no bargains made; no negotiations made. . . . The fever is broken; but the patient is in a sort of syncope, exhausted by the violence of the disease and the severity of the remedies."

In London, the arrival in mid-June of news about the suspension aroused lenders, who understood that maturing American debt now could be redeemed only for more paper rather than gold. "The Americans have proved too cunning for us," said the *Times of London*, "and European creditors may go whistle for their money."

Even in the United States there was popular anger at the banking establishment. But the fact was that the United States contained more debtors than creditors, and for debtors, suspension promised momentary relief. Suspending banks did not close immediately: they merely stopped honoring promises to exchange their paper for specie. Suspension allowed the banks and other businessmen to avoid disposing of assets at fire-sale prices, and to settle their debts in an orderly way. Still, business remained very slow for the

FIGURE 7. Mock Six Cents Banknote, August 1837. This note parodies the small-denomination notes that proliferated after the banks' suspension in May 1837. It mocks several of the Democrats' most prominent hard-money advocates. At the top is a quotation from Andrew Jackson's Farewell Address in March 1837: "I leave this great people prosperous and happy." Source: Library of Congress.

rest of 1837. Anyone who had specie hoarded it. The country was flooded with shinplasters—small-denomination notes of doubtful reliability that took the place of coin in everyday transactions.

Overseas, the Bank of England laid the groundwork for a mild recovery. By December 1837, its policies had produced the desired effect and its reserve of bullion had been replenished to nine million pounds, the highest level in five years. Consequently, the bank's directors reversed course and lowered its discount rate throughout 1838. Money, which had been scarce in London only a few months earlier, was once again "abundant and cheap." The directors did not know that they were laying the foundation for an even greater disaster the following year.

In the United States, the crucial question in early 1838 was when the American banks would resume honoring demands for payment in specie. In New York, the suspending banks were in violation of their state charters, and a one year legislative reprieve was scheduled to expire in May 1838. But it was dangerous for any small group of banks to resume honoring demands for specie alone. American banks faced a complex task of coordination, aggravated by the lack of a central bank or strong Treasury Department which could impose a common solution. Eventually, the New York banks resumed business in May 1838, fortified by a loan of one million dollars in specie from the now-flush Bank of England. Most other American banks resumed by August 1838.

By the fall of 1838, the American economy appeared to be undergoing a complete recovery. With the market interest rate in London down to almost 2 percent, British investors once again turned to the United States. "Large sums of money [were] invested in American securities. Bonds of all kinds . . . were poured upon the English market and found eager purchasers." Price levels in major American cities were beginning to approach what they had been two years earlier, and the Liverpool price for cotton was also better. In his annual address in December 1838, Van Buren treated the panic as though it were history. "The general business of the community, deeply affected as it has been, is reviving with additional vigor," Van Buren told Congress. "Confidence has been restored both at home and abroad, and ease and facility secured to all the operations of trade."

Van Buren spoke too soon. The difficulty, once again, was the fickle health of the Bank of England's reserve. After January 1839, it began another rapid decline. In the first quarter of the year, the reserve fell from nine to seven million pounds, and in the next quarter it fell again to four million pounds. This sudden drop was partly, although not entirely, the result of revived British investment in American securities. A larger difficulty was British weather.

Favorable conditions had produced ample harvests in Britain in 1832–1835, but the harvests of 1836–1837 were indifferent, and the 1838 harvest was the worst in twenty years. The year was cold and damp. Domestic food stocks were depleted and Britain was required, for the first time in years, to import large amounts of wheat and flour to feed the home market. The weather in 1839 was also poor—it snowed in London in May—and the harvest again disappointing. More wheat and flour was imported in 1839 than had been imported in the seven years of 1831–1837. As the country's balance of trade deteriorated, the drain on the Bank of England's reserve accelerated. It was not until May 1839, though, that the bank took firm action to protect its stock of bullion. Because it had delayed so long, its policy had to be severe. In August, the discount rate was raised to 6 percent, a rate unprecedented in the bank's 144-year history.

The bank's critics were furious over its delay in taking steps to protect the reserve. "How long," asked the *London Morning Chronicle,* "are the public to be at the mercy of a corporation which, when it suits their purpose, encourage speculation in every article to an extravagant degree, when they ought to make money scarce, and then as suddenly adopt restrictive measures when they have lured people out of their depth?" But the bank had little choice at that point but to put the brakes on hard. Its reserve was now down to three million pounds. "A great alarm pervaded society," Walter Bagehot later wrote. Faced with the imminent exhaustion of its bullion supply, the bank was humiliated by the need to negotiate an emergency line of credit with the Banque de France.

The brief reprieve for financial markets in Britain and the United States was over. Pressure for money was felt sharply in London throughout August and September. Conditions in the commercial discount market were "nearly as bad . . . as well they could be," the *Times of London* reported on September 2. There was "extraordinary pressure upon the money market," New York's *Courier and Enquirer* said. "The banks have no confidence in each other—there is no good feeling, no concert of action between them." At the same time, the price of cotton was collapsing again. This, too, was a product of the poor harvests. By 1839 the price of wheat in Britain was 80 percent higher than it had been in 1835. There were comparable increases in the price of other foods. For working-class households, whose income went mainly to food, this meant a sharp reduction in the money available for cotton goods and other manufactures. By the spring of 1839, many British mills were already reducing their work hours. This in turn implied a reduction in demand for American cotton. Cotton sold at about 15 cents a pound in 1835–1836, but was below ten cents by April 1839. The price would remain depressed for a very long time because of the excessive capacity in cotton production and manufacturing created during the boom years.

The Bank of the United States was caught out by this sudden change in economic conditions. In 1836–1837 it had borrowed heavily in Europe to preserve its own liquidity and to aid other American banks and merchants. To earn the money needed for repayment, it had launched a complex scheme to speculate in cotton. The bank calculated that if it could buy enough cotton from distressed growers at the relatively weak prices of 1837, then it could manipulate the price in Liverpool. Now it was the British, rather than Jacksonian Democrats, who complained about "a concentrated money power . . . [building] a dangerous practical monopoly." At first the venture appeared to succeed, and it was continued into 1839. When cotton prices began to decline, however, the bank's agents were caught with a large stockpile of unsalable cotton.

The bank's scheme was public knowledge in Britain. As the market turned, financiers in London understood that the U.S. bank was in trouble and began to restrict its access to credit. In July and August 1839, the bank undertook an even more desperate gamble to save itself from insolvency. It sold large amounts of short-term promissory notes to American investors, and allowed the proceeds from those sales to accumulate as deposits in New York banks. On August 26–27, the bank made sudden demands for withdrawal of the deposits in the form of specie. The aim was to force the New

York banks into suspension, and use this general suspension as a pretext for putting off the U.S. Bank's own creditors.

The plan backfired. New York was able to meet the bank's call for specie, and did not suspend. A few weeks later, though, the vast amount of short-term notes issued by the U.S. Bank would come due. The bank scrambled to raise funds in Europe—"Life or death to the Bank of the United States is the issue," the bank's agent in London confessed. But the bank still could not meet demands for payment, and itself suspended on October 9. Other banks in the mid-Atlantic states, the South, and the West soon followed. Only New England and New York avoided suspension. Elsewhere, almost 90 percent of banks had either suspended or collapsed entirely by January 1840.

The Bank of the United States never recovered from its October suspension. Its reputation, battered by its manipulations in the preceding months, was destroyed completely over the next year. Besieged by lawsuits by its creditors, the bank itself sued Nicholas Biddle for misappropriation of funds, while the state of Pennsylvania attempted to try Biddle and other former officers for conspiring to commit fraud. The bank attempted to resume specie payments in January 1841, could not sustain the effort, and failed completely three weeks later. There was, the bank's directors said, "a feeling of hostility to the institution . . . so great as to render the undertaking hopeless."

The rest of the country's banking industry made start-and-stop efforts at resumption as well, but did not succeed until late 1842. By then, two hundred banks had closed entirely. In the interim, economic activity ground to a halt. Money became scarce, and prices and trade declined precipitously.

The suffering began within weeks of the October suspensions. "The distress in the country is very great," said a correspondent from Mobile, Alabama, in January 1840. "This state of things here is unprecedented." "Business is at a stand," the *Ohio State Journal* wrote in early March 1840. "All, every interest, are on the verge of ruin." Commodity prices in Cincinnati had already dropped 30 percent. There was no hope this time that the United States would be saved by an impulse from the British economy. It too, was sliding into a depression, although not so severely as in the United States. More bad harvests, excessive capacity in cotton manufacturing and other sectors, confusion in Bank of England policy—all of this combined to frustrate the possibility of a quick recovery in Britain. And there was little demand for American cotton, or hope of support from British investors. The First Great Depression had begun.

❧CHAPTER 2

The States' Crisis

        The First Great Depression had a profound effect on the structure of government in the United States, and above all, on state government. This may seem odd to a modern reader. Today, when we think about problems that have an international aspect—such as the management of a crisis within the North Atlantic economy—our impulse would be to assume that they would fall within the sphere of federal responsibilities. To understand the crisis of 1836–1848 we must put this preconception aside. At that time—indeed, for most of American history until the Great Depression of the 1930s—the responsibilities and apparatus of federal government were small relative to those of the states. Moreover, it was the actions of state governments, rather than the federal government, that caused a rapid deterioration in relations with the United Kingdom.

    The problem was straightforward. In the 1830s, many American states borrowed heavily from British investors to finance canals, railroads, banks, and other projects. The states could not repay these loans when the economy collapsed unless they established new taxes, which they refused to do. And so many states defaulted. Outraged British investors, lacking any effective remedy in American courts, hurled angry rhetoric instead, and sent lobbyists to state capitals to campaign for repayment of their loans. Tempers rose on both sides of the Atlantic. And state governments were faced with a choice: should they levy new taxes or simply repudiate their debts?

Here was a direct collision between the ideal of political sovereignty and the expectations of the international financial markets. The 1820s and 1830s were a period in which voting rights were expanded significantly, and self-rule was glorified. State governments, responding to these political changes, adopted popular but ill-considered programs for economic development. And now they were being called to account by angry lenders. The question was whether legislators and voters were prepared, as a matter of honor or self-interest, to accept restrictions on their recently won political liberties.

The struggle within state capitals illustrates several of the major themes of this book. It shows how quickly an economic crisis is transformed into a political and social crisis, in which established political alliances are wrenched apart and matters of economic interest are tinged with questions of honor and national pride. It also shows how, in an open economy, domestic and international politics become thoroughly entangled. Indeed, the federal government was almost a bystander in the debate over state debts, one of the hottest issues affecting U.S. international relations during the First Great Depression. And as many American and British observers said at the time, the struggle within state capitals raised a basic question about the balance of liberty and order. Would American states insist on their political autonomy, or bow to the demands of international financial markets? This debate had an effect on the architecture of state governments that is still evident today—a lasting reminder of a time when the United States held a smaller and more vulnerable place in the global economic order.

◆ Defaulting on State Debts

> We must repudiate all the bonds. All morality does
> not consist in keeping faith in dollars and cents.
>
> —*Democratic Expounder* (Marshall, Michigan),
> November 17, 1841

An important consequence of the economic crisis was the complete destruction of the credibility of American state governments in international financial markets. In the few years before the Panic of 1837, state governments borrowed an extraordinary amount of money from investors in Europe. In the span of eighteen months, between July 1841 and December 1842, many defaulted on their loans, and some repudiated their obligations entirely.

To understand why state governments were borrowing so much, it is necessary to challenge the widely held idea that American governments have always hewed to the doctrine of laissez-faire and taken a very restrictive view of their role in guiding economic development. This was not true of state governments before the economic crisis of 1836–1848. In fact, it was the crisis itself that caused state governments to repudiate an activist role.

Before the crisis, there were two ways in which state governments were engaged in economic development. The first was through the construction of internal improvements, or what today we call transportation infrastructure. State governments financed and built roads, canals, and railroads which they considered to be essential to settlement and trade. The second mode of state action, particularly in the South and West, was through state-supported or state-owned banks. Operating with capital that was partly or entirely provided by state government, these banks provided credit to facilitate commerce and support expansion by farmers and plantation owners.

Federal policy—or more precisely, confusion in federal policy—encouraged state action. The federal government had a lukewarm attitude toward support of internal improvements, particularly under Democratic presidencies, primarily because such actions would set a dangerous precedent for intervention in the internal affairs of the southern states. A similar animus toward centralized authority caused President Jackson to move against the Second Bank of the United States. Inaction at the center meant that pressure for governmental support of economic development was directed principally toward state capitals. Even southern Democrats, hostile to the idea of federal action, were open to the idea that state governments should "promote both the general welfare and economic growth." The result was extensive, uncoordinated, and often rivalrous state action.

This behavior by state governments was encouraged by ready access to foreign capital. Borrowing abroad was politically easier than financing through taxation. The spectacular success of the Erie Canal, and the apparently unstoppable boom in real estate, seemed to prove that state loans could be repaid easily with transportation revenues and banking profits. European investors, tantalized by the promise of high returns backed by government guarantees, eagerly purchased state bonds.

Until early 1839, no one had a clear idea of how much state governments were borrowing. It was at that point that the Comptroller of New York, A. C. Flagg, reported on his survey of other state officials. His conservative estimate of the trend was staggering. In the decade running from 1820 to 1830, state governments had borrowed a total of just twenty-six million dollars. In the next five years, new borrowing rose to forty million dollars.

And in the next three years—1836 to 1838—borrowing exceeded one hundred million dollars. In a very short period, American states had accumulated obligations roughly equal to the combined national debt of Russia, Prussia, and the Netherlands.

As the economy teetered in 1839, apprehensions about this mountain of state debt grew. In December 1839 a London bond trader, Alexander Trotter, published a long report warning that many state projects were unlikely to produce enough revenue to support loan repayment: "The time will probably come, and seems now to be approaching, which is to determine whether, in a case of a partial or total failure of the expectations of the projectors of the various schemes on which the states have entered, those states so circumstanced will be willing to uphold their credit by submitting to taxes." Investors were cautioned about the "rapid strides which democratic principles are making in the United States." Most voters, Trotter said, would neglect the "true interests" of their state and refuse to shoulder new taxes.

American and British financiers tried to bolster flagging confidence in state bonds. Encouraged by Nicholas Biddle and Samuel Jaudon, president and London agent of the Bank of the United States, and aided financially by the Barings Bank of London, Massachusetts Senator Daniel Webster made a three-month visit to England in mid-1839. The *New York Herald* predicted that the trip would "have a beneficial effect on the sale of stocks." But Webster also had a personal interest in going to London. He wanted to sell his own investment in fifteen thousand acres of western land, including parcels at the entrance of the new canal which the state of Illinois was building to connect the Illinois River and Lake Michigan—"a point of great centrality," Webster said to Jaudon, that "must inevitably become a most important place."

Webster assured British investors that default "would be an open violation of public faith, which would be followed by the penalty of dishonor and disgrace; a penalty no state would be likely to incur." He also sold almost two hundred thousand dollars of his own property during his visit. However, the market for American securities continued to soften. It was shaken badly in February 1840 when Pennsylvania—regarded as one of the more solid states—missed payments on its loans. There was "surprise and consternation" in London until news arrived on the next steamship that the state had borrowed from American banks to pay its British creditors.

In a final attempt to bolster the market, Barings Bank proposed that the federal government should give investors a guarantee against the default of state bonds. A federal guarantee, Barings said, would assure the continued flow of British capital into the United States. Although Barings' proposal received a friendly reception in the American Whig press, it was savaged by Democrats as a scheme to cover the losses of foreign bankers. The Democrat-controlled Senate passed a resolution condemning calls for the federal assumption of state debt obligations in March 1840.

In July 1841, state finances finally collapsed. The sequence of state defaults began with Michigan's failure to meet its scheduled payment on state debt. This was different than Pennsylvania's delay fifteen months earlier, because it would be years before Michigan would resume payment, and only after investors had been forced to write off a substantial part of the state's obligations. In the next seventeen months, seven other states and one territory (Florida) would follow. By December 1842, one-third of the Union was refusing to meet obligations to overseas lenders.

Michigan, the first to default, was also the newest state in the Union. Admitted in January 1837, the state had a population of 175,000, most of whom had arrived in the territory in the preceding three years. "Michigan fever" was raging in 1836; in that year, more public land was sold to settlers in Michigan than had been sold in the entire country in 1833. Michigan's new constitution explicitly directed the state government to encourage internal improvements and put a duty on the legislature "as soon as may be, to make provision by law for ascertaining the proper objects of improvement in relation to roads, canals, and navigable waters."

The priority for state legislators was to build routes across the lower Michigan peninsula, allowing quick transit from Lake Erie to Lake Michigan. The debate was whether to make the transit by rail or canal, and at what latitude to make the crossing. In March 1837, legislators sidestepped both controversies by authorizing a cross-state canal and three cross-state railroads—in sum, four transits, comprising almost one thousand miles of rail and canal, within a one-hundred-mile band of largely unsettled territory. The estimated cost for the projects was five million dollars: a substantial amount given that the taxable property in the state was valued at only forty-three million dollars. (This estimate of costs proved to be too low, by millions.) However, Michigan's legislators did not intend to finance the improvements through taxes. Following the model of the Erie Canal, they would borrow the whole amount, and rely on canal and railroad revenues to cover the payments.

The timing of Michigan's venture was not good. Panic struck the American financial markets in March 1837, and when Michigan Governor Stevens T. Mason arrived in New York City to negotiate a loan, he found no interested investors. Reports from London and Amsterdam were equally bleak. It was not until June 1838, when the economy began to recover, that

Michigan was able to arrange for the sale of its bonds. It contracted with the Morris Canal and Banking Company, a prominent New Jersey bank led by a cousin of Nicholas Biddle, to act as its agent. Over the next six months the company gave the state 1.3 million dollars that it had raised from investors. At sunrise on July 20, 1838—"a day which will be recollected by the people of Michigan as the proudest that ever happened," according to the *Detroit Journal*—cannon were fired to celebrate the commencement of the cross-state canal.

However, the economic recovery of 1838 was faltering, and in the fall of that year, Governor Mason made a fatal error. The Morris Canal and Banking Company reported that the attitude of British banking houses toward American securities was "very gloomy" and that it was impossible to sell Michigan bonds on the terms set by the state. But Morris Canal itself, in combination with the United States Bank, took a better view of the market, and were prepared to buy all of the remaining 3.7 million dollars in bonds at par. The two banks promised to pay for the bonds by installments over four years. "It became a question," Mason told the Michigan legislature in January 1839, "whether this contract should be accepted, or our works of internal improvement be arrested." In March 1839, Mason took the offer.

Unfortunately, the eastern bankers had misjudged the market. The fragile condition of the United States Bank became clear in October 1839 when it announced that it was no longer capable of redeeming its obligations by payment of specie. Governor Mason sent the state's banking commissioner to Philadelphia to unwind the March contract and retrieve the state's bonds, but it was too late: the bank had already given the bonds to English and Dutch bankers as security for loans. The bank failed in February 1841 without making its payments to the state. The Morris Canal and Banking Company also sold its allotment of state bonds but failed to make payments to Michigan.

By the end of 1840, Michigan was in a predicament. Obviously it did not have the money promised to it by the two banks. Other revenue, mainly receipts from the limited parts of the Central and Southern railroads already completed, had declined sharply. The state had taken steps to reduce spending. The legislature abandoned the canal and northern railroad, and contractors were given state-issued notes or land grants to settle accounts. Nonetheless, the Michigan treasury was empty. When the first payment of interest on the five million dollars of state bonds came due on July 1, 1841, Michigan defaulted. It missed payment again in January 1842.

Within the state, there was mounting hostility toward the idea of honoring debt for which the proceeds had never been received. In February 1842, legislators who favored repayment advanced a resolution renouncing the "doctrine of repudiation" but were outvoted. The House of Representatives promised only that it would satisfy "just demands against the treasury . . . at as early a day as possible." A week later, the legislature declared that Michigan would not honor any bonds for which the state itself had not been paid.

Indiana, Michigan's neighbor, also defaulted in July 1841. It was an older state—admitted to the Union in 1816—with a longer-running interest in internal improvements. When the Erie Canal was completed in 1825, Indiana legislators began planning the Wabash and Erie Canal, which would link the Maumee and Wabash rivers and allow travel from Lake Erie to the Mississippi. Construction on the Wabash and Erie began in 1834.

However, Indianans harbored grander ambitions. In 1836, the state legislature adopted the Mammoth Internal Improvement Act, which proposed to cover the state with a lattice-work of other canals, roads, and railroads. Like the Wisconsin program, which ribboned the lower peninsula with three railroads and a canal, the Mammoth system was the product of legislative logrolling. The bill passed because it contained a project for every significant constituency, all to be commenced at the same time. "What were the scenes enacted in this city of Indianapolis immediately upon the passage of that bill!" an Indiana legislator recalled. "There was a general rejoicing; every pane of glass in the city was illuminated; and the population turned out on the streets as upon a great holiday. Upon the occasion of the exhibition of fireworks in different parts of the State, two or three persons were killed. A sacrificial offering! A few days after this a grand ball was given in honor of the passage of the bill, at which there was music, feasting, and dancing."

The euphoria did not last long. Following the usual path, Indiana financed the Mammoth Act with ten million dollars in bonds. Many were sold to the Morris Canal and Banking Company, which passed them on to the London market. There were allegations of corruption in the placement of the loan—one of the responsible Indiana officials was also a stockholder in Morris Canal, and received a commission from the company—but this was not the only difficulty with the financing arrangements. As in Michigan, Morris Canal had promised to pay the state for the bonds in installments, and when it collapsed, Indiana was still owed over two million dollars.

As state revenues plummeted, Indiana fell into crisis. Nearly all work on the canal and rail projects ground to a halt, and the state began paying contractors with state-issued treasury notes rather than cash. Meanwhile, state legislators temporized on tax increases. Indiana was in better shape than

Michigan, with three times the population and taxable property, but here, too, there was widespread antipathy to tax hikes. In 1839 the legislature actually cut property taxes in half to provide relief to voters. "Our citizens should be favored as much as possible," the newly elected Democratic governor, Samuel Bigger, said in December 1840, "until the pressure of their own debts shall be removed." The legislature was forced to reverse the tax reduction in 1841, but found that taxes were now being paid almost entirely with the state's own treasury notes, which were useless for paying bondholders.

The main device for making payments to bondholders, the legislature decided, would be more borrowing. Unfortunately, the market was not prepared to accept new Indiana bonds for anything near their face value. The Mammoth bonds were trading for sixteen cents on the dollar. Selling new bonds at such a deep discount would have caused the state debt to skyrocket. Indiana chose instead to default on its existing debt.

Governor Bigger insisted that Indiana was not repudiating its obligations to bondholders. There was an important distinction, he said, "between the blameless inability to pay and that fraud which avoids an honest debt." Bigger also reminded Indianans of the corruption that had tainted the placement of the loan and claimed that the state had been "the victim of preconcerted imposition and fraud." And investors were guilty too, Bigger claimed: after all, Indiana could never have borrowed recklessly if credit had not been so easily available.

Like the other states, policy on internal improvements in Maryland was driven by anxiety about the loss of position to neighboring states, as well as the refusal of the legislature to make difficult choices among proposed works within the state. The threat posed by other states was obvious. The Erie Canal had made New York City the main center for inland trade on the eastern seaboard, and the Pennsylvania legislature had responded with rail and canal projects that would link the port of Philadelphia to the Ohio River at Pittsburgh. Some comparable plan was needed to make the Chesapeake Bay a plausible alternative as an eastern entrepôt for inland trade.

The first of two major works supported by the Maryland government was the Chesapeake and Ohio Canal. The plan was to make the Potomac River navigable from its mouth on the Chesapeake Bay to Cumberland, in western Maryland, and then to connect Cumberland to the Ohio River at Pittsburgh. The scheme was not new. The Chesapeake and Ohio Company began laboring on the project in 1828 with capital invested by the federal, Maryland, and Virginia governments. However, the work was more difficult than expected, and by 1834 the company was bankrupt. The Jackson administration was hostile to more aid and the project limped on with a two million dollar loan from the state of Maryland.

Businessmen in Baltimore, further north on the Chesapeake Bay, regarded the canal as a threat to their city's own ambitions as a center of trade. They supported an alternative plan: the construction of a railroad running from the headwaters of the Ohio River eastward to a terminus at Baltimore. The state legislature matched its investment in the canal project with an equally large purchase of stock in the Baltimore and Ohio Railroad Company, which also began construction in 1828. The railroad fared better than the canal but still needed further infusions of capital from state legislators.

In 1836 this policy of equal treatment was taken a step further. The canal company, again facing bankruptcy, appealed for more aid from the Maryland legislature. It was estimated that three million dollars would be needed to complete the first phase of the project to Cumberland. Reluctant to accept the complete loss of their earlier investments, legislators authorized the new financing. But legislative politics demanded that equal assistance should be given to the railroad, along with two million dollars for other public works—a total of eight million dollars in new support.

The initial plan was for the state to sell its own bonds and use the proceeds to buy shares or bonds of the canal and railroad companies. However, the state delegation sent to London, Amsterdam, and Paris in June 1837, scarcely weeks after the initial panic, found no buyers for the state's bonds. Back in Baltimore, the delegation resorted to an alternative plan: they swapped the state's bonds to the canal and railroad companies in exchange for their shares and bonds. Throughout 1838 and 1839 the companies themselves sold the bonds in the United States and Europe, often at substantial discounts. Barings Bank was the main agent for the sale of Maryland bonds. It assured investors that the projects would be profitable and that, in the worst case, Maryland taxpayers would buckle down and accept new taxes.

By 1841, the state of Maryland was fourteen million dollars in debt, with interest obligations of six hundred thousand dollars a year, roughly two-thirds of the whole state budget. The expectation had been that the income from the state's canal and railroad holdings would be large enough to cover these charges, but actual income from those investments in 1841 was only fifty thousand dollars. The shortfall was too massive to be solved by reducing government spending. The state legislature authorized modest property taxes, the first since 1824, but lacked any capacity to collect them. The state borrowed until the market refused to accept any more bonds, and finally defaulted in October 1841. It would not resume payments on its public debt until January 1848.

Arkansas also defaulted in October 1841, the first southern state to do so. Arkansas was admitted to the Union in 1836, shortly after Michigan, and like Michigan it had a constitution that directed the state legislature to play an active role in economic development—this time, by chartering two state-supported banks. The State Bank of Arkansas was the financial agent of the state and had the duty to make loans "in each county, in proportion to representation," while the Real Estate Bank of Arkansas would "promote the great agricultural interests" of the state. The two banks were authorized to raise three million dollars in working funds by selling state-guaranteed bonds.

This was regarded as a riskless proposition. As a legislative committee explained in 1836, the banks were essentially a money machine for the state: "It has been the policy of other States, to procure means from foreign capitalists. . . . It is believed that the State could borrow any desirable amount of capital at an annual charge of five per centum, if not upon better terms. The capital being loaned at eight per centum, being three per centum in favor of the State . . . will produce an accumulation sufficient to redeem the whole in less than twenty years." The President of the Real Estate Bank assured the legislature in 1837 that it would "never be called upon to pay either the principal or interest of these bonds." The bank's assets included mortgages on land that was "the very best in the United States, in a region of the country where the production of cotton must ever make them more valuable."

"The gentlemen who organized this bank," an Arkansas financier said in 1906, "were ignorant of the fact that the banking system had received a shock from the effects of which it did not fully recover for several years." The initial plan had been for the banks to sell their bonds on the London market, but this was not possible in 1837. When conditions improved in 1838, most of the bonds were sold to a New York bank, the North American Trust and Banking Company. By October 1839, the Arkansas banks were already in distress and struggling to pay the first installment of interest on these bonds. Desperate for liquidity, the Real Estate Bank sold most of its remaining bonds to North American Trust at a discount, in violation of state law.

North American Trust re-sold most of its Arkansas bonds to British investors, promoting them as securities "of a very high order . . . having the faith and property of a young, vigorous, and triumphant state." By 1840, however, investors were frustrated by the Arkansas banks' failure to make regular interest payments. By early 1841, the two banks were in default.

(Both were liquidated by the legislature in 1843.) The banks refused to raise funds by moving against their own defaulting mortgagors because the mortgaged property was almost worthless. Attempts to make interest payments with more bonds were rebuffed by bondholders, who turned to the state government instead, demanding that it should honor its guarantee of the debt.

Governor Archibald Yell refused to satisfy the bondholders. A firm Jacksonian, Yell was elected in 1840 on the promise to break the "heartless tyranny" of the banking establishment over the common people. In October 1841, he told bondholders that the state's guarantee was voided because the Arkansas banks had misled the legislature and violated state law. "You mistake the character of the people," Yell wrote to a British banker who had received Real Estate Bank bonds from the North American Trust, "if you flatter yourself that they will calmly submit to be taxed to pay the bonds hypothecated to stocks jobbers, to enable the bank to carry on her speculations without the authority of law and in express violation of her charter." "This doctrine of Yell's," the *Times of London* retorted in January 1842, "goes by the scientific name of repudiation."

Illinois also defaulted in October 1841. The state had already stopped work on the Illinois and Michigan Canal. This was the project that Daniel Webster, selling his own land to investors in London in 1839, had promised would make much of the property so valuable. Illinois also suspended all of its other public works, but this was not enough to avoid default.

The improvement scheme had been substantial. In February 1837, the Illinois legislature authorized the construction of a north-south railroad that would connect at its head to the Illinois and Michigan Canal, as well as a ladder of east-west railroads that would link to the north-south spine. The state was authorized to borrow eight million dollars for the improvements, all of which were to be undertaken simultaneously. This was like Indiana's Mammoth Act, adopted a year earlier. Illinois went a step further, also promising to invest three million dollars in two state banks, sharing Arkansas' hopes of easy profits by borrowing cheaply overseas and lending at home. Governor Joseph Duncan, an opponent of government-run public works and banking, vetoed the whole scheme but was overridden by state legislators.

The panic upset the state's plans for selling its eleven million dollars in bonds. In July 1837 Duncan used the crisis as an argument for repealing the improvements law, but legislators were solidly opposed. ("So here ends, we hope forever, the opposition to our noble system of improvements," declared the Springfield *State Register*. Abraham Lincoln was among the representatives who voted against Duncan's veto and his call for repeal.) Duncan's successor, Thomas Carlin, said privately that he was "clearly convinced . . . of the utter failure of the Internal Improvement System," but he hesitated to challenge legislators openly. In 1838, the legislature authorized another million dollars for public works. State officials labored to obtain loans in New York and London, usually agreeing to accept less than par value for its bonds.

Carlin finally urged the legislature to halt construction in December 1839, and in January 1840 it reluctantly acquiesced. The state was already saddled with ten million dollars of debt and six hundred thousand dollars in annual interest charges—an amount six times the ordinary expenditure of the state. Throughout 1840 and 1841, the state legislature fiddled. It tried to sell state lands, paid contractors with state bonds, and arranged short-term loans in New York and London to cover interest payments. By October 1841, the state had run out of options, and defaulted on its bonds. At public meetings across Illinois there were calls for open repudiation. In his last message to the state legislature in December 1842, Governor Carlin warned creditors that it would be impossible for Illinois to honor its debts: "All the channels of trade are completely obstructed, and the vitality of business seems almost extinct. . . . The products of the country cannot be disposed of for cash at any price. . . . To increase the rate [of taxation] at the present time would be to inflict general embarrassment and distress, and to impose upon the people a burden which they could not possibly endure." Carlin said that it was impossible for the state to make arrangements even for the payment of interest on the state debt. The state's creditors would have to accept that they would never see the return of the full principal on their loans.

The Florida Territory pursued economic development primarily through support of banks. In 1835, the territory authorized a government guarantee for a half million dollars of new borrowing by the Bank of Pensacola, so that the bank itself could buy stock in the newly chartered Alabama, Florida and Georgia Railroad. Between 1833 and 1838 it also authorized the new Union Bank of Florida to raise working capital by selling three million dollars of territorial bonds. The main purpose of the Union Bank was to support the expansion of plantations, and as in other southern states this was regarded as a simple and riskless enterprise. After the crash, a prominent Floridian recalled the logic: "You want to know how it operates? . . . [A] man can mortgage his land or negroes; draw from the bank two-thirds (in money) of their value, which will be reinvested in more land and negroes. One or two crops of cotton will redeem all obligations to the bank; so you see that it is the best thing afloat; a man can just go to sleep and wake up rich."

In June 1838, the president of the Union Bank sailed for Europe to sell the last and largest issue of Florida bonds to investors in London and Amsterdam. It was strongly supported by the Bank of the United States, which assured investors that the Florida bonds were "as solid and desirable a security as any in the market." Daniel Webster vouched for the territorial legislature's authority to guarantee the bonds. The American bankers promised that the property mortgaged by their borrowers was conservatively assessed, and certain to increase in value. "In every way the present bondholders are amply secured," the financial correspondent for London's *Morning Chronicle* concluded in February 1839. "Florida, no doubt, is a very rising and prosperous country."

In fact, the Pensacola and Union banks were badly mismanaged. Appraisals of the value of mortgaged property were vastly inflated. Borrowers themselves often wasted their loans, as a legislative committee observed in 1840: "To become suddenly rich, to become off-hand the proprietor of lands, negroes, houses and equipages . . . was to enjoy in reality the vision of fiction." The Pensacola Bank defaulted in January 1840, while the Union Bank struggled on until January 1842. Then European lenders turned to the territorial government for relief.

But Florida's legislators refused to help. The territorial government that approved the guarantees had consisted solely of a presidentially-appointed governor and a small elected council. In 1838 the council was replaced by a larger and bicameral legislative branch. This change amplified the populist impulse against financiers and also gave legislators a pretext for refusing to honor the guarantees. The territorial government that gave commitments to investors, the new House Judicial Committee explained in 1840, was really an agent of the federal government and not an instrument of the sovereign will of Floridians. Attempts by the territorial government "to act for and in the name of the People of Florida, are usurpations," the committee said. "They can be of no binding obligation." Both houses of the Florida legislature affirmed their stance in February 1842: The territorial legislature was never "invested with authority to pledge the faith of the Territory . . . all pledges of the public faith so granted are null and void."

The most rancorous dispute over state debt came in Mississippi. Foreign investors were still reproving the state for its conduct—and seeking remedies in court over its delinquency—almost a century later. Trouble came to Mississippi because of its support for state banks. In 1830, it chartered the Planters' Bank, and purchased most of its equity with two million dollars in government bonds. In January 1837, the Mississippi legislature authorized a second institution, the Union Bank, to be supported by up to fifteen million dollars of state bonds. The Mississippi constitution barred the state from issuing debt unless the next legislature, to be elected in November 1837, adopted the same bill. The panic, which interceded in March 1837, did not cause voters or legislators to pause, and in January 1838 the bill was approved a second time.

The new Union Bank sold five million dollars in Mississippi bonds to the Bank of the United States in August 1838. When news of the sale was received in the state capital, "the multitudes were wild with a delirium of joy. Bonfires and illuminations were the order of the day, or rather of the night, while great guns, the rattle of drums, the blare of trumpets and the shouts of the frantic multitude made night absolutely hideous." Most of the bonds were sent to Europe, either sold to investors or given as security for loans to the Bank of the United States.

In Mississippi, the public's mood was susceptible to violent swings. Only a few years earlier, the same multitude that now celebrated the Bank of the United States' purchase of Mississippi bonds had voted overwhelmingly for Andrew Jackson, the bank's nemesis. In late 1839, the public's mood swung again, as the Mississippi economy and the two state-supported banks collapsed. Governor Alexander McNutt responded to the changing political atmosphere. McNutt had signed the bill establishing the Union Bank in 1838, as well as the bonds sold to the United States Bank. By the end of 1839, however, McNutt was attacking the Planters' and Union Banks for malfeasance, demanding their liquidation and warning that the state might not honor its guarantee on bonds sold by the banks.

McNutt's campaign against the banks escalated over the next year. In March 1840, he issued a proclamation declaring that the state would not recognize bonds sold by the Union Bank, on the grounds that the bank had violated terms of sale set by the state. In January 1841, McNutt restated his commitment to repudiation. The people of Mississippi, he said, would never elect representatives who were prepared to levy the taxes required for repayment. And in any case the dispute on repayment was really one between the Mississippi banks and their foreign creditors, such as the Rothschilds. The Union Bank, McNutt told legislators,

> has hypothecated these bonds, and borrowed money upon them of the Baron Rothschild; the blood of Judas and Shylock flows in his veins, and he unites the qualities of both his countrymen. He has mortgages upon the silver mines of Mexico and the quicksilver mines of Spain. He has advanced money to the Sublime Porte [the Ottoman

Empire] and taken as security a mortgage upon the holy city of Jeru-salem and the sepulchre of our Savior. It is for this people to say whether he shall have a mortgage upon our cotton fields and make serfs of our children. Let the baron exact his pound of flesh of Mr. Jaudon and the Bank of the United States, and let the latter "institu-tion of our country" exact the same of the Mississippi Union Bank. The honor, justice and dignity of the people of this state will not suf-fer them to interfere in the banker's war!

The dispute came to a head in May 1841, when both Mississippi banks ceased payments on their bonds. In July, McNutt told the Dutch investment house Hope and Company that the state "will never pay the five millions of dollars of state bonds issued in June 1838, or any portion of the interest due." McNutt approached the state elections of November 1841 as a referendum on repudia-tion and was rewarded with a legislature that was overwhelming hostile to repayment. In late March 1842, the packet ship *Oxford* brought news to Liv-erpool that Mississippi legislators had voted for repudiation five weeks earlier.

Pennsyvlania's default was the most spectacular. By the end of 1841, the state had accumulated a debt of forty million dollars, far more than any other state. Interest costs alone were almost two million dollars a year, while total state revenues were less than one million dollars.

Before the crisis, Pennsylvania had been absorbed in a fatal competition with New York State for the control of inland trade. The success of the Erie Canal, historian Avery Bishop wrote in 1907, "necessitated the commence-ment of similar works in other states for the sake of their own self-preservation." Between 1826 and 1835, the state borrowed twenty-five million dollars to build a network of roads, railroads, and canals that would run from the port of Philadelphia in the east to the Ohio River at Pittsburgh. But New York had geographical advantages that "made defeat inevitable to Pennsylvania from the beginning." Even in 1835 the state was not earning enough from its improvements to cover its interest charges.

The Panic of 1837 disrupted state finances and caused a brief delay in in-terest payments, and in 1838 the state treasurer warned the state government that Pennsylvania was again running into deficit, but legislators continued to borrow. President Jackson's battle with the Bank of the United States cre-ated a perverse incentive for state legislators to do so; when the bank sought a state charter to replace its expiring federal charter in 1836, Pennsylvania state legislators seized the opportunity to extract a promise from the bank that it would buy an additional six million dollars in state debt.

Earlier than many other states, Pennsylvania tried to raise taxes to cover its mounting interest costs. By 1842, total tax revenue was almost twice what it had been in 1835, but this was still far too little to restore the state's finances. The state also resorted to other tactics to avoid collapse. In April 1840, legislators compelled banks with state charters to lend three million dollars to cover the state's deficit, but the banks themselves were near collapse. A year later, the state treasury began paying many of its creditors with small-denomination relief notes, which were often returned to the state for payment of taxes and did little to improve its ability to pay overseas lenders.

By the end of 1841 the state was desperate. Philadelphia merchant Sidney Fisher wrote in his diary in early December that "the doctrine of repudiating state debts is spreading rapidly, is spoken of openly and boldly defended by many presses and leading politicians." A public meeting at the Philadelphia courthouse later that month passed resolutions denying that Pennsylvanians were under any "moral, legal or political obligation" to repay the "so-called state debt." In early 1842, the state met interest payments by scavenging from the assets of the Bank of the United States, which had collapsed in January. By August 1842, the treasury had nothing but its own relief notes, and Pennsylvania finally defaulted. "The substance of our State is swallowed up," wrote a correspondent to the local newspaper in Smethport, Pennsylvania, "and repudiation stares us in the face."

Louisiana was the last of the nine defaulters and, after Pennsylvania, the largest, with twenty-four million dollars in outstanding debt by 1842. Most of this was sold in Europe to support three state-chartered financial institutions: the Consolidated Association of Planters, Citizens Bank, and Union Bank. The banks were hard hit by the economic crisis but as late as November 1842 the *Times of London* commended all three for "struggling on in the payment of their dividends." Governor Andre Roman, the *Times* reported, had promised lenders that they would "never have to repent their confidence in the state."

The *Times*' commendations were misplaced. The newspaper did not know that the state government had forced the Consolidated Association and Citizens Bank into liquidation in October 1842. In January 1843, British investors learned that neither bank was capable of continuing payments on its bonds. The Union Bank staggered on until the middle of 1844, when it notified the Barings Bank that it could not repay the principal on bonds coming due in November of that year. British investment banks took the position that the state government ought to have honored the obligations on state bonds immediately after the banks defaulted. Louisiana legislators disagreed, insisting that the investors' first recourse had to be against the assets of the liquidated banks. The legislature then compromised the prospects of recovery from the banks by allowing plantation owners to redeem mortgaged properties on preferential terms. Governor Roman tried to reassure bondholders. "Louisiana will not shrink from the call that will be made upon her," he said in January 1843. "The purity of her honor must be maintained." In London, however, Barings Bank told investors that the state's actions were "disastrous" for holders of its bonds.

No other states defaulted after January 1843, but the damage that was wrought in the preceding year and a half was extraordinary. In 1839, Daniel Webster had assured British investors that no state would risk the "penalty of honor and disgrace" by defaulting on their bonds. Now nine governments, responsible for two-thirds of all the American government debt in private hands, were routinely missing interest payments, attempting to sidestep creditors, or flatly repudiating their obligations. Across the Atlantic, investors were outraged.

◄ Disgrace in Europe

Yankee Doodle borrows cash,
Yankee Doodle spends it,
And then he snaps his fingers at
The jolly flat who lends it.
Ask him when he means to pay,
He shews no hesitation,
But says he'll take the shortest way,
And that's repudiation!
   (*Literary Gazette*, London, January 1845)

As American state governments tumbled, the mood in the world's financial center soured. "I was in England when the intelligence was received, and the shock was felt, of your failing to pay the dividends on your bonds," James Hamilton told a crowd of Mississippians in 1843. Hamilton, a former governor of South Carolina, had been in London as an agent trying to sell bonds for the new republic of Texas. No one would buy them. The capital was seized was panic. Hamilton was accosted by an aged British pensioner who had put his savings into Mississippi bonds. "I assured this veteran, with a gush of sensibility equal to his, that every farthing of the Mississippi bonds, interest and principal, would be paid, *as sure as there is a God in Heaven.*" Hamilton was mistaken; Mississippi would never pay.

"Great bitterness of feeling is very naturally felt" by the mass of investors in American bonds, the American minister to London, Edward Everett, reported. "Many have by their investments lost all the earning of active life and the fund on which they relied for their support in old age. That this feeling should find vent in the popular press is natural." The *Times of London* reported that "[a]n American gentleman of the most unblemished character was refused admission to one of the largest clubs in London on the sole grounds that he belonged to a republic that did not fulfill its engagements. . . . It is not too much to expect that the example will be followed in other establishments. No distinction, as we understand, has been made as to the State to which an individual may belong, but the whole United States are looked upon as equally tarnished."

That defaulting states would be barred from financial markets was to be expected. But non-defaulting states—and the U.S. government itself—were alarmed by the prospect that they, too, would be denied loans. Shortly after the first defaults, President John Tyler delivered his first annual address to Congress, urging overseas investors to recognize that each state was autonomous, and "should in no degree affect the credit of the rest. . . . [T]he foreign capitalist will have no just cause to experience alarm as to all other State stocks because any one or more of the States may neglect to provide with punctuality the means of redeeming their engagements."

The address, quickly reproduced in London, had no effect. Joshua Bates, head of American trade at Barings Bank in London, confided to the bank's agent in Boston in December 1841 that British investors "in their anguish are crying out against *all* American stocks, and we shall never be able to sell any more. . . . I have come to the conclusion (which had best be concealed perhaps) not to sell any more American stocks. . . . I believe it will only be wasting our time to have anything to do with them." Barings' principal competitor, the House of Rothschild, was even cooler on American securities. Anthony de Rothschild, a partner in the London branch of the family's bank, urged his brothers to sell all U.S. investments. "Let us get rid of that blasted country—as much as we profitably can. It is the most blasted & the most stinking country in the world—& we must get rid of it."

Some Americans believed that British investors were deliberately imposing a rule of collective responsibility on American governments; that is, consciously punishing non-defaulting states for failing to bring defaulters into line. Everett also believed this was the case, and there was evidence to support his view. Shortly after Florida's threat of repudiation, a provincial newspaper in the United Kingdom warned other state governments to "remonstrate and prevent the perpetration of such an act of injustice. . . . We may just throw out to them a hint, that capitalists on this side of the water will not readily distinguish between such States as have supported their credit faithfully and honestly, and those which have repudiated their bonds." The *Times* agreed. "It is quite in vain for the honest portion of the United States to assert that because they have had no direct share in the guilt and turpitude of the repudiating States, therefore they are to stand clear. They are citizens of a country in which such acts are committed with impunity."

The more likely explanation for the behavior of British investors was ignorance of the distinctions among American bonds, or indiscriminate frustration about defaults. Barings' American agent, Thomas Ward, urged Bates in London to emphasize the disparities between state governments, but Bates replied that it was futile. "At a distance people do not see the local differences and argue that as Mississippi may repudiate her debt so may Massachusetts, and so the credit of all the States and that of the United States is involved in one common ruin." A British diplomat agreed that most investors simply did not discriminate between states: "There is necessarily much ignorance but there has not been, nor can there well be, any conspiracy." Even the *Times* conceded that most investors "never make themselves acquainted even with the broad distinction between the different states of a federal government. . . . This was very ignorant certainly, but still a very common ignorance among persons purchasing foreign securities."

The lowest point was reached in 1842, as the U.S. Government attempted to sell its own bonds to European investors. The federal government's record was impeccable: it paid off the debt accumulated from the War on 1812 on schedule, and had been largely debt-free for almost a decade. The American and British press viewed the sale of federal bonds as a test of the market. "Until that scrip pass current in Europe, the utmost exertions of the citizens of the United States to regain their credit will be ineffectual." It was "a trifling loan," said Edward Everett, but no one "in this great metropolis of the financial world" would subscribe to it. American agents went "a-begging through all of the exchanges of Europe" and eventually gave up in despair. The Rothschilds were especially cutting. "You may tell your government," said James de Rothschild, head of the family's Paris bank, "that you have seen the man who is at the head of the finances of Europe, and that he has told you that you cannot borrow a dollar, not a dollar." The version of this story which circulated in London was even more emasculating. "They cannot go to war," Rothschild was reported as saying, "because they cannot borrow a dollar."

What began as a problem of credit soon blossomed into a matter of high culture. The British romantic poet William Wordsworth led the way. In December 1839, Wordsworth confided to an acquaintance in Philadelphia, Henry Reed, that "several of my most valued friends are likely to suffer from the monetary derangements in America." Wordsworth's own family had invested in Mississippi bonds. "There is an opinion pretty current among discerning persons in England that, Republics are not to be trusted in money concerns, I suppose because the sense of honour is more obtuse, the responsibility being divided among so many. For my own part, I have as little or less faith in absolute despotisms, except that they are more easily convinced to keep their credit by holding to their engagements." Wordsworth was already drafting the poem *Men of the Western World*, soon published as one of his "sonnets dedicated to liberty and order":

> Men of the Western World! in Fate's dark book
> Whence these opprobrious leaves of dire portent?
> Think ye your British Ancestors forsook
> Their native Land, for outrage provident;
> From unsubmissive necks the bridle shook
> To give, in their Descendants, freer vent
> And wider range to passions turbulent,
> To mutual tyranny a deadlier look?

The poem appeared in New York in April 1842, hailed in a literary journal as "the free utterance of a painful emotion, the solicitude that liberty may be degenerating here into licentiousness." What Wordsworth said mattered to the American literati—Ralph Waldo Emerson had recently written that "the fame of Wordsworth is a leading fact" in American literature—and many understood him as a poet who was sympathetic to the American project of democratic rule. Consequently, *Men of the Western World* was a jolt which many struggled to accommodate. The Boston poet Park Benjamin penned a sympathetic reply:

> If Pennsylvania refuse to pay,
> If Indiana name a distant day,
> If Illinois and Mississippi act
> Like brave defaulters, and confess the fact,
> If Maryland suspend on either shore

Her legal payments twenty years or more—
Not they, except in name, the judgment bear,
Though on their brows the slavish brand they wear.
We are accused, *our* fame and honor lost,
And they are swindlers at the country's cost.

This echo did little to staunch Wordsworth's frustration. In 1843 he wrote to Seargent Prentiss, a Whig politician in Vicksburg, to lament his family's losses on Mississippi bonds:

> The personal interest which I attach to it is not solely on account of the sum of money that is at stake, as the condition of the proprietors, a brother and sister of Mrs. Wordsworth, are advanced in life, and one has a large family; and both, owing to various misfortunes, are in very narrow circumstances. The other owner is my only daughter, who is married to a gentleman that has been very unfortunate also. . . . Nothing remains for the suffering parties but patience and hope. . . . In matters like this, time, as in the case of my relatives, is of infinite importance, and it is to be feared that the two individuals, for whose comfort payment is of the most consequence, may both be in their graves before it comes.

To Reed in Philadelphia, Wordsworth wrote that he was especially disturbed by the default of Pennsylvania:

> Theirs is one of the richest countries in the world, so that the whole resolves itself into a question of morality. An immense majority of the educated inhabitants desire nothing more earnestly than that the debt should be provided for, but their opinion is overborne by the sordid mass, which will always have a considerable influence over a community whose institutions are so democratic as yours are. . . . I mourn . . . for the disgrace brought upon, and the discouragement given to, the self-government of nations by the spread of the suffrage among the people.

Wordsworth, now the Poet Laureate of the United Kingdom, penned another sonnet on order and liberty in 1845, this time with more pungency. In *To the Pennsylvanians*, Wordsworth wrote:

> All who revere the memory of Penn
> Grieve for the land on whose wild woods his name
> Was fondly grafted with a virtuous aim,
> Renounced, abandoned by degenerate Men

For state-dishonour black as ever came
To upper air from Mammon's loathsome den.

By 1845, though, this was mild stuff. Another pillar of the Anglo-American literary establishment had already made a more sensational assault on the Pennsylvanians. Sydney Smith was an Anglican cleric, a canon of St. Paul's Cathedral in London, a Whig reformer, and one of the most highly regarded writers of his age—"the wittiest man in England," according to one American journal. Smith was also the unfortunate owner of Pennsylvania bonds, and in April 1843 he published a petition to the U.S. Congress for relief against "an act of bad faith which has no parallel, and no excuse." Americans, said Smith, has emboldened the enemies of democratic institutions across Europe:

> The Americans, who boast to have improved the institutions of the old world, have at least equalled its crimes. A great nation has been guilty of a fraud as enormous as ever disgraced the worst king of the most degraded nation of Europe. . . . Sad is the spectacle, to see you rejected in every state in Europe, as a nation with whom no contract can be made, because none can be kept; unstable in the very foundations of social life, deficient in the elements of good faith, men who prefer any load of infamy, however great, to any pressure of taxation, however light.

Smith's petition was reprinted across the United Kingdom. A prominent Tory magazine needled the reformer for losses suffered at the hands of America's "swindling democrats." *Punch* published a poem ostensibly submitted by a correspondent in Larceny Lane, Pennsylvania:

> There's Sydney Smith, poor foolish man,
> Keeps up a ugly feelin',
> And tries to prove our matchless plan
> Of borrowing is—stealing!
> But let the critter rant away,
> We'll try again to-morrow;
> Whoever dreamt we meant to pay
> The money that we borrow?

Smith's petition was also taken up *forte* by the U.S. press. American opinion was riven. Many in the commercial and intellectual elite who cherished their cross-Atlantic ties were stung by Smith's criticism but prepared to admit its truth. It helped that Smith was regarded as a sympathetic liberal—an "old protector of the country," as an American magazine said. Smith, the *Bankers' Magazine* concluded, had delivered "a most severe, though just castigation." But the popular press was generally hostile. In August 1843, the *Times'* American correspondent reported that Smith's petition had produced "violent ebullitions of anger and spit from those journals who, in order to live, must cater to the passions of the multitude."

Smith's American critics made three ripostes. The first was that he had falsely slandered democratic institutions; after all, other states were still punctual in their payments, and there were many examples of monarchies that had defaulted before. The second reply was that Smith was simply a disgruntled gambler. British bonds were more secure but paid half the return; Smith must have known that "the income [from Pennsylvania bonds] was greater because the security was less." In truth, though—and this was the third retort—Smith probably had not been careful in investigating precisely where he was sending his money. Indeed, it seemed clear that many Britons simply did not understand how the American federation worked. They appeared to regard it just as they viewed their own government: unitary and highly centralized. Although Tyler had made it clear in his 1841 address that the federal government was not responsible for state debts, Smith, who was better informed than most, still directed his petition to Congress rather than the state capitol in Harrisburg.

The same error was made by Smith's compatriots, who imagined that Americans in non-defaulting states might feel a sense of shame or have the power to induce defaulters to change their ways. "I find myself involved, with the rest of the nation, in indiscriminate censure," wrote a Bostonian, "because some of those who unite with us under the same government, in Pennsylvania and Mississippi, are delinquent. Still, I have no power to act there . . . [It cannot] be expected . . . that one state will pay for another, or that the nation will pay for either. When the money was lent, these distinctions were clearly perceived, and a higher rate of interest was required and allowed." An American correspondent to the *Times* agreed that the federal government could not "interfere with the states in any effectual way. . . . As to national disgrace, [Americans] do not understand it, for theirs is no national feeling; and a citizen of the State of New York considers it no reflection upon *his* State, that Mississippi repudiates."

Smith wrote privately in late 1843 that "[m]y bomb has fallen very successfully in America, and the list of killed and wounded is extensive. I have several quires of paper sent me every day, calling me monster, thief, atheist, deist, etc." In public, he continued to throw grenades. "I never meet a Pennsylvanian at a London dinner without feeling a disposition to seize and divide him," Smith wrote in the *Times* in November 1843:

> to appropriate his pocket handkerchief to the orphan, and to comfort the widow with his silver watch, Broadway rings, and the London Guide which he always carries in his pockets. How such a man can set himself down at an English table without feeling that he owes 2*l*. or 3*l*. to every man in company, I am at a loss to conceive. . . . The truth is, that the eyes of all capitalists are averted from the United States. The finest commercial understandings will have nothing to do with them. . . . Great and high minded merchants loathe the name of America.

Furthermore, Smith said, the United States had crippled its foreign policy through improvidence. "The warlike power of every country depends on their Three per Cents. . . . In the whole habitable globe [the Americans] cannot borrow a guinea, and they cannot draw the sword, because they have not the money to buy it." Smith clearly had heard of James de Rothschild's taunt to the Americans a year earlier.

Now the controversy escalated into a matter of high diplomacy. The following week, the *Times* published a retort from Duff Green, a "rough, coarse, red-faced" American working as an informal emissary of President Tyler in London. Green accused Smith of stirring up sentiment for war against the United States and warned that Americans would be ready for conflict, even if they were unable to borrow in Europe: "It may be true that the Governments of Europe cannot go to war without having made arrangements with the wealthy bankers in question; but such is not the condition of America." Smith dismissed Green's warning. "What do I mean by war?" he replied. "Not irruptions into Canada—not the embodying of militia into Oregon, but a long tedious maritime war of four or five years' duration. Is any man so foolish to suppose that Rothschild has nothing to do with such wars as these?"

The jibes were being reprinted throughout the United Kingdom and the United States, and finally Edward Everett, the U.S. minister in London, visited Smith to conciliate. Everett, Smith said, almost persuaded him that Pennsylvania would honor its debts—but it did not matter, because Smith had already sold the bonds at a sixty percent discount. And so his war of words ended.

Another British writer carried on. Throughout 1843, Charles Dickens had been publishing installments of his novel, *Martin Chuzzlewit*. The story was already being reprinted in the United States. In the September 1843 installment Chuzzlewit, a budding architect, is defrauded by an American agent promoting a city very much like Cairo, Illinois, which Dickens had visited the previous year. The two look at a lithograph of the fictional city of Eden:

> A flourishing city! An architectural city! There were banks, churches, cathedrals, marketplaces, factories, hotels, stories, mansions, wharves; an exchange, a theatre; public buildings of all kinds, down to the office of the *Eden Stinger*, a daily journal; all faithfully depicted in the view before them.
>
> "Dear me! It's really a most important place!" cried Martin.
> "Oh! It's very important," observed the agent.
> "But, I'm afraid," said Martin, glancing again at the Public Buildings, "that there's nothing left for me to do."
> "Well, it ain't all built," replied the agent. "Not quite."

Martin Chuzzlewit, the *Democratic Review* reported in October, was "spiteful and malignant . . . [and] thoroughly vile." But Dickens was not done. In early December 1843, only days after Smith's final sally against Duff Green, Dickens published his novella, *A Christmas Carol*. There is a passage in the story in which Ebenezer Scrooge reaches for a phrase to describe a worthless commercial note. It is, Scrooge decides, "a mere United States' security."

Shackling the States

> A burnt child dreads the fire, and this state has been most dreadfully burned.
>
> —John Pettit, delegate to the Indiana state constitutional convention, November 1850

By the end of the 1840s, most of the defaulting states had resumed payments to bondholders. Pennsylvania resumed in 1845, Illinois in 1846, Indiana in 1847, and Maryland in 1848. Louisiana resumed on some of its debt in 1844, although it never acknowledged bonds issued to support the state's plantation banks. Michigan eventually honored bonds for which it had received the full principal, but insisted that holders of other bonds would be paid only thirty cents on the dollar. Two states—Mississippi and Florida—remained solid for repudiation. Arkansas was practically in this camp as well: it did not acknowledge liability for most of its debts until after the Civil War.

European investors were warming again to American government debt, although still with a significant premium for the risk of default. Pennsylvania 5 percent bonds that had been trading in London for thirty-five cents on the dollar in September 1842 were trading at eighty cents in June 1849, while Indiana bonds were up from twenty cents on the dollar in June 1842 to fifty-two cents in March 1849. The federal government had no difficulty in selling bonds in Europe to finance its war with Mexico in 1846–1848. The diehard repudiators were still locked out of the financial markets, however.

The states' resumption of payments played an important part in reviving the market for American government securities in London and Amsterdam, but the states took additional steps that had the effect of restoring the confidence of overseas investors. In fact, the economic crisis had triggered large changes to the organization of state governments, and not only among the defaulting states. This was reflected in constitutional and statute law, and also in political culture, as Americans drew lessons from the economic debacle. Foreign investors themselves played an important role in producing this painful but substantial transformation in the American political order.

One aspect of this transformation was a shift in the tax policy of state governments. Before the crisis, states drew most of their revenue from their investments in banks and improvements, land sales, and fees charged to businesses. Throughout the country there was "sullen resentment" against property taxes, and as a consequence most state governments avoided them whenever possible. In Maryland, where there was an "overwhelming prejudice against direct taxation," property taxes had been eliminated in 1824. An editorialist observed in 1843 that citizens of Maryland "had hardly known what a state tax was, for a generation." Nor was Maryland alone: many other states lacked property taxes as well. During the boom, the widely-held ideal of a "tax-free system of state finance" seemed within reach.

In most states, the crisis broke the back of public resistance to the systematic application of property taxes. Typically, legislators began with modest tax levies, and only increased them when revenues provided inadequate to service debts. This hesitation frustrated bondholders, but even critics of the defaulting states conceded that it was probably unavoidable: "Both parties have found, when in power, what, indeed, any party must always find, that there are always great obstacles in the way of a large and sudden increase in taxes. No people will submit to it willingly. It requires time to convince them of its necessity and policy; some time is necessary to enable them to accommodate their affairs and resources to the new demand."

Eventually, though, a comprehensive shift in state financing did occur. In both defaulting and non-defaulting states, the burden of property taxation and the share of state revenue drawn from property taxes increased markedly in the 1840s. The ideal of a "tax-free system" was shattered.

The levying of new property taxes had implications for the organization of government. The actual amount of property tax revenue in Maryland between 1841 and 1844 was only half of what Maryland legislators had expected, largely because of the state's inability to enforce the law. The task of collecting taxes belonged to city and county governments, which had been given more autonomy over the preceding two decades. Few local officials pursued the job aggressively, and several counties refused to collect property taxes at all. Public meetings were held across the state to protest taxes that "oppress the people beyond their power of endurance." In 1844, legislators reluctantly increased the state government's own power to collect revenues. The governor was authorized to appoint his collectors in delinquent counties, and penalties for resisting taxes were raised. Collections improved, although protests against "ruinous taxation" continued across the state.

Enthusiasm for state-driven projects to spur economic development also waned. At first this was a pragmatic response to budget crises rather than a careful reappraisal of the government's role. States such as Illinois and Indiana quickly stopped work on canals and railroads because they could not afford to pay contractors, while Louisiana and Arkansas forced state-supported banks into liquidation to curtail further losses. Some governments also privatized state-owned projects in an attempt to settle their debts, although few could be sold for significant amounts. Michigan exchanged two of its railroads for disputed state bonds. Pennsylvania also sold its stocks in canals, railroads, turnpikes, and banks, recovering one-third of what those investments had cost.

Maryland offered to satisfy bondholders by giving them the state's interest in canals and railroads, but the bondholders refused. However, the very fact that Maryland was prepared to divest its holdings showed that the rage for state-supported enterprises was fading. In 1851, Maryland's constitution was revised to prohibit state involvement "in the construction of works of internal improvement, or in any enterprise which shall involve the faith or credit of the State." The reformed Maryland constitution also prohibited the borrowing of money unless state legislators authorized new taxes that were adequate to repay the debt. Five other defaulting states also adopted new constitutional debt limitations. Indiana, with the most extreme restriction, proscribed borrowing entirely except in case of war. The other state constitutions imposed a dollar limit on debt, established special procedures to approve borrowing, and often banned state guarantees for debt issued by private corporations.

It was not just the defaulting states that adopted such restrictions. Eight other states that had been part of the Union at the onset of the economic crisis adopted limitations on borrowing, and two more came close to adoption. "I wish to see State Government brought back to its simple and appropriate functions," said a delegate to Ohio's constitutional reform convention in June 1850, "to protect the rights of the citizen, without governing too much." Seven of the eight states that joined the Union between 1845 and 1861 had restrictions as well (Florida, an unrepentant repudiator, was the exception). Two of the new states—Oregon and Kansas—prohibited state involvement in internal improvements entirely, just as Maryland had. By the eve of the Civil War, popular understandings about the role of state government had undergone a radical shift. The economic crisis put an end to the internal improvements movement and produced a new set of limitations that "made *laissez-faire* the law of the land."

What induced state legislatures to make such fundamental changes? Aggrieved lenders sometimes can go to court to force borrowers to meet their obligations; however, this option was not available to lenders who held the bonds of American state governments. They were blocked by the doctrine of sovereign immunity: the principle, as Chief Justice Roger Taney later explained, that a sovereign government "cannot be sued in its own courts . . . without its consent or permission."

Daniel Webster had warned the Barings Bank in 1839 that it was usually impossible to go to state courts to force payment on bonds. Only two states—Mississippi and Arkansas—actually permitted suits in state courts against the government, and even in these states the remedy was limited. In Mississippi, judges were popularly elected and seemed unlikely to be friendly to creditors, while in Arkansas a case could be initiated only if bondholders put their bonds in the custody of state officials, which no bondholder was prepared to do.

The situation seemed to be a little better under federal law. Article III of the U.S. Constitution purported to give federal courts the jurisdiction to hear cases involving disputes "between a state and citizens of another state" and also "between a state . . . and foreign states, citizens, or subjects." However, the Eleventh Amendment of the Constitution prohibited federal courts from hearing cases against states that were brought by "citizens of another state, or by citizens or subjects of any foreign state." The two constitutional provisions were obviously contradictory. As Chief Justice John Marshall explained in an 1821 Supreme Court case, this was largely because state governments, heavily indebted after the Revolutionary War, had reacted fiercely when creditors began turning to federal courts after the adoption of the Constitution in 1787. The very purpose of the Eleventh Amendment, ratified in 1795, was to block lawsuits against states by debt holders in federal courts.

In July 1843, Nicholas Biddle, by now separated from the defunct Bank of the United States, publicly suggested a way by which investors might get around the doctrine of sovereign immunity, which relied on a crucial distinction in wording between Article III and the Eleventh Amendment. Article III acknowledged that federal courts could hear disputes between two states or between a U.S. and foreign state, while the Eleventh Amendment only precluded suits brought by *citizens* of other states or foreign states. It would be possible, Biddle said, for another government to acquire bonds from its citizens and then pursue a case in U.S. federal courts on their behalf. If the bondholding government won its case, federal authorities would be compelled to take action to enforce the judgment against the defaulting state by seizing and selling state property. Biddle argued that there was precedent for such federal intrusion: in 1794, President Washington had sent an armed force of thirteen thousand men into Pennsylvania to enforce the collection of federal taxes.

Biddle's plan was never executed. Among bondholders he had little credibility. As the *Times of London* said, he was "notorious for his management of a concern which ruined nearly everybody who came in contact with it." Whether federal judges would have tolerated the argument is also in doubt. As Chief Justice Marshall said in 1821, the Eleventh Amendment did not explicitly preclude suits between governments because "there was not much reason to fear that foreign or sister States would be creditors to any considerable amount." Furthermore, federal courts might have regarded Biddle's plan as a connivance which defeated the purpose of the Eleventh Amendment, and they might have balked at the prospect of rendering a judgment that could require the deployment of a mass of federal troops to enforce it.

There was a final complication with Biddle's scheme: the British government would not intercede on the bondholders' behalf. In 1841, the House of Rothschild asked the British Foreign Secretary, Lord Palmerston, for help in its dispute with the state of Mississippi. Palmerston refused, saying that British subjects who buy foreign securities "do so at their own risk and must abide the consequences." Palmerston's successor, Lord Aberdeen, was equally recalcitrant, telling investors in March 1843 that the British government had "no concern with the securities in question and no power to compel payment of the sums required." It was government policy, Aberdeen later explained, "to abstain from taking up as international questions the complaints made by British subjects against foreign governments which have failed to make good their engagements."

Embassies, like courts, provided little relief to angry creditors. American diplomats were sympathetic but unhelpful. The reality was that the Tyler administration did not regard the defaults as a responsibility of the federal government. This was made clear when a group of nine hundred investors petitioned Edward Everett, the U.S. minister in London, in February 1843. "By far the larger portion of us are persons in the middle ranks of life," the petitioners said, "officers on half-pay, superannuated clerks, retired tradesmen living on small means, aged spinsters, widows and orphans." They wanted only "simple justice," and asked Everett to put their petition before President Tyler and the U.S. Congress. Everett believed that the states were bound as a matter of honor to pay their debts, but said that he had no authority to convey the petition in his official capacity. "The general government is not a party in the contracts of the separate states," Everett said. "The subject of the memorial does not fall directly within the president's province."

A group of sixty Dutch investors petitioned Christopher Hughes, the American chargé d'affaires in The Hague, three months later. Among them was Adriaan van der Hoop, head of the powerful merchant bank Hope and Company, which had helped to finance the Louisiana Purchase forty years earlier. Hughes "received the deputation with the greatest politeness . . . [and] said pretty explicitly that he was himself convinced of the justice of the complaints contained in the petition." Even so, Dutch investors were rebuffed even more firmly than their British counterparts. Hughes was instructed by the State Department to tell the bondholders "in the most formal and explicit terms, as the clear and unalterable determination of the general government, that it will not consent to be held, in any wise, or to any extent, responsible for any default, actual or eventual."

Lacking recourse to courts or the help of federal authorities, foreign lenders were driven to campaign for repayment directly in state capitals. "The sole resort," a Boston lawyer advised investors in 1842, "is a supplication to their justice or an appeal to their fears." Overseas bondholders were not alone; there were also domestic bondholders, and many American businessmen, who shared a desire to reverse policy in the defaulting states. But a remarkable feature of the campaign against default is the extent to which it was shaped and financed by foreign investors. Default impelled them to become active participants in domestic American politics.

In Pennsylvania and Maryland, the bondholders' campaign was led by

Thomas Ward, Barings' agent in the United States, and financed by a common fund established by many of the major London banks. Ward and his deputies negotiated directly with state legislators and paid thousands of dollars in campaign contributions and gifts to friendly politicians. Ward's principals in London professed "instinctive horror" of some tactics used in the two states and reminded Ward that the London banks could not be seen interfering openly in state politics. Ward promised discretion. But he also reminded London of the "humiliating fact" that American politicians sometimes "must be bought and paid for even in the highest of causes."

The bondholders' campaign extended beyond the statehouse. A Barings historian says that Ward also launched "what might be termed a campaign of propaganda." Prominent authors were recruited to write anonymous articles in favor of repayment and newspaper editors were paid to publish them. One contributor was the writer Alexander Everett, brother of the U.S. minister in London; another was Benjamin Curtis, a Boston attorney who was appointed to the Supreme Court in 1851. "We wrote Maryland right," said John Latrobe, a Baltimore lawyer hired to oversee the bondholders' efforts in that state. The rhetoric was high-flown. The choice confronting citizens of defaulting states, Curtis said, was one between honor and disgrace.

Ward even enlisted clergymen to make the bondholders' case. One ally was Francis Wayland, a Baptist pastor and president of Brown University, and a leading economist of the antebellum period. Wayland blended prudential and moral arguments. His 1841 textbook on political economy warned that governments which lost market confidence could borrow only at "a ruinous premium" if at all. From the pulpit, Wayland declaimed that each citizen of a defaulting state would be marked with the "stain of dishonesty" unless he had done all he could to "reassure the world that the national honor is inviolate."

In Michigan, the spokesman for the major London banks was Charles Butler, a New York lawyer with good connections to businessmen in the northwest. Butler arrived in Detroit in January 1843 and immediately began two months of close negotiations with the governor and legislators. "Very, very busy days," Butler wrote to his wife. "It is a regular lobbying campaign." Butler reprised his role as mediator in Indianapolis in the winter of 1845, where he was

> incessantly engaged, night and day, and hardly find time to eat or sleep. . . . I cannot give you any ideas of my labor here. They are greater than anything I have ever before undertaken and more various. I have

to talk with and see the members, have to take care of the printers, . . . attend on committees, keep in with the Whigs and Democrats, counsel and advise both parties, and be all things, to all men.
Above all, I have to keep my temper, which is the hardest work of all.

A devout Christian, Butler anguished about lobbying on Sundays, because
"repudiation and Sabbath breaking ought to go together as national sins."
Faith tinged Butler's entire approach to mediation. He eschewed some tactics used by Ward in the eastern states and even avoided direct appeals to the
state's material interests. He conceded that some politicians would be brought
to the negotiating table because the Michigan economy would wither without access to capital. However, Butler relied mainly on the "paramount
moral obligation involved . . . if the moral feeling be only rightly stimu-
lated, the pecuniary relief will soon and cheerfully follow. It is not the mere
question of dollars and cents." Butler was helped by a young Indianapolis
preacher, Henry Ward Beecher, who warned parishioners against the vice
of default: "When a whole people, united by a common disregard of justice, conspire to defraud public creditors, and States vie with States in an
infamous repudiation of just debts . . . then the confusion of domestic affairs has bred a fiend, before whose flight honor fades away. . . . Need we
ask the causes of growing dishonesty among the young, and the increasing
trustworthiness of all agents, when States are seen clothed with the panoply
of dishonesty?"

The bondholders' agents were exhausted by their experience in negotiating with defaulting governments. In correspondence, they affirmed the
dismal view of democratic politics already prevalent in the financial houses
of London. In Michigan, Butler found the legislature "an impulsive body . . .
[with] queer notions of matters of things. . . . It is *all* a lottery." Indiana was
no better, with "heartless, unprincipled politicians" determined to bury
great matters of state in "the most trifling local politics." The bondholders'
agents in Illinois were even more severe. "You are little aware of the corrupt
morals of the low, stealthy, base intriguing politician of the west," they
wrote to London in 1845. "The demagogues . . . are numerous; and like the
carrion crow set watching for a dead carcass. You must expect from them
every species of intrigue, falsehood, and baseness." Another letter to Barings
Bank explained:

> Among public men the great art seems to be to learn what means may
> be most effectually employed to sway the public mind and gain over it
> the ascendancy which will produce favorable results at the polls. False-
> hood, misrepresentation, erroneous reasoning and all such appliances

designed to rule public opinion have in such a country a greater chance of success than in most places because of the thousand obstacles in the way of pursuing and correcting what is false and erroneous.

These grim appraisals were probably premature. Even as they were written, many state governments were reluctantly preparing to levy new taxes and recognize outstanding debts. Moreover, the nation was on the cusp of a remarkable shift in elite and mass opinion about the role of state governments. This was evidenced in the debates within the constitutional conventions that produced such a wave of restrictions on state power between 1846 and the onset of the Civil War.

Only a decade earlier, most Americans had shared the Jacksonian belief in the capacity of democratic polities to govern themselves well. "We have an abiding faith in the virtue, intelligence, and full capacity for self-government, of the great mass of the people," stated the *Democratic Review* in 1838. "We are opposed to all self-styled 'wholesome restraints' on the free action of the popular opinion and will." The drive within constitutional conventions to establish limits on borrowing and state involvement in internal improvements was widely and accurately understood as a challenge to this belief. In Indiana, a critic of restriction complained that it was "palpably subversive of the self-evident principle that the will of the majority must govern." A Kentucky delegate protested that his state convention was posed to undermine "the great representative principle in our system of government." "The people are the source of power," said an Iowa delegate, "[i]f the people send foolish men here to represent them and make laws for them, who will spend their money for them unnecessarily, it is their business, not ours. We are not sent here to guard and watch the people, and place a check upon them and prevent them from acting for their own good."

By the end of the 1840s, this had become a minority view. The overwhelming weight of opinion ran in favor of constraining popular sovereignty. Within constitutional conventions, the very idea that state action could bring prosperity was now widely disparaged. "Every man dreamed that he was about to reach a new *El Dorado*," recalled a Maryland delegate in 1851. "These works were to bring upon us a flood tide of prosperity and advancement, which was to know no ebb." An Iowa delegate also remembered "these dreams of wealth, this Utopian doctrine, that we can legislate and vote ourselves rich." But these dreams had, in most cases, yielded nothing but half-completed projects and crushing taxation. "De Witt Clinton has been overrated," said an Ohio reformer in 1851, remembering the New York governor who championed the Erie Canal, the model for so many other improvement schemes. "There was the choice of two modes of improving the country, and De Witt Clinton chose the worst, and mankind are prone, in many cases, to follow example without inquiry or investigation."

The crisis had shaken the public's confidence in the capacity of state legislatures to make sound policy. In addition, there was now a widespread tendency to portray the legislative process itself as tainted by self-interest and corruption. In a sense, this unburdened voters themselves of responsibility. "It was not the people who committed the blunder, but the Legislature, and the Legislature was governed by a system of log-rolling," an Indiana delegate said in 1851. Improvement laws like Indiana's Mammoth bill of 1836 were routinely condemned as the products of "bargain and intrigue, of log-rolling and corruption." A New Yorker dismissed his own state's improvement plans as "a union of selfish purposes and improper objects." Legislators had connived so that all would receive some benefit for their own constituents, and then used their "seducing wiles" to persuade the public at large that the works would finance themselves.

Other reformers doubted that voters could be exculpated so easily. "The people called and demanded," said another New Yorker, "and the legislature yielded and obeyed." A former Kentucky legislator recalled that he had attempted to argue against a substantial improvement program, but "such was its popularity that the people were almost ready to hiss me from the lobby." A delegate to Michigan's 1851 convention said that "public sentiment demanded" the state's ill-fated five million dollar loan, "and the Executive and the Legislature had not courage to resist. It was what had grown up as public opinion, which in a few months would have been discarded."

A new sensibility about the irrationality of public opinion pervaded the conventions. Another former Kentucky legislator remembered that the country had been "inflamed with the internal improvement fever." The state's populace, agreed one of his colleagues, "were swept along with the current." Voters had been "tempted into flattering speculations," said a Maryland delegate, and then had turned wholesale against them. Public sentiment was volatile and could turn again: "Have we learned no lessons on that point?"

Arguments about the inviolability of popular sovereignty were invariably countered by a pragmatic appeal to the hard lessons of the economic crisis. Constitutional restrictions might be "shackles upon the power of the legislature," a Kentucky delegate conceded, but they were demanded by experience. Critics of Ohio's restriction tried to stigmatize it as an "iron rule." "I care not what you call it," responded another Ohioan. "If its insertion will promote the prosperity and happiness of the people of Ohio, I will vote for it." Constitutional restrictions were "the sheet anchor of the security of our State," agreed an Iowa delegate, "and we ought to cling to it."

"Self-government is no longer a theory, it has been demonstrated," said John Pettit, an Indiana delegate who had served in both the state and federal legislatures. And time had shown its frailties: "We have not that perfect confidence in ourselves . . . and we take our cool and calm moments to bind and restrict ourselves—to protect ourselves against the sudden and dangerous impulses of passion and prejudice. . . . It is to prevent the evils resulting from excitement and passion, that we take our calmer and quieter hours to bind ourselves and our fellow man."

Many states had, indeed, bound themselves in the years following the crisis. This was manifest in constitutional reforms and new tax policies, but a more important alteration, which both caused these changes and made them durable, could be seen in political culture. Humiliated by the experience of default or near-default, pressed by angry lenders, and oppressed by new taxes, states had abandoned the internal improvements movement. They had replaced their sunny views about popular sovereignty with a darker conception of the rationality of political processes. The economic crisis seemed to have taught them a lesson: that liberty without discipline was a formula for ruin.

CHAPTER 3

The Federal Government's Crisis

The panic in spring 1837 that marked the onset of the First Great Depression was rooted in a collapse of trust among financiers and businessmen. As in all panics, no one knew who was solvent and who was not. "A general distrust and want of confidence exists in reference to everybody," the American political economist Condy Raguet observed about early nineteenth-century panics. "Everybody is afraid to trust his neighbor." As a consequence, business ceases entirely. Trust holds the machinery of commerce together: when it dissipates, the machinery succumbs to disintegrating forces and flies apart.

Something similar could be said about the effect of the First Great Depression on national politics. The United States, on the eve of the Panic of 1837, was a fragile compound, composed of sections and classes with sharply divergent views about the role of central government in taxing, spending, and regulating. The negotiation of these differences was difficult even in the best of times, and sometimes punctuated by moments of resistance to central authority so fierce that they stoked fears about the survival of the union. Holding the nation together under such circumstances was a test of statesmanship. It required constant bargaining and the careful cultivation of good will, and often resulted in legislative pacts or mutual understandings that, as Frederick Jackson Turner would later observe, bore "a striking resemblance . . . [to] treaties between European nations in diplomatic congresses."

Prosperity made it easier to negotiate such pacts. Sharing gains from a growing economy was a less difficult task than dividing losses from a shrinking economy. When times were hard, it became more difficult to keep the peace in Washington. A process similar to the collapse of trust among businessmen was repeated, this time in the sphere of politics. Good will collapsed, old animosities were revived, and delicately wrought truces were unwound. As a result, the depression years became a long, painful test of the federal government's capacity to manage sectional and class conflict. The nadir came in 1842, five full years after the panic, and coincidentally at the same time that Charles Dickens visited the capital. His dire impression of Washington was harsh but not exceptional. The machinery of government, like the machinery of finance and commerce, was flying apart. The preservation of political order, of the barest capacity to make and enforce law, had become a paramount concern.

If there was one subject on which a majority of Americans agreed, at least at a high level of abstraction, it was the desirability of territorial and commercial expansion. The United States was understood to be a rising nation, blessed by Providence, with a special claim on much of the North American continent, and an aspiration to serve all of the world's markets. Even during the First Great Depression, and sometimes because of it, it was possible to stoke expansionist fervor among Americans. But here was another instance in which American statesmen were required to manage carefully the impulses of a sovereign people. The country's main rival for territory and markets—Britain—was also a critical trading partner, the principal source of its overseas investment, and a military superpower, with a navy and army which the financially distressed American government could not hope to match. Foreign policy in these years involved the delicate and sometimes distasteful reconciliation of soaring popular ambitions with hard realities about the distribution of power within the international order.

❧ Gridlock in Washington

> We observe . . . a great nation agitated upon its whole surface, and at its lowest depths, like the ocean when convulsed by some terrible storm.
>
> —Henry Clay, June 1840

Martin Van Buren entered office in 1837 thinking that his presidency would be concerned mainly with the restoration of calm and cohesion within the

Democratic party after the strife of the Jackson years. It was soon obvious that events would upset his plans. The economy tottered throughout March and April, and Van Buren wrestled inconclusively with the question of what, if anything, the federal government could do to provide relief. New York merchants sent a delegation of sixty to Washington to petition for withdrawal of the Specie Circular, on the theory that this would relieve pressure in the markets. Van Buren wavered privately but decided to stand by Jackson's policy.

Staying the course ceased to be a tenable policy after the collapse of the New York banks on May 10. Within days the Whig opposition was lambasting the administration for its inaction. On May 15, Van Buren called on Congress to convene a special session in September. But what Van Buren would recommend to Congress at that time remained unclear. The *Washington Globe*, the administration's newspaper, reflected the confusion within the White House. Throughout May its editorial line was "remarkably erratic and inconsistent," a rival Whig paper complained, "as if for the express purpose of baffling conjecture . . . and taking no little pains . . . to contradict, or mystify, or explain away, in each day's publication, what had been put forth the day before." Some of the president's supporters became frustrated with the drift in policy. There was a need to act with "unshaken firmness," Pennsylvania Senator James Buchanan warned Van Buren in June. "The next step which we take as a party in relation to the public revenue, if it should not be successful, will prostrate us and re-establish the Bank of the United States."

Van Buren was not only preoccupied with the public impression of White House vacillation. The federal government also faced a budget crisis. All of its revenue was deposited in state banks, most of which had suspended, and some of which had failed. The federal government "has not a dollar of gold or silver in the world!" the Whig *National Intelligencer* exclaimed in May. The *USS Independence*, scheduled to carry Van Buren's ambassador to St. Petersburg, was reported to be marooned in Boston harbor, lacking the coin needed to pay its crew. By December, the Treasury had a nominal balance of thirty-four million dollars but only one million dollars actually available to finance government operations. One-fifth of the total balance was probably lost because of bank defaults.

By midsummer, Van Buren had settled on a plan: the creation of a new method for managing federal money called the Independent Treasury system, or sometimes the sub-Treasury system. If approved by Congress, federal revenue would be collected, held, and disbursed by the federal government's own agents, rather than state banks. To use the phrase that would dominate federal politics for the next decade, there would be a complete "divorce of bank and state." As the Independent Treasury withdrew its funds from state banks, it would also surrender its last instrument for influencing their behavior.

The Independent Treasury plan had been refined by William Gouge, a Treasury official who was a ferocious critic of paper money. The federal deposits had spurred reckless lending by state banks, Gouge argued, while the utility of deposits as a lever for controlling those banks was overrated. The only certain way of imposing a check on overbanking was by completely withdrawing federal support. In any case, Gouge thought that the federal government had no business regulating banks that were created under state law. "It is the duty of the government and people of each state," Gouge said, "to bring the institutions of that state into order." Gouge urged a hard line on reform. If the Independent Treasury plan was not adopted quickly, the country would face disaster "greater than would be occasioned by a contest with the most powerful nation on the globe." "The war between specie and paper money is now fairly begun," Gouge warned in June 1837. "There may be many traitors, and many trimmers, but there can be no neutrals."

Van Buren, like Gouge, was a states' rights man, and therefore reluctant to extend federal regulatory powers over the banks. And the Independent Treasury system also seemed to offer better security for federal funds. The boldness of Gouge's plan also had political advantages. It would play on popular revulsion over bank abuses and suspension. It would also help to shift blame for the Panic of 1837 away from the government and onto the banks. Bankers had abused their power, and therefore they would be ostracized: that was the essential message of the Independent Treasury scheme. "Our opponents charge the difficulties . . . to the government," said Connecticut Senator John Niles, an ally of the President, in July 1837. "We charge them to the banks. This is the issue between us."

A casual observer might have expected that Congress would act quickly on the Divorce Bill, as the Independent Treasury plan was soon known. The Democrats had majorities in both chambers of Congress: 35 of 52 Senate seats, and 128 of 242 House seats. But the impression of party dominance was misleading, especially in the House. While radical Democrats— sometimes known as Locofocos—supported the bill, many conservative Democrats who supported state banks were repulsed by it. It was "warfare against the banking institutions of the country," said Senator Nathaniel Tallmadge, a New York Democrat, "no more or less than a war upon the whole banking system."

The opposition Whigs were also firmly opposed to divorce. Some saw the crisis as an opportunity to campaign for the revival of the federal Bank of the United States. The bank itself, continuing its business under a charter from the state of Pennsylvania, was working assiduously to build resistance against the Independent Treasury and support for its own restoration. There was "an opportunity of making a political movement," the bank's president, Nicholas Biddle, said in private correspondence. "A coup d'état worth trying." But it was wholly implausible that Democrats, conservative or radical, would betray Jackson by restoring the bank.

"The present prospect may thus be briefly summed up," wrote a correspondent for London's *Morning Chronicle* on September 16, when the special session was only twelve days old. "The sub-treasury system will not, in all probability, be carried into effect, because a majority of the Lower House appears averse to the scheme. And a national bank cannot be carried into effect for a similar reason. Congress, in such a case, being unable to act efficiently upon either of the two schemes that have excited so much attention, will . . . be compelled to adjourn without providing any substantial remedy." As expected, Congress adjourned in mid-October, with the Divorce Bill laid over until the session scheduled to begin in December. Businessmen on both sides of the Atlantic hesitated as they waited for clearer signs of what Congress might do. "Our trade is lamentably dull," a Liverpool newspaper reported in November 1837. "Until the result of the sub-Treasury policy shall have been exactly ascertained, and generally known, we can anticipate no change, and shall venture no opinion. In trembling expectation we must 'bide our time.'"

In December, Van Buren again appealed to Congress for quick action on his proposed legislation. "It is obviously important . . . to the business and quiet of the country that the whole subject should in some way be settled and regulated by law . . . at your present session." But the dynamics which precluded action in September operated with even greater intensity in December, creating a debilitating uncertainty about the direction of federal policy. "The effect of this bill upon the money-market is operating very injuriously," the *Times of London*'s American correspondent wrote in February 1838. "It has again created a kind of panic, and that panic, be it more or less, will be kept up until the question is in some way settled. . . . This state of uncertainty as to what character the bill will ultimately assume is as injurious as the bill itself could be if passed in its worst form."

Wrestling over the Divorce Bill continued for months. With Congress' adjournment looming, a final attempt was made in June 1838 to win a majority for the bill in the House of Representatives, again without success. Two weeks later, Congress adjourned until December. Many businessmen were happy to have a few months free of anxiety over what Congress might do. "The breaking up of Congress has given great relief to the mercantile community," a New York newspaper reported in August 1838. "So long as sub-Treasury schemes were suspended over the public there was no confidence. The result being known there is a better feeling manifested." That feeling was shared across the Atlantic. Finally, the *Times of London* told its readers, there was an end to "the uncertainty and discouragement resulting from the . . . apprehended measures of the Government."

Over a year had passed since the panic. Van Buren had gambled on bold action and lost, producing nothing more than political contention and business frustration. His administration had also been absent from the negotiations among state banks about the date on which they would resume honoring demands for payment of specie. This delicate problem of coordination was eventually resolved by the summer of 1838. The economy appeared to be regaining its feet, and this weakened enthusiasm for a reprise of the Independent Treasury debate in the next session of Congress.

It was also clear that the issue had not played well for the Democrats in many state elections, merely splitting the party and unifying the business community behind the Whigs. "I beg you in the most emphatic terms to close up this most vexatious question now," a party leader in Virginia wrote to Van Buren in July. "The schism in our party may produce the direst results." Whigs swept the state in that year's elections.

Van Buren repeated his case for the Independent Treasury system in his December address to Congress, but in such tepid language that his opponents assumed the idea was dead. Van Buren had "abandon[ed] all idea of proceeding with the sub-Treasury scheme," London's *Era* newspaper reported that month. American bankers were already responding with more liberal lending, "and the result is a considerable extension of orders [to the United Kingdom] for manufactured goods . . . [and] a renewed stimulus to many branches of trade." New York's Whig Governor William Seward told state legislators in January 1839 that "[t]he gloom which had spread over our country [since 1837] has passed away, and the enterprise of our people is resuming. . . . The angry passions which availed themselves of that disastrous time . . . to disseminate pernicious opinions, and to bring forward measures of rash and intemperate legislation, have subsided."

The revival of good feeling ended with the second wave of bank suspensions in the fall of 1839. Once again, at the start of Congress' next session in December, Van Buren made an appeal for the Independent Treasury plan. The presidential election was only a year away, and Van Buren needed a clear platform, just as he had in the summer of 1837. The air of crisis played in his favor. So, too, did the discrediting of the Bank of the United States after its collapse in October, and the defeat of a handful of conservative Democrats in mid-term elections.

Still, the passage of the Independent Treasury Act was a close-run thing. A correspondent for London's *Examiner* wrote in late June 1840 that it was "very doubtful" that the Independent Treasury bill would ever become law. The bill had received early and solid approval in the Senate, as it had in previous years, but an affirmative vote in the House did not come until July 3, 1840, only days before Congress' adjournment. Van Buren delayed signing the bill so that it would become law on July 4, 1840. The law was like "a second Declaration of Independence," said Representative Edmund Burke, a New Hampshire Democrat. "[It is] one of the most important measures in its results and consequences, that was ever presented for the action of a democratic assembly."

In New York City, twenty thousand Democrats gathered in Battery Park's beer garden for a rowdy celebration of the new law. A sixty-four gun salute—one for each year since independence—was fired to celebrate the nation's freedom from "the money power, the aristocracy of the rich against the poor." "The scene was highly exhilarating," one correspondent said. "The sun shone brightly, the wind blew freshly; flags were flying, children crying, men whorrahing, drums beating, cannons roaring, petticoats flying hither and thither, glasses rattling, but brandy punch and gin slings swilling, then more cheers, and guns and drums and trumpets! Oh, it was what one honest, but hard spoken Locofoco called it, 'a hell of a day for the democracy!'"

Later, a "great meeting of merchants" in New York City congratulated the Van Buren administration for finally settling the controversy over the Independent Treasury. "Having greatly suffered in our mercantile pursuits, from the long contest of parties on that question . . . we cannot deem it consistent with the interests of any department of business to renew a conflict so injurious to the stability of commerce." But other businessmen were less sanguine about the future. The *Times of London*'s American correspondent anticipated in August 1840 that timid investors would "hoard their funds" until they could see how the new law was likely to affect trade. Others thought that the law would be repealed if the Whigs won the November election. "Everything on this side of the Atlantic continues as much depressed as ever," a merchant wrote from New York to England in late summer. "There is great want of confidence, and people seem to have made up their minds to do nothing until the presidential question shall have been settled one way or the other. The Sub-Treasury Bill has passed . . . and as yet has made no difference in the existing state of things. . . . I look upon the re-election of Mr. Van Buren as very doubtful."

The country was already embroiled in the wildest presidential race in its history. The Whigs had finally built a solid party machine and acquired from the Democrats an understanding of mass electioneering. ("They have at last learned from defeat the art of victory," lamented the *Democratic Review*. "We have taught them how to conquer us!") They confronted a Democratic party exhausted by years of incumbency. "Little Van," as the Whigs called him, did not have the charisma of Andrew Jackson. He was, as the Whig campaign song said, a "used up man."

He was also known as Martin Van Ruin, overseer of a devastated economy. Unemployment, falling prices, debased currency, collapsed banks—all of this had happened on Van Buren's watch, and an angry public would not allow him to escape the blame for it. Whigs assailed the Independent Treasury law, which the Democrats made the main plank of their campaign. A Whig journal warned that it would reduce American workers to "the degradation . . . which still oppresses the laboring classes in the old world." At the same time, the party avoided clear but potentially divisive statements about their own policies, and allowed despair to grind away at Democratic support. Van Buren, it was said, cared little about the hardship that had fallen on the country. American workmen "almost perish for lack of bread," complained Whig Representative Charles Ogle, while the president dined on gold plate in "his marble palace, amid luxurious appliances, with well-paid salary."

The country braced for violence as Election Day drew near. Two years earlier, in Pennsylvania, tensions between Whigs and Democrats ran so high that Governor Joseph Ritner appealed to Van Buren for federal troops to restore order. (Van Buren refused, and Ritner called out the militia instead.) "The greatest excitement prevails, men's minds are wrought up to a state of frenzy," wrote the Whig merchant Philip Hone on the day before the 1840 vote in New York City. "A gang of several thousand Locofoco ruffians paraded through the streets last night with clubs, and assaulted and drove off several of the Whig processions. The police seem to be afraid to oppose the majesty of Democracy."

The next day, a thousand of New York's Locofocos assaulted a Whig headquarters on Canal Street, shattering all of its windows. In a Locofoco riot in Baltimore, "bricks flew like hail, and a number of shots were fired." In Cincinnati, a small Whig mob had the upper hand, attacking the offices of a Democratic newspaper. Philadelphia's mayor was one of several people injured in a futile attempt to stop a Locofoco charge on the city's Whig headquarters. From Lockport, Illinois, there were reports of "a row of such a serious nature as to call for the militia, who fired upon the rioters, and three Irishmen were shot dead."

The Whigs had anticipated that the dire economic conditions would boost voter turnout. "We have many recruits in our ranks from the pressure of the times," Harrison had said in February 1840. But the sheer mass of voters that arrived at the polls in November was still surprising. It is estimated that 80 percent of adult white males voted in the election of 1840, a turnout never before seen in the United States. In the previous three elections—including the election of 1828, which brought Andrew Jackson to power—turnout averaged only about 57 percent. The 1828 election has been described as a hinge point in American history, "a mighty democratic uprising," because Jackson was buoyed by the support of men no longer bound by property restrictions on voting. (In 1824, only 27 percent of adult white males had cast a ballot.) But it was not until 1840 that most Americans who acquired the right to vote through these franchise reforms actually exercised it. Economic distress breathed life into voting rights. Almost 40 percent of ballots in 1840 were cast by first-time voters.

By mid-November it was clear that Van Buren had been soundly defeated. "General Harrison will be our next President, if he lives until the fourth of March next," said the *Hudson River Chronicle* on November 10. "Nothing but death can prevent this glorious result." The Democrats' control over the House of Representatives and Senate was broken as well.

With the election over, hope for a final resolution of the Independent Treasury controversy was again revived. "However the question be settled," the *Philadelphia Ledger* said as votes were being counted,

> the result will be confidence in the certainty of business. . . . During the last two years . . . the whole country has been agitated by the Presidential election. . . . The result being uncertain, some have been afraid to engage in new enterprises; others, already engaged, have been afraid to prosecute their business with due vigor; and others, terrified by apprehended results, or perplexed by uncertainties, have retired from business. . . . Who can calculate the loss of productive industry, and the moral degradation which this contest has produced? . . . But the contest is now at an end, and whatever be the end, the country will be relieved from a great evil. . . . [T]he country may congratulate itself upon the settlement.

The *Ledger* thought it likely that the Whigs would simply reconcile themselves to the Independent Treasury, recognizing that there was no support
in the country for the restoration of the Bank of the United States. The
newspaper was not alone in its view. "The Independent Treasury Bill has
now passed into the law of the land," said the *Democratic Review*, "beyond
the probable reach of serious danger to its permanent establishment."

Henry Clay had other ideas. Within a month he introduced a resolution
in the Senate calling for repeal of the Independent Treasury law, saying that
the election was tantamount to a referendum that came down squarely
against its continuance. Clay perceived the opportunity to revive a national
bank. Harrison, he believed, was pliable, and could be persuaded to accept
a bank bill if the new Whig majorities in Congress endorsed it. Clay regarded himself as the true "mayor of the palace," one critic said.

Harrison, aged and frail, caught pneumonia after delivering a long inaugural address in bad weather and died in early April 1841. Vice President
John Tyler acceded to the highest office and seemed at first to be as accom-
modating as Harrison had promised to be. He, too, regarded the 1840 election as a vote against the Independent Treasury. But Tyler also acknowledged
that the American public had supported Jackson when he opposed the re-
chartering of the Bank of the United States in 1832, and that the subse-
quent practice of keeping federal funds in state banks had been broadly
condemned as well. "What is now to be regarded as the judgment of the
American people on this whole subject I have no accurate means of determining," Tyler told the new Congress in July 1841, inviting it to propose a
solution to the quandary.

In fact, Tyler had firmer opinions on the subject than he suggested publicly. Like Clay, he was opposed to the Independent Treasury, which he
thought gave the president too much control over the management of federal money. But Tyler was also opposed to a revival of the Bank of the
United States. He considered the bank to be unconstitutional, and twenty
years earlier had railed against its "long catalogue of crime." Furthermore,
Tyler had endorsed Jackson's 1832 veto of the bank's charter. In truth he was
scarcely a Whig at all. Tyler joined the party after a falling out with Jackson
in 1832, and was added to the 1840 ticket in a cynical effort to attract Southern voters. He was, as many Whigs called him, the Accidental President.

The Whigs were about to fracture even more violently than did the
Democrats under Van Buren. In the first week of August, Congress sent
Tyler two bills. The first repealed the Independent Treasury Act of 1840.
Tyler signed it into law on August 13. The second bill established a new
Fiscal Bank of the United States, with most of the powers of the old

national bank. The Constitution allows ten days for the president to veto legislation, and Washington sat in "anxious suspense" as it waited for Tyler's decision. On August 16, Tyler vetoed the bill. Whigs in Congress were outraged. That night a drunken mob shouting "Huzza for Clay!" protested at the White House with blunderbusses, drums, and trumpets. "The President and his friends prepared to meet them with such weapons as were on hand," Tyler's son recalled. "But the crowd repaired to a neighboring hill, where they burnt the President in effigy." Where there was not anger, there was simple confusion. The old law had been overturned but nothing adopted in its place. "We are not yet sure what system of treasury policy now actually exists," the Washington correspondent of the *Farmers' Register* reported on August 18. "We are on the eve of most important political changes, if not of party revolution. . . . Most important events *must* soon occur, though no one yet may foresee what will be the great result."

In Washington, moderate Whigs attempted to bridge the rift between Tyler and the party caucus. But Tyler sent confused signals about the terms on which he would sign a bill, and hardliners in Congress continued to push for more than Tyler could accept. A second bill to establish a bank—now called the Fiscal Corporation of the United States—was passed on September 3. Tyler returned a second veto on September 9.

All pretense of unity between the president and the Whig majority in Congress now evaporated. On September 11, all of Tyler's Cabinet resigned—except Daniel Webster, who remained as Secretary of State. Two days later, as the twenty-seventh Congress finished its first session, fifty members of the Whig caucus announced that they no longer regarded Tyler as their party leader. Effigies of Tyler were hung across the country. In Albany, New York, his likeness was strung from the flagstaff of the Whig headquarters, with a sign that read "Tyler the Traitor." After a day it was "cut down, drawn, and quartered, after the regular old fashion." Meanwhile, the Democratic press assaulted Whigs at both ends of Pennsylvania Avenue. "They possess an overwhelming majority in Congress," observed an opposition newspaper in Plattsburgh, New York, on the eve of the legislature's adjournment. "And yet scarcely a single measure has been carried through. . . . [The Independent Treasury] has been repealed, and what has been gained by so doing? . . . Is not everything thrown into confusion worse confounded? Is not trade suffering from the wicked movements of these mad and reckless politicians?"

Tyler stumbled forward with a new Cabinet. When Congress reconvened in December 1841 he proposed another model for a limited national bank, now called the Exchequer Board, but Whigs in Congress were in no mood for reconciliation. "There is no longer the shadow of a hope" for passage of new banking legislation, the *Times of London* reported in early 1842. Whig fratricide combined with the conventional inter-party rivalry to create a toxic atmosphere on Capitol Hill. Disgust with the "confusion and tumult" in the House pervaded the popular press. The *Baltimore Clipper* asked whether members of Congress "can really possess American hearts— there being, apparently, so total an indifference to the interests of the country. . . . [M]easures of the greatest importance are all contemptuously passed over with neglect, that members may employ themselves in paltry disputes about questions of order, or indulge in vile political harangues. . . . [T]hey are doing more to bring republican institutions into disrepute, than could be effected by all the monarchical writers of Europe."

The gridlock in Washington had the unexpected effect of finally assuring some stability in federal policy on its relationship with state banks. Perversely, the policy that was now locked in place was one that had been established by Jackson following the removal of deposits from the United States Bank in 1835, and subsequently condemned by both Democrats and Whigs alike: an "unlegalized system" that relied mainly on state banks as custodians of federal funds.

This Jacksonian policy persisted for three years, until the political order in Washington was completely overturned. Repulsed by the gridlock in Washington, voters fled the Whigs in mid-term elections, and the party lost its majority in the House of Representatives. But Democratic representatives who gathered in Washington in 1843 still confronted a Whig majority in the Senate, and a president who threatened to veto any bill that restored the Independent Treasury. Not until March 1845—with Democrats controlling the House and Senate, and a Democratic President, James Polk, settled in the White House—was it again possible to contemplate reform.

"As long as these folks are sitting in Washington we don't know from one day to another what's to take place and we are kept in constant excitement," a New York stockbroker complained in early 1846. But the new Democratic phalanx in Washington was less fractious than the Whigs had been. Polk signed legislation reestablishing the Independent Treasury in August 1846. This time the reform would stick: the Independent Treasury remained in place until it was supplanted by the Federal Reserve System in 1913.

The final votes in Congress proceeded on strict party lines. Still, the debate was less rancorous than it had been during Van Buren's presidency. Polk's administration was more pragmatic than Van Buren's. In August 1846 the United States was at war with Mexico, and it needed loans from American financiers to pay for its troops on the Rio Grande. The Whig press mocked Polk's Treasury Secretary, Robert Walker, as he appealed to Wall Street for aid:

> [The Polk Administration] rode into power on the cry of "Divorce of Bank and State" . . . [and is] now exerting all of its financial science and address to induce the banks or bankers to lend that same Government several millions of dollars. If you were to read only some of the organs of this Executive, you would suppose that a virtuous abhorrence of all banks, or dealings with banks, was the ruling idea of the "powers that be," and the next you hear of Secretary Walker is round among the banks, cap in hand and smile on brow, modestly asking these "corrupt" and "soulless" monopolies [for] five or six millions . . . to be disbursed in New Orleans, Texas, and scattered broadcast over the rugged steps of Mexico.

Polk had already approved conciliatory measures, such as a law that allowed merchants to defer the payment of duties on warehoused imports. This, British newspapers reported, "had a very favorable effect upon prices of fancy stocks, and upon commercial matters generally." Later, Walker made clear his willingness to support financial markets by buying bonds with government gold on favorable terms, even if the new Independent Treasury law had to be bent to do it. By "loosening the screws a little," the *Milwaukee Sentinel* said, Walker "afforded some relief to the business circles in New York." "Mr. Walker has become what Mr. Nicholas Biddle was alleged to be," said the *New York Tribune*: "[He is] the Money King. He can make money 'tight' or 'easy' by raising his finger. . . . Our business men would go to wreck, only he won't let him." A formal divorce might have been finalized, but even Democrats were not averse to friendly cohabitation between bank and state.

A decade had lapsed since Van Buren first proposed the Independent Treasury plan. In the intervening years, both Democrats and Whigs had made the case for bold reform, and warned of disaster otherwise. Neither faction had got its way, and neither proved right in its prophesies of disaster. The economy had rebounded. Insolvent banks were swept away; many states adopted stricter banking laws; and banks themselves followed more conservative practices. Other factors, some of the most important of which lay far beyond American shores, also encouraged a resumption of trade.

This did not mean that the federal stalemate was benign. For a decade the federal government largely absented itself from any role in repairing the financial system—even the soft role of persuasion and coordination among state governments and banks, which would have been acceptable to many Democrats who opposed the restoration of a national bank. Economic distress produced polarization between and within both major parties. The result was almost entirely negative: ten years of bile and rancor, political instability, and business uncertainty.

❧ The Fraying National Compact

> The union of the country is factitious, and is becoming less real every day. Every day the difference between the North and South is becoming more prominent and apparent. . . . Such a Union is one of interest merely, a paper bond, to be torne asunder by a burst of passion or to be deliberately undone whenever interest demands it.
>
> —Sidney George Fisher, April 1844

In the years following the Panic of 1837, Washington was seized not only with the question about where federal revenues should be put for safekeeping, but also with the related and larger question of taxing and spending. This was a subject that provoked sectional differences so intense in the early 1830s that they seemed to threaten the union itself. By the end of Jackson's presidency, Congress had negotiated a compact on taxing and spending which seemed to reconcile the North, South, and West. But this compact hinged on the persistence of good economic times. As the economy declined, and federal revenues evaporated, old animosities came quickly to the surface.

Jackson had the good fortune of being president at a time when the economy was growing and the fiscal position of the federal government was excellent. After the War of 1812, Congress had imposed large tariffs on British textile imports. These tariffs were broadened in 1824 and again in 1828. By the end of the 1820s the average tariff on dutiable imports was more than 60 percent, by far the highest level in American history. The result was an extraordinary surge in federal revenues. In the first term of Jackson's presidency (1828–1832), income to the federal government massively exceeded its expenditures—by an average of 75 percent over the whole four years.

With the federal Treasury bursting, it was easy for the Jackson administration to pursue several popular policies. One of these was the elimination of the federal debt. In 1828 it was the federal government, rather than the state governments, that owed most of the public debt of the United States.

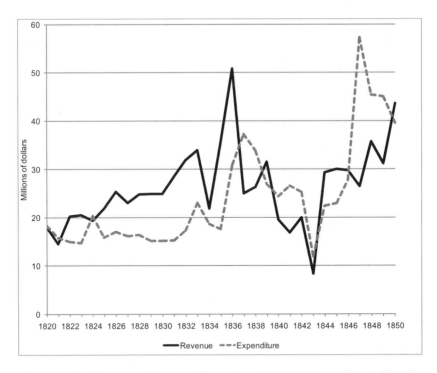

FIGURE 8. Federal Government Revenue and Expenditure, 1820–1850. Source: *Historical Statistics of the United States Millennial Edition Online*, hsus.cambridge.org/.

Federal debt had ballooned because of the War of 1812 and lingered for a long time afterward: at the time of Jackson's election in 1828, it was still about seventy million dollars—regarded at the time as a massive sum. The persistence of the federal debt was, in Jackson's eyes, evidence of moral and political failure. Jackson "*hated* debt," his biographer James Parton wrote in 1859. The national debt was "incompatible with real independence," Jackson said in his inaugural address. Jackson promised that his administration would eliminate the debt by 1835. "We shall then exhibit the rare example of a great nation, abounding in all the means of happiness and security, altogether free from Debt."

Jackson was not alone in his disdain of federal indebtedness. His ally Thomas Hart Benton also considered the national debt "a burthen upon the American people." And John Quincy Adams, trounced by Jackson in the 1828 election, nonetheless agreed on the need for "total emancipation of the nation from the thraldom of a public debt." "The total extinguishment of the debt," Adams said in 1832, was "a fundamental maxim in the system of public credit of the United States."

President Jackson achieved his goal on the schedule that he had projected in 1831. In January 1835 Treasury Secretary Levi Woodbury announced that the outstanding federal debt had been almost entirely eliminated. The United States had "earned a distinction entirely exclusive and characteristic. . . . [It] is the only government on earth that has ever paid to the last cent its national debt." Jackson's supporters organized a gala banquet in Washington to celebrate the country's liberation. "Our public debt is cancelled," Thomas Hart Benton told the celebrants. "There is more strength in these words than in one hundred ships of the line, ready for battle, or in a hundred thousand armed soldiers." (Time would show that this was not quite right: what really mattered, from the point of view of national defense, was the capacity to borrow rather than the existing level of debt.)

The health of the federal budget also allowed Jackson to pursue a conciliatory path on the contentious question of tariffs. On this subject, a transient consensus had been replaced by deep and violent divisions. The tariff of 1816 had broad support throughout the country. Even southerners endorsed the tax, for three reasons: because the federal government clearly needed revenue to reduce the debt produced by the War of 1812; they had hopes that it would stir industry in southern states; and they shared an apprehension about another conflict with the United Kingdom. John Calhoun endorsed the 1816 tariff, arguing that a nation that was so dependent on foreign trade with the dominant maritime power could not "stand the shock of war."

This consensus on tariffs quickly evaporated, however. The threat of war diminished. Southern hopes about the growth of infant industries faded, and were replaced by an understanding of the South's growing dependence on British manufacturers as the main market for cotton and other crops. Southern states opposed the extension of tariffs throughout the 1820s with increasing virulence. By the end of that decade, tariff policy was understood in the South as a matter in which its economic interests were directly opposed to those of the North. This was, of course, simplistic; the attitudes of northerners and westerners toward the tariff were neither uniform nor consistent. Still, the perception of a simple opposition encouraged secessionist impulses in the South. "We shall ere long be compelled to calculate the value of our union," said Thomas Cooper, the president of South Carolina College, in 1827. "Is it worth our while to continue this union of States where the North demands to be our masters and we are required to be their tributaries?" Many southerners questioned whether the federal government had authority to levy tariffs that were mainly intended to shelter northern industries.

By the midpoint of Jackson's first term as president, the South was at the flashpoint. Virginia Congressman Charles C. Johnston came to Washington in December 1831 convinced that the next session of Congress "would form a crisis in which the political destiny of this Government would be determined, either for evil, or for good, for years to come." John Quincy Adams warned northerners that "they must relieve the South or fight them." Congress attempted to conciliate. A new law that lowered tariffs in 1832 undermined militancy in many southern states, but not in South Carolina, where a state convention declared the tariff laws to be unconstitutional and threatened to secede if the federal government attempted to enforce them. In Boston, former Senator Harrison Gray Otis felt "a gloom, foreboding & uncertainty respecting public affairs" not seen since the Revolutionary War: "That we shall have treason and insurrection in fact, I can no longer doubt." Jackson replied with a mix of threats and promises of further accommodation. In March 1833 Congress expanded the president's power to use force to collect federal taxes in South Carolina. But Jackson also asked Congress to lower tariffs even further. On the same day that it broadened the president's authority to force compliance, Congress adopted legislation that promised a gradual but substantial reduction of duties on imported goods, until all of the increases of the previous decade had been wiped away. These concessions defused the conflict in South Carolina. Southerners understood that by the date fixed in law—June 30, 1842—relief from protective tariffs would finally be delivered.

This compromise on tariffs, so vital to the preservation of peace, was made possible by the robust health of the federal budget. Two weeks after the nullification threat, Jackson publicly declared that high tariffs could not be justified "when the money is not required for any legitimate purpose in the administration of the Government." Of course, there were manufacturing interests that sought protection regardless of how the revenue was used, but their capacity to make a public case for tariffs was weakened by the reality of a large surplus. Supporters of protection were compelled to justify "the oppression of drawing money out of the pockets of the people for nothing, merely to accumulate it in the treasury." It was "the present state of the Treasury, the fact that our debt is paid" that made concessions possible, said Virginia's Representative Johnston.

The compromise tariff bill of 1833 provided only for a gradual reduction of duties, and federal revenues still exceeded expenditures by a large amount. Federal coffers were also being filled with profits from the sale of public lands. Land receipts doubled from 1832 to 1834, almost tripled in 1835, and nearly doubled again in 1836. In that year, the federal government actually reaped more from land sales than it did from tariffs. The Jackson administration was awash in cash.

One way of eliminating the surplus was to distribute it among the states. Distribution of excess revenue was an old idea, first advanced by Thomas Jefferson in 1805. It had been revived in the late 1820s, and was briefly favored by Jackson himself. Jackson quickly retreated from distribution as southerners complained that it would become a device for justifying continued high tariffs. But the 1833 compromise on tariffs was understood to be inviolable—"a sort of temporary annex to the Constitution, and consequently sacred"—and so by 1836 there was no possibility of eliminating the surplus by lowering customs duties. Moreover, the western states were becoming stronger advocates of distribution. Jackson had made clear that he opposed a federal role in building roads, canals, and other improvements that would benefit the western states. A distribution of the surplus, governors said, would at least allow the states to do what the federal government would not.

In June 1836, Congress passed legislation promising that the federal surplus available on January 1, 1837, would be divided and paid in installments to the states. Technically, the Treasury retained power to retrieve the money deposited with states, but this was widely understood as a pretense to avoid the appearance of pure distribution, which Jackson seemed more likely to veto. "It is evident," the governor of Kentucky told state legislators, "that the intention of Congress was to make a permanent distribution rather than a temporary loan to the States." Jackson signed the bill under pressure from Van Buren, who feared that a veto would damage his prospects in the November election.

On the morning of Van Buren's inauguration in March 1837 it could be said that there was a national compact, forged through a decade of hard argument, that reconciled the conflicting interests of the different sections. Northern manufacturers had the assurance that protective tariffs would be maintained for the next five years. The South had an assurance that a policy of low tariffs would eventually be restored. The western states may have been disappointed by Jackson's opposition to federally sponsored improvements, but they had the promise of distribution as a consolation. And all of this would be done without incurring an odious federal debt. But this compact was fragile. It all hinged on the health of the Treasury, which collapsed after the Panic of 1837. Revenue from land sales and tariffs plummeted. Federal income in 1837 was half what it had been the preceding year, and the federal government confronted its first substantial deficit since the War of 1812.

The first casualty of the collapsing Treasury was the policy on distribution. The Treasury had calculated that thirty-seven million dollars was available for distribution, and by the fall of 1837, three of the promised four installments had been paid to the states. The final payment was due in October, but by late summer the federal government was unable to pay its ordinary expenses, much less the nine million dollars still due to state governments. "It is not easy to see," said Raguet's *Financial Register* in August 1837, "how the government can carry on its affairs without holding back from the states the October instalment." Within weeks, Congress revised the law to delay payment of the fourth installment until January 1839. It was obvious by late 1838 that the federal government still lacked the ability to pay, and in December Congress postponed the last payment indefinitely.

State governments, convinced that the federal government would continue payouts, were caught flatfooted. In December 1838 the governor of Pennsylvania urged the state legislature to increase appropriations even though Congress had just deferred payment. The legislature increased spending and forced the newly state-chartered Bank of the United States to provide a short-term loan based on a planned repayment in April 1839 out of the anticipated proceeds of the fourth installment. When Congress deferred the installment indefinitely, Pennsylvania was left with an uncovered liability equal to one-third of its total current expenditures. Indiana, Michigan, Mississippi, and New York also borrowed against the anticipated fourth installment and found themselves short. New York Governor William Seward accused the federal government of a breach of faith. The Ohio legislature condemned the federal government for "intercepting" the fourth installment—an act not "justified by any want of the federal treasury, however urgent."

The reality was that federal finances were in miserable condition. In May 1838, Van Buren told Congress that there was only $216,000 in the Treasury: enough to finance government operations for only two days. The nation faced "serious embarrassment," Van Buren said. "The United States are in immediate danger of being unable to discharge with good faith and promptitude the various pecuniary obligations of the government." The hard reality was that the U.S. government would have to borrow to meet its obligations. Only months before, Democrats had celebrated the distinction of the United States as the only country on earth to be free of debt. "We had our dream of inexhaustible surpluses," said Senator Thomas Hart Benton, "and were waked up to the reality of an empty Treasury."

Democrats tried to avoid an admission that the federal government's happy, debt-free days were over. At first, the Van Buren administration asked Congress to authorize the issuance of treasury notes—small denomination paper that could be given to creditors instead of cash. Hardened Democrats were prepared to argue that, so long as the country was relying on treasury notes alone, it still had no national debt; treasury notes, it was said, were only a stop-gap to bridge a temporary decline in revenues. But many in Congress refused to accept the pretense of fiscal rectitude and protested that the Van Buren administration had done little to avoid borrowing. "There is not one single act of retrenchment performed or in progress," said South Carolina Senator William Preston. "There is no pretense of economy. . . . No one has proposed to cut off any branch of extravagance, and no party measure has been proposed to organize a system of economy."

Congress narrowly approved the issue of treasury notes in 1837. When conditions did not improve significantly in 1838, the Van Buren administration called for another issue, and Congress again relented. "Here now, is another emergency—another unexpected crisis," said Senator Preston. "I believe that the treasury habitually exists in a state of emergency—in a critical condition." This was not far from the truth. The Treasury routinely overestimated how much revenue it was likely to collect in the coming year, and then sought short-term financing to cover the deficiency. New issues of treasury notes were approved in 1839, 1840, and 1841. In that year, spending exceeded revenue by almost 60 percent.

After March 1841 the Whigs claimed control of the presidency as well as the House and Senate. The pretense of Democratic finance—that the federal government merely had short-term financing gaps, which could be bridged by treasury notes—was now abandoned. Congress authorized a twelve million dollar loan in July 1841 and another five million dollar loan in April 1842. Democrats, now in opposition, protested that Whigs were recreating the national debt that Jackson had so carefully erased. But Democratic credibility was worn away by the practice of the preceding four years. "It was the more manly course to openly ask a loan," said Whigs, "than to continue the issue of notes which must return to the treasury in a few weeks or months."

Even if the practice of deficit financing was now clearly reestablished, there were limits to how far it could be pursued. The European market was largely closed to the federal government and the American market remained deeply unsettled. Twice, Congress was obliged to loosen the terms on which government bonds could be sold. The interest rate paid on 1842 bonds was the highest since the War of 1812. Still, Whig policy brought a definite end to the Jacksonian drive against the national debt. By 1843, the federal debt was back to thirty-three million dollars, roughly what it had been in the early years of Jackson's presidency. "The brilliant prospect that had been held out, of the extinction of the national debt—which had been the fond vision of Jackson's administration—was shattered."

The compact continued to unravel. The plan for reduction of federal tariffs that had been agreed in 1833 was scheduled to reach its end by June 1842. There was to be a final, sharp lowering of tariffs in the last months of the plan, and after June 1842 it was understood that tariffs would be reduced to the minimum needed to finance the federal government's operations. In 1833, when the trade passing through customs houses was large and growing, this seemed to imply that the remaining tariffs would be very low. But by the end of 1840 it was already clear that trade was declining sharply, and that if tariffs were reduced to the levels expected by southerners, there would not be enough revenue to support current government spending. The Tyler administration struggled to restrain expenditures but could not keep up with the collapse in tariff revenue.

This was not the only reason why the compromise of 1833 was threatened. Distressed state governments, many in default on their debts, were pressing hard on the federal Treasury for relief. Although there was no longer a surplus that could be divided among the states, there was still a stream of revenue from the sale of public lands, which, while scarcely a fraction of what it had once been—income from land sales in 1841 was only one-twentieth of what it had been four years earlier—could still be claimed. The division of federal land revenues among the states was treated as a matter of high principle (the public lands were a national asset, it was said, and the profits from their disposition ought to be widely shared) and also of budgetary convenience: "a relief measure to the indebted states." In Illinois, which eventually defaulted in January 1842, voters were reminded that the state faced "unparalleled pecuniary pressure." The case for a new policy of distribution was declared to be "the clearest imaginable."

In the North, meanwhile, struggling manufacturers and workers were increasingly agitated over the looming elimination of protective tariffs. In April 1842, a national convention was held in New York's Broadway Tabernacle, the city's largest meeting place, to organize a Home League to campaign against free trade. "Thousands of mechanics and labouring men cannot obtain employment, and consequently cannot supply themselves with provisions sufficient for their comfortable support," wrote William Handey of Maryland. The "selfish and sectional" policy of the southern states—free trade—would make conditions even worse, as American workers were forced to compete with "the under-fed and over-worked labourer of Europe." Delegates at the Tabernacle meeting were warned that northern industry might even look for relief by exploiting the country's tense relations with Britain:

> Our manufacturers and laboring artisans will not now be content without protective aid. *War is protection to them.* They know it. . . . Is it to be supposed that if denied protection by the government . . . that they will not foment the causes of war, so rife at this moment, and bring about that forced state of protection which would at once afford them profit and employment? Low murmurings of this policy are already heard from discharged workers and want-appalled laborers.

Congress began its twenty-seventh session in March 1841 and its first impulse was to yield to the demands of states. A new land bill gave concessions to states in two ways. For frontier states, there was a guarantee that settlers who were squatting on public land could obtain legal title to their property at a reduced rate. Distressed states also won a promise that federal revenue from land sales would be distributed according to population. The main champion of distribution, Henry Clay, dampened southern hostility by promising that it would be suspended if it required higher tariffs after June 1842 than had been promised to the South in the compromise of 1833. The distribution law was signed by President Tyler in September 1841. Indigent states were already tallying the amount likely to be received from the federal government.

The land bill was generous to the states—too generous, in fact. There were already signs that the federal government would be unable to keep its promise to the West on distribution without breaching its promise to the South on tariffs. Only a week after signing the distribution bill, Tyler signed a bill to increase some tariffs which, although it did not itself violate the compromise of 1833, gave a signal about the rapid decline of the federal Treasury. By the end of 1841 Tyler had privately acknowledged that the federal government's own needs could not be satisfied without breaking the compromise. This implied that the policy of distribution would have to be suspended as well. In public, though, Tyler was circumspect. He told Congress that the federal government faced a deficit, that its attempts to borrow had met with modest success, and that Congress should consider some tariff reform, ideally one that did not unwind either the 1833 compromise or the 1841 distribution policy. In February 1842, Clay countered with a broader and more concrete plan: an explicit abandonment of the compromise and a guarantee that distribution would be continued.

Clay's proposal created convulsions in a Congress already riven over Tyler's vetoes of bank legislation. "That body is *incompetent* to legislate," Navy Secretary Abel Upshur complained privately. Tyler could find no way of saving the Treasury, except by completely halting all defense expenditures, and in March 1842 he finally conceded publicly that the compromise could not be upheld even if distribution was cancelled, as he thought it should be. He appealed to Congress to act quickly in "a spirit of mutual harmony and concession."

Neither Tyler nor Congress were truly in the mood for conciliation. In June, Congress sent Tyler a bill that delayed for one month the final tariff reductions promised in the 1833 compromise, and retained the policy of distribution. Tyler vetoed the bill, suspecting a northern scheme to perpetuate unnecessarily high tariffs, and instructed customs houses to execute the final reduction of duties that was scheduled for June 30. The Whig majority in Congress, enraged by the veto, sent a second bill to Tyler in August. It restored high tariffs and continued distribution permanently. Tyler vetoed the bill again. This was the fourth veto from Tyler in less than a year. Many Whigs began agitating for impeachment of the president, counting among his offences the "arbitrary, despotic and corrupt use of the veto power." Most Whigs in the House of Representatives favored impeachment, although there was not a large enough majority to begin a formal investigation.

"The unsettled state of the tariff question," as a British newspaper called it, was causing transatlantic trade to seize up and aggravating economic stagnation on both sides of the ocean. "The condition of the county is most appalling," London's *Morning Chronicle* reported on August 25, after news of the second veto arrived in Liverpool. "The Treasury is bankrupt to all intents and purposes." Finally, Congress succumbed to Tyler's requirements. At the end of August, it approved a bill abandoning the compromise of 1833 by raising tariffs, but also abandoning the policy of distribution, and this time Tyler signed it into law. The bill passed with a majority of one vote in the House of Representatives and one vote in the Senate. Northern representatives voted overwhelmingly for the law, while the South voted overwhelmingly against.

In the north, the new tariff law was credited with breathing new life into the ailing economy. "The Tariff of 1842 is doing wonders for us," wrote Calvin Colton, a protectionist pamphleteer. Mills and factories were reopening and canals appeared busier. A leader of the Home League said that the association could look on the tariff law "with no ordinary feelings of satis-faction. . . . The headlong career of the government in prostrating our most important interests to gratify the cupidity of European manufacturers, or to practically refute the visionary theories of nullifying abstractionists has been arrested." In the South, though, the "nullifying abstractionists" fumed. South Carolina's Calhoun said flatly that the South had been betrayed. For almost a decade it had honored the truce of 1833 by withholding demands for reduced tariffs, "and now, when the time has arrived, when it is our turn to enjoy its benefits . . . [the manufacturing interests] turn round, and coolly and openly violate every provision in our favor." In December 1842 the South Carolina legislature approved a resolution condemning the tariff law as a breach of faith and warned that it might turn again to nullification. However, nullifiers were persuaded to give the newly elected Democratic majority in the House of Representatives a chance to undo the legislation.

When Congress failed to act, southern anger grew. In July 1844 South Carolina politician Robert Rhett, later a member of the confederate con-gress, condemned the federal government as a despot and called for seces-sion. The 1833 compromise "was in fact a treaty, made between belligerent parties with arms in their hands," said South Carolina Governor James Hammond in November 1844. This treaty had been broken by the 1842 law and there was no reasonable ground, he concluded, for believing that the federal government would ever repeal it. "Our state is bound . . . to adopt such measures as will bring all her moral, constitutional, and if neces-sary, her physical resources in direct array against a policy . . . which impov-erishes our country, revolutionizes our government, and overthrows our liberties."

Distressed states were also left without aid. For the second time, a prom-ise of distribution from the federal government had been made and broken. With distribution now abandoned, some states revived the idea that the federal government should assume their debts. Pennsylvania and Maryland, both defaulters, were the loudest voices for assumption. But there was no appetite in Congress to provide the most troubled states with relief for the consequences of their own misjudgments. "If the states were relieved from their present difficulties," critics said, "they would in all probability get heav-ily into debt again."

The pressures that would eventually lead the country to civil war were evi-dent well before the Panic of 1837. The economies of North and South were following different paths, so that the material interests of the two sec-tions were increasingly opposed to one another. The populations of North and South were also growing at different rates, and this—combined with the rapid emergence of the West—generated uncertainty about the balance of political power, and in particular a growing sense of vulnerability in the South. These pressures were clearly at work in debates over the federal budget involving the basic questions of how money should be raised and spent.

In good times, when private wealth was increasing and the federal treasury was full, it was easier, although certainly not easy, to satisfy conflicting interests and allay regional anxieties. If business was good, the South could tolerate a delay in tariff reductions, and the North could stomach the eventual lowering of duties. The West might be disappointed by the federal government's inaction on improvements, but at least it was compensated for its disappointment. And all of these accommodations could be made without plunging the country into a debate about the virtues or evils of a federal debt.

Yet hard times sharpened the perception that economic policy was a zero-sum game: if one section was to succeed, another would need to be harmed. The decline in private wealth made it more difficult for businessmen and workers to accept the imposition of new losses, even for the sake of national reconciliation. The federal government, its treasury bare, and shunned by major lenders, could not conciliate by offering compensation to disadvantaged sections. Political rhetoric was inflamed and comity within political institutions, such as it was, declined. Crisis made the country seem a union "of interest merely, a paper bond," as the diarist Sidney George Fisher said, "to be deliberately undone whenever interest demands it."

◆ Losing the Arms Race

> What worse than senseless babbling must it be to any man capable of combining together two rational ideas, with a disgraced and insolvent treasury, to use the words *retrenchment* and *economy*, in the very act of presenting and recommending from the two military departments of government . . . a yearly expenditure, in PEACE, of at least fifty millions of dollars?
>
> —John Quincy Adams, November 1842

As the federal Treasury was drained, Congress struggled to restrain governmental spending. The entire system of budgeting conspired against it. Estimates about amounts needed in the coming year were initially produced by bureaus within the five executive departments (State, Treasury, Post Office, Army, and Navy). It was generally acknowledged that bureaus had incentives to inflate their requirements, to "make them larger than is necessary," as President James Polk later said, "calculating that they will be cut down and reduced by Congress." Bureau heads sent their requests to Cabinet secretaries, who were so short-staffed that they could do little but tally the requests and send the total directly to Congress. There was no central review of proposed spending for the whole of government; no presidential budget as we know it today. Eventually, in 1845, President Polk asserted his right to review departmental estimates before they were sent to Congress, but even Polk lacked the capacity to judge whether the requests were reasonable. A few years earlier, in 1839, Treasury Secretary Levi Woodbury had confessed to President Van Buren that he was unable to understand the departmental budgets and "judge which will best bear any reduction."

Congress tried but failed to do much better. The House of Representatives established a special Committee on Retrenchment to search for savings. It was chaired by a Virginia Democrat, Thomas Gilmer, who took his assignment so seriously that he became known in Washington as Retrenchment Gilmer. "Retrenchment fever ran high," John Quincy Adams recalled. But budget hawks in Congress were stymied by their inability to discern where reductions were possible. Adams found that Secretary of State Daniel Webster "manifested a very warm disposition for economy and retrenchment in the abstract, but an equally warm aversion to any specific reduction." When the Retrenchment Committee asked departments to identify possible savings in 1842, "the response was a general request for more clerks."

Congressional self-interest also complicated the task of retrenchment. Representative Thomas Arnold caused "excited debate" in the House of Representatives in July 1842 when he proposed a reduction in pay and travel expenses for members of Congress. The bill was shelved, and Arnold's repeated attempts to revive it became a standing joke on Capitol Hill.

Congress was equally ambivalent about making cuts in the Post Office Department. Other than defense, the Post Office was by far the most costly program in the federal budget, although the cost was usually defrayed by the department's own revenues. Easily three-quarters of the federal workforce consisted of Post Office employees, and even this statistic underestimated its true size, because it overlooked the two thousand contractors who were hired to carry the mail by sulky, coach, steamboat, and rail.

The Post Office was the country's central nervous system: the conduit by which business was done, news carried, and politics managed. The growth of its network—the steady increase in the number of post offices and miles of postal routes—was carefully monitored as an index of the health of the nation as a whole. "There is no more striking illustration of the rapid growth of the United States than the rate of increase of the post offices and the mail routes," the *Baltimore American* said in 1832. "We have just reason to be proud of the capability of a young country which has done so much in its infancy." Profits from postal operations were reinvested in expansion of the network. When the economy boomed, the Post Office flourished. In 1835–1837, postal revenue exceeded expenditure by 20 percent, and Congress approved an unprecedented extension of services, particularly in rural and frontier areas. Between 1836 and 1840, postal routes grew as much as they had in the preceding two decades. The Post Office, the Postmaster General said in 1840, "enjoyed the advantages of an excited state of business." By then, however, the Post Office was saddled with much higher costs and sagging revenues. The department plunged into deficit after the Panic of 1837; by 1840 it had exhausted its savings and needed a subsidy from Congress.

The decline in Post Office revenue was not just a result of reduced business activity. The department also faced competition from private carriers who, unburdened by the need to subsidize rural and frontier routes, offered better rates to customers on the urbanized east coast. Existing law purported to give the Post Office a monopoly over mail delivery and in 1840 the department attempted, for the first time, to prosecute its competitors. The results were devastating for the Post Office. Courts interpreted the law so strictly that the ban on competition was effectively gutted, and customers flocked to private carriers.

For some of its defenders, the predicament of the Post Office seemed to mirror the troubles of the country at large. One of the country's major institutions, long a symbol of national growth and integration, was at the point of collapse. Private carriers, and the citizens who took advantage of their cheaper rates, appeared to be set on "destroying the post-office ultimately altogether." Francis O. Smith, a Jacksonian from Maine, warned that the country faced "the possibility of an *utter overthrow* of the whole system of mail arrangements." The Post Office was soon "the subject of more public discussion than any other department of the public service," according to James Whiton, a Boston merchant. There was deep resistance within Congress to a whole-scale reversal of the expansion that had been undertaken in 1836–1838, but neither could Congress afford to give large subsidies. The Postmaster General warned that the department could not sustain itself unless some action was taken. One remedy was to strengthen the statutory ban on competition, but advocates of private enterprise balked at strengthening the government's "odious monopoly" over postal services.

Finally, in 1845, Congress cracked. Unwilling to countenance a substantial reduction of postal routes, it gave the Post Office an ironclad monopoly on letter mail. (This bitter medicine was sweetened with the promise of a significant reduction in the postage rate for letters.) The suppression of private competition would "put an end to all interference with the revenues of the department," said the author of the 1845 legislation, Democratic Senator William Merrick. The Maryland senator regarded the law as a moral necessity as well. Despite the unfavorable court rulings, Merrick thought that it should have been clear to Americans that the Post Office was always intended to have a monopoly. Those who turned to private carriers had engaged in "the unblushing violation and open defiance of the laws . . . [and] shown themselves to be destitute of all patriotic or moral outrages." Strengthening the postal monopoly was not just a matter of dollars and cents; it was also a matter of preserving the social order.

In the field of defense, budget pressures compelled even more painful tradeoffs. In the second Jackson administration, expenditure on the army and navy accounted for more than half of all federal government outlays. Jackson took power in 1829 skeptical about the need for defense spending, but circumstances demanded a change in thinking. The nation's territory, and a vast oceanic commerce, had to be secured. By 1842, the main obstacle to expansion of American defenses was not primarily ideological. The country wanted a stronger military, but now they could not pay for it.

The regular army, as it stood in 1835, was small and weak. With seven thousand men, it had not changed much in size for fifteen years. The force was "a mere fragment," the *North American Review* said in 1832, "scattered in small detachments over an immense frontier." By contrast, the British Army, which had been dramatically reduced after the Napoleonic wars and was, in 1835, at its lowest point in the nineteenth century, still had over one hundred and thirty thousand men at arms. Of course, British troops were dispersed across a vast empire. Even so, Britain had a policy after the War of 1812 of maintaining a ready garrison along the Canadian frontier that was comparable to the whole of the American army.

Conditions in the American army were grim. Most troops were posted in miserable and dangerous frontier outposts. The biggest base for the U.S. Army in 1835 was Fort Gibson, in Arkansas Territory, whose five hundred soldiers were occupied mainly with the resettlement of Indians from the east. Fort Gibson was said to experience the hottest temperatures of all American posts, and it had been built in a place on the Neosho River "most conducive to the evolution of malaria." In 1834–1835, there were 142 deaths at the post, mainly from fever. "The location . . . is not the best that could have been made," the Army's surgeon general conceded. But other posts were similarly dangerous. It was not surprising that desertion rates among enlisted men were high. Even officers trained at the Military Academy at West Point were reluctant to stick with the service. There was no system for retiring older officers and therefore little chance for promotion, and during the boom years there were alluring opportunities in private business. From 1835 to 1836, over one hundred officers (out of an officer corps of only seven hundred) handed in their commissions.

Military service, the *Army and Navy Chronicle* complained, was held in contempt by Congress. To a large degree this was a matter of deliberate policy. Many Americans believed that a large standing army was "dangerous to the safety of a republican form of government." Jackson himself said in 1829 that the citizen militia, organized by the states but available for federal service, should be "the bulwark of our defense. . . . A million of armed freemen, possessed of the means of war, can never be conquered by a foreign foe." And there was, of course, no immediate threat to the nation; even on the northern border there was, in 1835, no warning of hostilities with the British. So a tightfisted Democratic administration kept its spending on the army to a minimum.

This policy changed at the end of 1835. In Florida, Seminole Indians were resisting the Jackson administration's attempt to resettle them west of the Mississippi, and in December of that year a party of Seminole warriors attacked a column of 110 army regulars, killing all but two. Attempts to counter the uprising with militiamen failed and in April 1836 the American commander, General Winfield Scott, asked Washington to send reinforcements—"3,000 good troops (not volunteers)." Militiamen, said Scott, were ineffectual "in a distant war like this . . . after the zeal of the first week or two has subsided." Supporters of the militia were offended, but the regular army was expanded. On average, it comprised eleven thousand troops over the next five years. Spending on the U.S. Army reached levels not seen since the War of 1812.

It took six years for American troops to contain an uprising of less than two thousand Seminole warriors. Martin Van Buren, president throughout most of the campaign, insisted in 1840 that the fight was prolonged by "causes beyond the control of the government." But others saw the long struggle as an indictment of the federal military establishment and proof that the country needed a larger and better organized army. "This Florida war ought to be a lesson," a British traveller observed. "The arm of the Federal Government is too weak to reach its own confines." John Tyler's new Secretary of War, John Spencer, urged Congress to maintain army appropriations even though the Seminole War had ended. In the winter of

1841–1842, however, Congress was in no mood to take Spencer's advice. Revenue was "declining fast," Pennsyvlania Democrat Joseph Fornance told the House of Representatives. The War Department had undertaken "extravagant expenditures when the Treasury was full," but now, without any substantial threat to U.S. territory, it was time to reverse course. In August 1842, Congress reduced the authorized strength of the army by one-third. Spending was cut again in 1843. In 1844–1845 expenditure on the army was little more than what it had been during the first Jackson administration, fifteen years earlier.

Even the Military Academy at West Point came under assault. The school had always been resented by Jacksonian Democrats, who thought it aristocratic and anti-republican. But fiscal distress gave power to a new argument against the institution: it also wasted "a vast sum of money." In 1842, congressional Democrats blocked funds for the Board of Visitors, a supervisory body that habitually issued reports favoring the academy. The following year, they advanced a resolution to abolish the school entirely. The resolution failed, but the House Ways and Means Committee agreed that Secretary Spencer should "plan for the gradual reduction" of the academy's budget. West Point had narrowly dodged extinction.

Retrenchment in the navy proved more difficult. As it stood on Martin Van Buren's inauguration day in March 1837, the U.S. Navy comprised twenty-one active ships. At the head of the fleet was the USS North Carolina, a three-masted vessel almost two hundred feet long, with ninety-two cannon arrayed on her three decks. The North Carolina was a ship-of-the-line, a floating fortress designed to participate in the great broadside battles that determined control of the oceans in the early nineteenth century. She was grand but aging, originally authorized by Congress after the War of 1812, and launched in 1820. On inauguration day she arrived in Rio de Janeiro, halfway through a five-month voyage to join the navy's Pacific squadron at Callao, Peru.

After the North Carolina, in order of firepower, came five frigates. The Constitution, with forty-four guns, launched in 1797, and almost scrapped in 1830 for unseaworthiness, was in the Mediterranean. The Constellation, also launched in 1797, was cruising in the Caribbean. The Potomac, built after the War of 1812, was returning from Brazil, two days out from Norfolk Navy Yard. The Brandywine, launched in 1825, was returning from a three-year tour in the Pacific. The Columbia, the newest of the frigates, launched in 1836, was lying at Norfolk and preparing for her first cruise to Asia. Supporting these six big ships were fifteen smaller vessels, like the eighteen–gun sloop *Boston*, sailing with the *Constellation* in the Caribbean. There was also the twelve-gun schooner *Shark*, which with the *Constitution* constituted the whole American force in the Mediterranean, and the ten-gun brig *Dolphin*, which aided the *Potomac* off the east coast of South America.

This small American fleet had massive responsibilities. In the Pacific, for example, the naval presence of the United States would shortly be bigger than ever, comprising the ship-of-the-line *North Carolina*, two sloops, and two schooners. "A considerable addition to our force," Navy Secretary Mahlon Dickerson boasted. But these five ships were expected to protect American interests over "all of the west coast of America," as well as the Pacific's entire expanse from the tip of the Aleutian Islands south to Antarctica. A tour from the navy's base in Peru to San Francisco, and then to Hawaii, and back to Peru, was twelve thousand nautical miles of sailing. Sailors assigned to the Pacific squadron were away from home for at least four years.

In the two decades before the Panic of 1837, American naval policy had swung back and forth. The War of 1812 triggered a naval build-up. In 1813, Congress authorized the construction of four large warships, all of which were launched within the next six years; in 1816, it approved the construction of another nine ships-of-the-line, as well as a dozen frigates. "The sentiment in the mind of every citizen," President James Monroe said in March 1817, "is national strength." By 1821, though, this sentiment had waned. An economy-minded Congress balked at the expense of building and maintaining a fleet of large ships, and over the next four years the naval appropriation was a third less than what it had been in the six preceding years. By 1824, all of the large ships authorized in 1813 had been taken out of service. Of the nine large ships approved in 1816, only one was on active duty. Two were out of service, and the remaining six remained on the stocks—largely completed but not launched.

The theory was that these stored or nearly completed ships could be readied for combat quickly. With lack of maintenance, though, this ghost fleet deteriorated. In 1826, a British naval officer, Frederick de Roos, was startled by the condition of the *Ohio*, docked in Brooklyn, which had been launched in 1820 but never put into active service. "I was filled with astonishment at the negligence which permitted so fine a ship to remain exposed to the ruinous assaults of so deleterious a climate," Roos wrote. "She has only been built seven years, and from want of common attention and care, is already falling rapidly into decay." In Philadelphia, de Roos saw the massive hull of the *Pennsylvania* lying on the stocks. With 104 guns, and displacing three thousand tons, it would have been the largest fighting ship in the world. But six years after the laying of her keel, the *Pennsylvania* was still not complete. It became the object of derision within the British Navy. Americans were "a little puffed up" by their victory in the War of 1812, the permanent secretary of the British Admiralty said mockingly in 1838, and began building the *Pennsylvania* "on the principle of the tower of Babel—to 'make themselves known.'" In 1838 the ship was still not in service, and the British were about to launch the even larger, 110-gun, *HMS Queen*.

The policy of restraint, if not neglect, on military spending continued after the election of Andrew Jackson, whose ambivalence extended to the navy as well as the regular army. The lack of a strong fleet might cause "partial injuries and occasional mortifications," Jackson conceded in 1829, but in the end the militia would always save the homeland. Rather than building new ships, the navy was directed to stockpile timber and other materials so that in a moment of emergency it could build vessels as required. In this way the federal government attempted to avoid the heavy cost of building and maintaining a large fleet.

The shortsightedness of this policy was increasingly clear by Jackson's second term. The United States had the largest commercial fleet in the world after Britain, and like Britain it wanted to expand its commerce with new markets such as China. This required a navy that could suppress piracy and impress governments with which the United States wanted to make treaties. The navy eventually developed a measure of its capacity to protect the commercial fleet: the number of guns on its warships that were available to protect each one hundred thousand tons of the country's commercial fleet. By this "guns-per-ton" measure, the United States was far weaker than any of the European powers.

The country also became concerned about the possibility of war with France. Jackson, angry over France's failure to pay compensation for American commercial losses during the Napoleonic wars, told Congress in December 1834 that the United States might be compelled to retaliate by seizing French shipping. French parliamentarians reacted furiously and the two countries seemed to be on the edge of conflict throughout 1835. A friend of Jackson's called this "the most dangerous moment" of his administration. The reality was that France had a vastly larger navy than the United States, with thirty big ships in service, another thirty laid up but available for service, and more than a hundred smaller sailing ships and armed steamers on active duty. "Suppose for one moment that our late differences with France had terminated in a war," the *Army and Navy Chronicle* wrote in 1836, after the dispute was resolved. "It would be madness to close our eyes to the truth.

Our trade and our navy must have been instantly swept from the ocean by the overwhelming superiority of the French marine."

Jackson ended his presidency with a call for Congress to strengthen the navy to protect commerce and "give to defense its greatest efficiency by meeting danger at a distance from home." No more would the militia serve as the bulwark of national defense. Shaken by the war threat, Congress had already increased naval appropriations by 60 percent, allowing for the launch of the *Pennsylvania,* the rehabilitation of the *Ohio,* the construction of two frigates, and an experiment with three-armed paddle-wheel steamers.

But this enthusiasm for naval expansion was quickly checked by the onset of the economic crisis. Pressed for revenue and unwilling to borrow, Van Buren was content to maintain the status quo. In 1841 the navy was larger than it had been a decade earlier, but still woefully smaller than European fleets. In a series of articles published anonymously from 1840 to 1841, Lieutenant Matthew Maury described a force that was overstretched, disorganized, and demoralized. In 1838, the captain of the *Independence,* "mortified at his own weakness," had been compelled to beg for the release of American merchantmen seized by French warships maintaining an illegal blockade against Brazilian ports. Off the African coast, British cruisers tacitly rebuked "the inertness of the American government" by intercepting American vessels engaged in the illegal slave trade. National honor demanded reform, Maury said. "With a commerce full-fledged, spreading her wings on every sea and sailing before every breeze on the ocean, a larger Navy with a new organization is loudly called for."

In September 1841, the navy got its fiercest advocate in years when President Tyler appointed Abel Upshur as his new Secretary of the Navy. Upshur was a Virginia Whig, an Anglophobe, and a staunch proponent of territorial and commercial expansion. "Times were never more propitious for the Navy than they now are," wrote the *Southern Literary Messenger* in January 1842. "It has a friend in its present head, who will give tone to its enfeebled state, and let its wants be known."

Within weeks of his appointment, Upshur sent Congress a plan for the increase of naval power. The department itself should be completely reorganized, Upshur said. The Board of Navy Commissioners, a cumbersome oversight device set up during the War of 1812, would be replaced with five bureaus specializing in different aspects of navy operations. Steps would be taken to improve professionalism in the service, including the establishment of a naval academy to match West Point. And the fleet would be substantially enlarged. Upshur asserted in December 1841:

It is now the settled policy of the Government to increase the Navy as rapidly as the means at its disposal will admit. . . . [W]e cannot safely stop short of half the naval force of the strongest maritime power in the world. . . . We might reasonably hope to repel from our shores any maritime power, with only half its force in ships. With less than this, our fleets would serve only to swell the triumphs and feed the cupidity of our enemy. It is better to have none at all than to have less than enough.

Not only was this an ambitious goal, given the massive superiority of British naval forces, it was a goal that became more ambitious every day, because the British were themselves racing to maintain dominance over the French. Upshur wanted to lock the United States into a global arms race. John Quincy Adams thought that Upshur's plan was absurd. To execute it, he said, the United States would have to quadruple its naval budget. Upshur had proposed only a 50 percent increase in navy expenditure in 1842. Still, this would have been the largest navy appropriation since independence.

Like War Secretary Spencer, Upshur confronted a Congress that was struggling to match expenditures with plunging revenues. "Is now the time to enlarge the navy?" asked New York Democrat Fernando Wood. "The wheels of Government but yesterday stood still, and the machinery of the Executive was stopped, for want of a small pittance to proceed. . . . But yesterday, the public faith was hawked up and down Wall and Chestnut Streets, an humble suppliant to *British capitalists* for favor. . . . Out of money, out of credit, embarrassed and financially disgraced—is this the chosen opportunity to appropriate the millions asked?"

Even Whigs balked at the request. The House Ways and Means Committee, chaired by Millard Fillmore of New York, pressed the Navy Department for savings. "To all their enquiries as to where retrenchment might be made, they received the reply 'nowhere'," Fillmore reported to the House in May. "The Department insisted that the whole amount was indispensable."

Upshur's request for a naval school comparable to West Point was felled by retrenchment—not surprisingly, given the assault on West Point itself. Otherwise, though, Upshur had more success than War Secretary Spencer. The proposal for reorganization of the department succeeded precisely because it promised to save "*many millions* from waste." In the end, Upshur obtained much of the money that he sought for expansion of the fleet. In December, Tyler announced plans to improve the readiness of vessels in storage and add several new "ships of a small class." However, this modest expansion did not proceed smoothly. The paddle-wheelers *Mississippi* and

Missouri were put into service but with disappointing results. The ships devoured coal and in early trials proved unable to attain their anticipated speed. In April 1842, the *Missouri* ran aground during a trial run on the Potomac, and sixteen men died in the attempt to dislodge her. Upshur decided that the two ships were "altogether too expensive for service in a time of peace," and that they should be taken out of commission. The *Missouri* was saved from that indignity: while docked in Gibraltar in August 1843, she caught fire and sank after her magazine exploded.

Disaster struck the steamer *Princeton* six months later. Launched in September 1843, the ship was ground-breaking in its design. The world's first screw propulsion warship also had an engine that ran with greater efficiency than any in the British fleet. Its armament included a massive wrought-iron gun, the thirteen-ton Peacemaker designed by Robert Stockton, who boasted that the gun had "an effect terrible and almost incredible." The *Princeton* was anchored at Washington in February 1844, where it was visited by crowds of enthused Americans. On the last day of February, Stockton invited President Tyler, Upshur (now Secretary of State), Navy Secretary Thomas Gilmer (the former chair of the House Committee on Retrenchment), and three hundred other guests onto the ship for a tour of the Potomac. During a firing demonstration, the Peacemaker exploded, killing Upshur, Gilmer, and six others. Tyler narrowly escaped death.

The *Princeton*, once a reason for celebration, was now the cause of national mourning. A Washington paper reported that the White House was again "a receptacle of death," as it had been when President Harrison died in 1841:

> Instead of one, five bodies were now laid out in the east room of that fair mansion. . . . [G]athered within its gloom the blackened and bloody remains of a most frightful tragedy—the bodies of five intimate friends of the President, two of them his Cabinet associates, all hurried out of existence. . . . The bodies were then hearsed [to the Capitol]. . . . The immense crowd was perfectly mute in its march. . . . The sweeping trains of crepe that blackened the closed windows and doors of the buildings on the way gave, altogether, the most saddened and impressive aspect of woe every worn by this city.

Despite these setbacks, the U.S. Navy did grow as a result of Upshur's policies. By 1846 it had one ship-of-the-line on active duty, the *Columbus*. With enough time, another eight of the stored or incomplete ships from the class of 1816 could be readied for war. In addition, there were now twenty-five other warships on duty. "Never," said one writer, "had the United States

FIGURE 9. *Awful Explosion of the Peace-Maker on Board the U.S. Steam Frigate Princeton.* Lithograph published by N. Currier, New York, 1844. Source: Library of Congress.

possessed so powerful a fleet." Still, the American navy was vastly outgunned by its British and French counterparts, as a table produced by the Navy Department in March 1846 showed (Table 1). Britain had seventeen ships-of-the-line in service, seventy-five in reserve, and another two dozen under construction. It also had six steam frigates in service and was building another twelve. The United States was far short of Upshur's goal of a force equal to half of the British Navy. Indeed, it was not even approaching that goal: the firepower under construction in Britain in 1846 exceeded the whole of the existing or planned American fleet. A consolation—and in the end, not a small one—was that Americans could crush the feeble Mexican navy.

Table 1   Size of Navies by Number of Guns, 1846

	IN SERVICE	OUT OF SERVICE	UNDER CONSTRUCTION	TOTAL
United States	1,155	576	614	2,345
United Kingdom	4,583	9,933	3,165	17,681
France	4,293	1,120	3,515	8,928
Mexico	42	—	—	42

❧Reconciling with the Superpower

> Here are two nations in the worst possible humor
> with each other, ready, with only a little more
> provocation, to go to war.

—Nicholas Biddle, July 20, 1843

If there was one policy on which most Americans agreed, it was this: territorial and commercial expansion. Since the early days of the republic, American leaders had regarded this as a special mission, blessed by God. The United States was "a rising nation," Thomas Jefferson said in 1801, "spread over a wide and fruitful land, traversing all the seas with the rich productions of their empire." In its first half century the nation doubled its territory and built a substantial commercial fleet. Even after the Panic of 1837 there seemed to be no dampening of enthusiasm for the "extension of our Empire," as John Tyler called it. New York Governor William Seward believed that the popular passion for expansion was irresistible: leaders might try to direct it, but it could not be subjugated. "We are the nation of human progress," wrote John O'Sullivan, editor of the *Democratic Review*, in 1839. "Who will, what can, set limits to our onward march? Providence is with us, and no earthly power can."

This was hubris, as Americans in more sober moments were compelled to concede. Britain, not the United States, was the world's dominant power. "John Bull," said the American editor Park Benjamin Sr., "scatters his garrisons and his frigates to all points of the compass." The British had as many troops garrisoned on the northern American border as the United States had dispersed across the whole of its territory, and their navy was massively larger. Moreover, the United Kingdom was the principal market for American exports and the main provider of capital. Jefferson might have negotiated the Louisiana Purchase, but it was a British bank, Barings, that financed it. The United States was in a peculiar position, jostling for territory and market access with another power that had substantial military and economic advantages.

The American predicament was aggravated by the economic crisis. Distressed southern planters could not afford a disruption in the cotton trade. Bankers, businessmen, and governments could not afford a curtailment of credit. The federal government, its treasury empty, could scarcely afford an arms race. And yet popular enthusiasm for expansion did not abate—on the contrary, nationalist calls for the "extension of empire" had a special appeal to a nation ground down by hard times. The task for American leaders was managing this collision between the aspirations of a sovereign people and hard economic and military realities.

There was a parallel between the predicament of national leaders dealing with matters of territory and markets, and that of state leaders wrestling with default. In both cases there was a conflict between what a newly enfranchised citizenry professed to want, and what—given the country's place in the order of nations—could realistically be achieved. In Washington, the management of this tension was a difficult job that often produced contradictory results. Sometimes American politicians would amplify popular opinion, and sometimes seek to suppress or manipulate it. Sometimes they would bluster against the British, and sometimes they would conciliate. In the end, though, most understood that the crisis had compromised the pursuit of American destiny. Expansionist sentiment could not be allowed to produce a direct conflict with the military and economic hegemon.

The Panic of 1837 was accompanied by a security crisis on the northern border of the United States. In November 1837 a rebellion against the British colonial government broke out in the province of Lower Canada, now Quebec, followed a few weeks later by a rebellion in Upper Canada, now Ontario. Both were quickly suppressed and many of their leaders fled into the United States. Here they found broad public support. In Buffalo, in mid-December, rebel William Lyon Mackenzie addressed an enthusiastic throng, inviting Americans to join him in another assault on the colonial government. A "patriot army" of American sympathizers, numbering in the hundreds, was soon formed in upstate New York. "Your cause is popular here," Albany postmaster Solomon Van Rensselaer wrote to his son, a leader of the patriot army, in December 1837. "War with England may grow out of it."

A few days later, a British raiding party attacked and sank the *Caroline*, a steamship used by the rebels to supply their camp on an island in the Niagara River. At the time of the attack the *Caroline* was moored on the American shore of the Niagara, and one American was killed in the assault. Soon the whole border was seething with what the New York *Herald* called the "settled determination of vengeance." Buffalo's mayor warned President Van Buren that "the civil authorities have no adequate force to control these men, and unless the General Government should interfere, there is no way to prevent serious disturbances." In Michigan, rebel sympathizers took weapons held within the Detroit jail and threatened to seize another cache at Fort Gratiot. More guns were stolen from an American arsenal near Lake Champlain.

In 1837–1838 New York was a Democratic state; anti-British sentiment was prevalent within the Democratic Party; and, of course, Martin Van Buren was a Democratic President. But Van Buren quickly grasped that the country could not wage war against Britain. He tried to steer a middle course. Van Buren demanded reparations for the attack on the *Caroline* and asked Congress for appropriations to improve border defense. At the same time, however, he issued a proclamation that promised the country would not interfere in Canadian affairs, advised state governors to arrest rebel sympathizers, and directed General Winfield Scott to visit the border and use his influence to maintain order. The British ambassador, Henry Fox, told London that Van Buren's aim was to maintain peace on the frontier.

Many of Van Buren's followers were flummoxed by his policy. Missouri Senator Thomas Hart Benton said that Van Buren lost "much popular favor in the border states from his strenuous repression of aid to a neighboring people, insurging for liberty." An editor of the Democratic *Washington Globe* wrote to a rebel leader that the party viewed Van Buren's policy "WITH DEEP, DEEP MORTIFICATION. At heart there is not a northern or western Democrat . . . who does not regret it. . . . [T]here is a magazine of burning patriotism now buried in the bosom of the democracy, that wants but a single spark to set it in an active flame. . . . But what would you have us do now? . . . We have NOTHING TO GAIN by a war with Great Britain." That view was most strongly held by Democrats from the plantation states, who believed that war would be disastrous for the cotton trade.

In fact, though, Van Buren's capacity for "strenuous repression" of the border states was limited. This was so even after Congress passed a neutrality law that gave new powers to act against rebel supporters. State and local officials hesitated to act firmly. The federal military presence consisted of little more than Scott's small entourage: the U.S. Army, consisting of only a few thousand soldiers, was mainly employed in fighting Florida's Seminole tribe. In May 1838, American citizens seized and burned a British steamboat, the *Sir Robert Peel*, and in November another rebel force made a foray across the upper St. Lawrence. Ambassador Fox conceded that Van Buren was "sincerely striving, as far as so weak and feeble a Government can be said to strive for anything—to fulfill its natural duties." But Fox was skeptical about the president's control over events. "In this country, it is not the Govt. that governs. How they are eventually to keep themselves out of a war with Great Britain, I hardly see."

On the frontier between Maine and New Brunswick, Van Buren's control was tested even more severely. The exact border had never been clearly established, but conflict had been avoided because of the slow pace of settlement. This changed in 1839, when Maine sent a party to clear the disputed land of British trespassers. New Brunswick's colonial government arrested the Maine party and threatened that it would use force to hold the territory. Maine's legislature responded in February 1839 by sending ten thousand state militiamen northward. Maine's governor warned Van Buren about suppressing a conflict with the British. "Should you go *against* us upon this occasion—or not espouse our cause with *warmth* and *earnestness* and with a true *American feeling*, God only knows what the result will be *politically*." In Washington, Congress stoked the fires by authorizing the president to call out fifty thousand troops if needed to repel the British.

Once again, Van Buren sought the middle ground. He endorsed Maine's claim to the territory and at the same time assured Fox of his desire to avoid hostilities. But Maine's state militia ignored Van Buren's call to disband while the two nations worked out a plan for resolving the dispute. General Scott was sent to Maine and won the grudging agreement of state leaders to a plan for withdrawal of American and British forces from the contested territory. An uneasy peace was restored.

By late 1840, however, the entire northern border was seething once again. In September, authorities in Buffalo arrested Alexander McLeod, a Canadian who was alleged to have killed an American during the attack on the *Caroline*. Van Buren rebuffed British protests about the arrest by insisting that he had no power to intervene in a prosecution under state law: after his defeat at the polls in November, Van Buren was content to delay action on the matter until the inauguration of his successor, William Henry Harrison. In the northeast, meanwhile, an attempt to allow voting in the U.S. election on disputed land revived conflict over the Maine boundary. By March 1841 several state legislatures had passed resolutions promising support to Maine to drive the British from American soil.

The two countries were again lurching toward war. Vice President John Tyler, summoned to the capital after the death of Harrison in April, said that "the peace of the country when I reached Washington . . . was suspended by a thread." Fox, the British ambassador in Washington, had instructions from London to leave the country if Alexander McLeod was executed. Andrew Stevenson, a Democrat still serving as the American representative in London, warned the new Secretary of State, Daniel Webster, that the British government was soliciting bids for transporting soldiers to Canada. "This country will not be quiet much longer," the head of American trade at Barings Bank in London, Joshua Bates, wrote in September 1841. "They are all ready with ships, steam and men, and a war with the United States would add very little to current expenditure."

The prospect of war alarmed the Anglo-American business community. As early as April 1840, Bates had cautioned Webster directly that the Maine dispute was "a matter of deep anxiety to all engaged in commercial transactions." Webster, with his close connections to the world of trans-Atlantic commerce, hardly needed to be persuaded about the need for peace. Soon after becoming Secretary of State, he began lobbying Britain's new Conservative government to undertake negotiations on the issues straining British-American relations.

By fall 1841, relations had become even more complex. Although Archibald McLeod had been acquitted, relieving pressure on the New York frontier, another issue had arisen. In November, British authorities in the Bahamas gave safe harbor to slaves who had mutinied on an American ship, the *Creole*, and killed one slaveholder. Southerners demanded the return of the slaves, but Britain's extradition treaty with the United States had expired in 1807 and the Bahamian court set them free.

The government of Prime Minister Robert Peel agreed that the decline of trans-Atlantic relations could have "consequences of the most disastrous nature" and in December 1841 appointed a special envoy, Lord Ashburton, to negotiate directly with Webster on the range of outstanding issues. (News of Ashburton's appointment arrived in Boston on the *Britannia*, with Charles Dickens, in January 1842.) Rarely are negotiations so obviously constructed with the aim of protecting commercial interests. Before his elevation to the peerage in 1835, Ashburton was known as Alexander Baring, "the prince of British merchants," and head of Barings Bank from 1810 until his retirement in 1830. He had an American wife, owned a million acres of Maine land (roughly one twentieth of the state, none of it disputed territory), and believed strongly that "the material interests of the two countries call loudly for peace and friendship." And his family's business had a close relationship with Webster. Barings Bank had kept Webster on retainer as a legal advisor and helped with the expense of his voyage to London in 1839. Webster's lobbying of the Peel government while secretary of state had been done largely through Barings. "I rather think this has been bro't about by Webster's letters to me," Joshua Bates wrote about Ashburton's appointment in January 1842. "But this must not be mentioned."

Some Americans believed that even during his service as secretary of state, Webster was "in the pay of the great English bankers, the Barings," and in London there were allegations that Ashburton paid Webster thousands of dollars to secure passage of a treaty. Allegations of a large payoff were eventually discounted, but Webster did receive other financial benefits from the Barings during the treaty negotiations. "I should like to have it in my power to help Webster a little bit if he should be much in want," Thomas Ward, Barings' Boston agent, wrote to London in April 1842. In June 1842, Webster asked Ward whether he could settle debts with Barings by giving the bank some of his land in the distressed western states. "I have a general impression that the land may not be very valuable," Ward told London. The London office agreed to the exchange in July 1842 without even enquiring about the property's actual worth.

The London stock market was immediately buoyed by the news of Ashburton's appointment to Washington. So was the American market. "No public man possesses a more correct knowledge of the trade between the two countries," wrote the New York correspondent for the *Times of London* in January 1842. "No man can estimate with greater accuracy the direful effects of a war between Great Britain and the United States than the former Mr. Baring. . . . He possesses in a high degree the confidence of the American merchants."

Commercial stability was important to Webster, but the American government also had more immediate reasons for pursuing a settlement with the British. The federal treasury was exhausted and the Tyler administration was struggling to finance its operations. In October 1841, Webster asked Ward whether Barings would manage a twelve million dollar loan that had been approved by Congress in July but could not be placed in the American market. Joshua Bates replied directly to Webster that Barings would handle the loan once "the result of Lord Ashburton's mission is known to be favourable." If Ashburton failed, Bates warned, "it will be *impossible* for anyone in the United States to negotiate a loan abroad."

As it had been for Van Buren, the challenge for Webster was assuring domestic support for any understanding that might emerge from negotiations with the British. With the consent of Tyler, Webster deployed what one of his allies called a "new mode of approaching the subject" of popular consent. Congress had given the president a fund to be used covertly "for the contingent expenses of intercourse between the United States and other nations." Webster used this money in a secret campaign to "adjust the tone and direction of the party presses and . . . public sentiment" in Maine. (Years later Tyler said that "the administration had no press in Maine to enforce its views . . . [and] merely wanted to be heard.") While Webster vehemently denied that newspapers were paid to publish articles favoring compromise with the British, his agents had persuaded the Portland *Eastern Argus*, the most prominent Democratic newspaper in the state, to abandon its belligerent stance and endorse negotiations with Ashburton. The *Argus'* articles were reprinted throughout the country, creating confusion within

Democratic ranks about the line that ought to be taken regarding the border dispute.

Webster also persuaded Ashburton that representatives of the Maine and Massachusetts governments should be allowed to participate directly in treaty negotiations. (Massachusetts was the original American claimant to the disputed territory; Maine was split from Massachusetts in 1820.) No agreement with the Ashburton would be durable if the states did not agree; in fact, Webster seemed to believe that it was the states, rather than the British, that were most likely to undermine a settlement. "Great Britain [should] consider that we cannot legislate as a unit as she can," Ward explained to London. Ashburton agreed to include the states, but soon grew frustrated at Maine's obstinacy and Webster's inability to manage the state delegations. In fact, Webster was attempting to soften the states' opposition by privately showing them evidence from earlier negotiations that supported the British claims to the territory.

Despite these troubles, the main elements of an accord were settled by early August. A new line for the northeastern border was drawn; terms were established about extradition and interference with American slave ships; and notes were exchanged expressing regret about the *Caroline* and McLeod incidents. Congress also passed legislation allowing the federal government to remove cases like McLeod's from state courts. For the second time during the financial crisis—the first was the passage of the neutrality law in 1838—Congress had strengthened federal powers over the states to preserve stability in its international affairs.

The Webster-Ashburton Treaty was ratified by the Senate within two weeks. Qualms about its terms were overwhelmed by the desire to revive a depressed economy. "Peace is the first of our wants, in the present condition of the country," said John Calhoun. "Our Government is deeply disordered; its credit is impaired; its debt increasing; its expenditures extravagant and wasteful. . . . Peace settled and undisturbed, is indispensable to a thorough reform, and such a reform to the duration of the Government." Many Americans agreed. "The treaty with Great Britain," said *Niles' Register* in late August 1842, "may prove the harbinger of better times."

The peace established by the Webster-Ashburton Treaty was immediately tested by conflict over the Sandwich Islands (now known as the Hawaiian islands). Still independent, and ruled by the King Kamehameha III, this island group was of immense importance to the United States. It offered the only harbors in the northern Pacific for the American whaling fleet, which by the early 1840s comprised well over one hundred ships. And, as an

American diplomat said in 1843, it was "impossible to overrate the importance of the Hawaiian group" as a way station for the burgeoning U.S. trade
with China, the Philippines, and Indonesia. American missionaries had also
established themselves on the islands.

However, the Americans were not alone in their interest in the archipelago. The British, the European discoverers of the islands, had diplomats
and merchants in Honolulu. They, too, understood that the island chain was
"placed so as to give its possessor complete command of the whale fishery
of the Northern Pacific." It also fit with a broader ambition for British dominance in the western Pacific. Britain had asserted sovereignty over New
Zealand in 1840 and forced access to Chinese ports at the end of the First
Opium War in 1842. France was struggling to keep up with the British,
establishing its own protectorate over islands in Polynesia in 1842. It also
attempted to make its presence felt in the northern Pacific. The French
frigate *Artemise* blockaded Honolulu in 1839 to protest the mistreatment of
Catholic missionaries in the Hawaiian islands.

Despite the substantial interests at stake, the Tyler administration remained cool to repeated appeals for protection from Kamehameha's court,
conveyed through American missionaries and businessmen. Secretary of
State Webster might have been reluctant to complicate negotiations with
Lord Ashburton by addressing the question of Hawaiian sovereignty. It was
only after the Webster-Ashburton Treaty was ratified, and a threat by Kamehameha's representatives that the islands might need to accept British
protection against French predations, that Webster and Tyler were persuaded
to act.

On December 30, 1842, Tyler sent a message to Congress stating that
the United States was "content with [the] independent existence" of the
Hawaiian government and "anxiously wishes for its security." Attempts by
other powers to take possession of the islands, Tyler added, "could not but
create dissatisfaction on the part of the United States" and would justify the
American government "in making a decided remonstrance" against such
action. At the same time, Tyler promised that the United States itself sought
"no peculiar advantages, no exclusive control" over the islands.

Some historians draw an analogy between Tyler's 1842 message and the
policy laid out earlier by President James Monroe, which warned Europeans
that interference in the newly independent states of the western hemisphere
would be regarded "as dangerous to our peace and safety . . . [and] manifestations of an unfriendly disposition toward the United States," justifying a
military response. But the comparison is inapt. The breadth and firmness of
Monroe's statement immediately impressed listeners, and the policy was

soon known as the Monroe Doctrine in the United States and European capitals. By contrast, the 1842 message did not become known as the Tyler Doctrine until historians gave it that name a century later. Tyler's warning was narrower in its reach and more equivocal about consequences.

The reason for this is straightforward. The Monroe Doctrine was mainly intended to deter Spanish and Russian intrusions in the New World. The United Kingdom had encouraged an American declaration and it was understood, if rarely acknowledged, that British naval power could be deployed to enforce it. In contrast, Tyler's message challenged a British interest. Many Britons believed that they had, "according to the custom of nations, an exclusive claim" to the islands. Moreover, it would be difficult for the United States to resist a British attempt to assert sovereignty. (An American naval commander reported that the islands "have no port that is defensible against a strong naval force.") As the *Times of London* editorialized, British acquiescence to Tyler's declaration would not flow "from want of right or any power to defend that right."

Kamehameha's agents in Washington certainly felt that they had got less than they hoped for from the Americans. Webster told them privately that Tyler saw no need for a treaty recognizing the islands' independence and establishing formal diplomatic relations. William Richards, one of Kamehameha's representatives, wrote in his diary that Webster said that "it was best not to do too much at once." Even while Tyler was making a public commitment to the islands, Webster was giving private assurances to the British government that the United States itself had no aspirations to control the archipelago. The American ambassador, Edward Everett, also told the British Foreign Secretary, Lord Aberdeen, that he had heard privately that the Hawaiians had invited the United States to annex the islands, but that "if the offer were made it was certainly declined." The former British consul to the Sandwich Islands also believed that an offer of annexation had been made to the Tyler administration but that Americans "saw that England would not permit such a glaring alienation of what, really, appertained to her."

American policy was certainly not driven by repulsion toward annexation in general. After all, President Tyler was an enthusiastic advocate for annexation of Texas, notwithstanding the fact that Mexico had claims on that territory. In December 1843, Tyler publicly mocked Mexican warnings that annexation would provoke a declaration of war against the United States. But confrontation with Britain was a different matter entirely. American policy toward the Sandwich Islands attempted to straddle the gap between the nation's expansionist tendencies and the prevailing economic and military realities.

The awkwardness contained within the policy became immediately obvious. In February 1843 a British warship, *HMS Carysfort*, entered Honolulu harbor. Its commander, Lord George Paulet, threatened to attack the town unless reparations were made for the mistreatment of British officials and citizens. Under duress, Kamehameha surrendered to Paulet and the British flag was raised over all the Sandwich Islands. Kamehameha appealed to London for a reversal of Paulet's actions, and to Washington for help in recovering Hawaiian sovereignty. News of Paulet's actions produced a wave of popular anger in the United States against the British. The *Democratic Review* called it "an act of sheer, simple, downright and outright spoliation . . . one of the most outrageous outrages that have ever disgraced even the foreign domination of that great maritime and mercantile tyranny." The *Merchants' Magazine* said that Paulet's action was motivated by "a settled and determination hatred to all that is American." Moreover, the provocation was universally understood as a test of the Tyler administration's policy toward the islands. "It remains to be seen," *Niles' National Register* said in June 1843, "whether the United States government will acquiesce in an usurpation so destructive to the fruits of American industry."

The Tyler administration said nothing to stoke Americans' anger over the British action. Secretary of State Legare, acting on Tyler's instructions, wrote to Everett, the American minister in London, that the United States had critical commercial and political interests in the islands, and that it "might even feel justified . . . in interfering by force" to prevent their falling into the hands of a European power. But Legare did not instruct Everett to convey this hedged threat to the British government. Instead, Everett was to use his "best endeavors" to enlist diplomats from France and Russia in a joint effort to dissuade the British government from following through with occupation.

By the time Legare's letter reached London, however, the British government had already defused the conflict. Not yet aware of the popular anger in the United States, Britain announced that Paulet had exceeded his authority in seizing the islands, and directed the Royal Navy to restore Kamehameha to power. Thus a test of the American commitment to Hawaiian independence was avoided. Legare's successor as secretary of state, Abel Upshur, wrote to British ambassador Henry Stephen Fox directly in July 1843. His letter conveyed relief as much as vindication, and another promise that the United States itself would seek no undue advantages for American citizens in the islands at the expense of Britain.

The tension between popular pressure for an aggressive foreign policy and commercial and military realities was illustrated even more vividly in the

conflict over the Oregon Territory, a wild region west of the Rocky Mountains comprising the present-day states of Oregon and Washington as well as
the Canadian province of British Columbia. The United States and Great
Britain were the only two powers with serious claims to the territory. Spain
had conceded any right to land north of California in 1819, while Russia abandoned any claim south of Alaska in 1825. But British and American claims in
the territory could not be reconciled. Until 1845, the Americans claimed all
land south of the 49th parallel. The British disputed the American claim
with regard to land that was south of the 49th parallel but north of the Columbia River. The contested region included the Puget Sound, the only
good port on the west coast other than San Francisco Bay and San Diego
Bay, both of which were still in Mexican hands. In 1818 and again in 1827,
the two countries agreed to defer a resolution of the dispute and establish a
joint Anglo-American occupation of most of the territory.

Time was running against the British. American migration into the region south of the 49th parallel was increasing, and although the total Anglo-
American population was still very small, the British were outnumbered.
American settlers were establishing primitive governmental institutions. A
trader with the Hudson's Bay Company warned London in 1845 that the
country was bound to pass into American hands in the absence of active British intervention, "as the overwhelming numbers of Americans who are from
year to year coming to the country will give an American tone and character
to its institutions which it will be impossible afterwards to eradicate."

The Oregon question was not seriously addressed during negotiations
over the Webster-Ashburton Treaty, mainly because both Webster and Ashburton believed that territorial disputes in the east deserved higher priority.
But once the treaty was finalized, both sides were ready to discuss a permanent solution to their problems in the west. In October 1842 Lord Aberdeen asked the Tyler administration to authorize negotiations about Oregon
between himself and Edward Everett, the U.S. representative in London.
Everett told Washington that he was convinced that the British were "really
willing to agree to reasonable terms of settlement." Indeed, Aberdeen recognized that the American demand for access to Puget Sound could not be
rebuffed. In November 1843, Everett suggested to Aberdeen a compromise:
a border that ran westward along the 49th parallel to the ocean's edge, and
then down along the main channel of the Strait of Juan de Fuca. The Americans would have Puget Sound, while the British would keep the whole of
Vancouver Island and easy access to Vancouver itself. Everett reported that
Aberdeen seemed open to this plan. A few weeks later, Aberdeen privately
instructed the British ambassador to Washington that Britain would be

prepared to consider this arrangement if the British had free access to American ports in Puget Sound and also to the Columbia River. In a brief conversation, Everett and Aberdeen came very close to the terms by which the Oregon question was resolved in a treaty signed by President Polk in June 1846. But the route by which the two countries arrived at this conclusion was complicated by American domestic politics, so much so that the two countries were, by early 1846, again on the verge of war.

At first the Tyler administration seemed receptive to negotiations with the British. Webster told the British ambassador in November 1842 that Tyler "concurred entirely" on the desirability of immediate discussions. "I wish to avoid . . . any action on our part which might bring us into collision with England," Tyler wrote privately in April 1843. To preserve good relations, Webster suppressed an 1842 report from a U.S. naval expedition that recommended a military occupation to consolidate American control of all territory up to the Alaska boundary. Yet no significant negotiations were undertaken in 1843. Webster complicated matters by pursuing an ultimately unsuccessful plan to have himself appointed as a special commissioner to London on the Oregon question.

Aberdeen hoped that the new British ambassador, Richard Pakenham, could begin negotiations after his arrival in Washington in February 1844. But the Oregon dispute was already entangled in the politics of the 1844 presidential election. The opposition Democrats saw an opportunity to make political capital out of the dispute. In January 1844, a convention of Ohio Democrats resolved that the United States should take "formal and immediate possession" of all of the Oregon Territory. At the national Democratic convention in Baltimore four months later, Ohioans won a platform statement that American title to the entire territory was "clear and unquestionable, [and] that no portion of the same ought to be ceded to England." The Democratic nominee James Polk promised that he would not allow the United Kingdom to "hold dominion over any portion" of the Oregon Territory. "The subject has given rise to so much excitement," Lord Aberdeen reported to Prime Minister Robert Peel in October 1844, that the prospects for constructive negotiation had evaporated.

Polk, elected president a few weeks later, regarded himself as an old Jacksonian with the plain and direct style of his mentor. "The only way to treat John Bull," he said, was "to look him straight in the face . . . [and take] a bold & firm course." And in his public statements, Polk appeared to do this on the Oregon question. In his inaugural address in March 1845, Polk again insisted that the country's title to all of Oregon was clear and unquestionable. Polk promised to use all constitutional means to assert the American claim. It was immediately clear, however, that this position would lead to conflict with the United Kingdom. Only hours after Polk's address arrived in London on March 27, the *Times* warned: "The territory of the Oregon will never be wrested from the British Crown, to which it belongs, but by WAR." On April 2, Prime Minister Peel and Lord Aberdeen agreed that spies should be sent west "to gain a general knowledge of the capabilities of the Oregon territory in a military point of view, in order that we may be enabled to act immediately and with effect in defense of our rights." British warships were ordered to the Oregon coast "to let the Americans see clearly" that British title would be defended.

On April 4, Prime Minister Peel reassured the House of Commons that his government was "resolved and prepared" to defend British rights if negotiations failed. The steamship *Caledonia*, scheduled to leave Liverpool for Boston earlier that day, was detained so that it could carry "the distinct and emphatic declaration of the British government on the subject of the Oregon territory," resoundingly endorsed by the British Parliament. It also contained a private letter from Aberdeen to Pakenham warning that "the time has come when we must endeavour to prepare for every contingency . . . we are perfectly determined to cede nothing to force or menace."

The news from Britain arrived in Washington at the end of April, provoking an equal and opposite reaction from expansionist Democrats. Senator Hopkins Turney of Tennessee said that some western Democrats "were almost mad on the subject of Oregon." Illinois Senator Sidney Breese reassured constituents that he would fight against the surrender of any part of the territory. "I am for the whole, and that statesman who shall advise the surrender to England of one foot of its soil or one drop of its water is a *doomed man*." Polk stoked the fires further in his December 1845 message to Congress, restating his "settled conviction that the British pretensions of title could not be maintained to any part of the Oregon Territory," and calling on Congress to withdraw from the 1826 convention that established joint occupancy. Tyler's policy, the Democratic newspaper *The Union* said, was "the whole of Oregon, or none."

If there had been any doubt in the White House that this policy would mean war with the British, it was dispelled in January 1846 by a message from Louis McLane, the new American ambassador in London. McLane had been asked by Secretary of State James Buchanan to meet with Aberdeen and determine whether Britain really was preparing for war over the Oregon question. McLane replied that it was impossible to establish exactly the real motives for British military maneuvers. But he added this warning:

> It is very clear that if a rupture with the United States should grow out of our present difficulties, this country will be as fully and effectually prepared for it at all points, and for all possible purposes, as if that, and that alone, had been the object of all her warlike preparations. She will be in a situation to act and strike as promptly and signally as she could have been with her energies directed to that end; and I feel it my duty to add, that not to expect, in case a rupture becomes unavoidable, that this Government, thus in complete armor, will promptly and vigorously exert her utmost power, to inflict the utmost possible injury upon our country and all its interests, would not be doing justice to such a crisis.

The prospect of war "stares every one in the face," *Niles' National Register* wrote in November 1845. The uncertainty had a devastating effect on commerce. Barings' London office told a South Carolina banker in December 1845 that trading in American securities was "paralyzed by the uncertainty about the Oregon question. There are no buyers and forced sales must be made at great sacrifices." (Barings' Boston agent, Thomas Ward, met with Polk to gauge his real intentions. Ward assured Polk that he was "my political friend & the friend of my administration," the president wrote in his diary. But Polk dismissed him as a stalking-horse for the British and said nothing to allay his fears.) The *Register* reported that money was also becoming scarce in the United States as "a very general anxiety" pervaded the market. In Indiana, Charles Butler, the New York lawyer who had been hired by London banks to negotiate over the state's default, worried that "the war feeling springing up among the people" would undermine his attempts to persuade state legislators to honor British-held bonds.

In New York, the aging Albert Gallatin, who had been secretary of the treasury under Jefferson and Madison, wondered how the war could be paid for, except through ruinous taxation. "The credit of the Union has been injured abroad by the failure of several of the States to fulfill their engagements. . . . No expectation can be entertained of being able to borrow money in Europe." An anonymous Philadelphia pamphleteer agreed. "How is our government to obtain the enormous funds requisite to carry on a war? . . . Monied men, for the most part, think very unfavourably of belligerent measures for the acquisition of Oregon." By 1846 it was not just moneyed men who were having doubts about Polk's hard line. The prospect of a disruption in economic relations with Britain also caused many southern Democrats to resist a hard negotiating position over Oregon. (It was easier for northwestern Democrats, Daniel Webster observed: "They have no cotton crops, and no ships.") A large majority of slave-state Democratic senators joined with Whigs in January 1846 to delay debate on Polk's call for a repudiation of the 1826 convention. A similar coalition of southern Democrats and Whigs emerged in the House. Senator Thomas Hart Benton, an ardent expansionist, eventually told Polk that he was prepared to settle for much less than the whole of Oregon. In May 1846 Polk's own vice president, George Dallas, urged him to forego "the abstract question of title" and negotiate with the British.

Some Americans wondered whether Polk was seriously prepared to fight Britain for all of Oregon: perhaps he was playing a clever game of bluff, which involved the deliberate deception of voters and legislators about his real intentions. It is doubtful that Polk was not being nearly so artful as some of his critics supposed. He genuinely believed that the United States was entitled to all of Oregon, and understood his obligation to the powerful constituencies who shared that view and helped to make him president. Writing in his diary in December 1845, Polk said that his "greatest danger" was being attacked domestically for surrendering the American claim to the whole of the territory. He worried that opposition to a compromise would be so strong that it "would have gone far to overthrow the administration." But Polk also understood that the British had drawn a line against cession of the whole territory—"Britain is fully committed on that point," Albert Gallatin wrote in 1846—and that the United States could not now afford a war with Britain, any more that it could in 1838.

In fact, Polk had already made one attempt to negotiate with the British. In July 1845, Polk sent a message to the British ambassador, Pakenham, offering to settle exactly at the 49th parallel. The British had repeatedly rejected this proposal over preceding years, and Aberdeen had told Everett in 1843 that a simple division at the 49th parallel was still untenable. Moreover, the offer was made so belligerently—accompanied by yet another assertion that American title extended to Alaska—that the offer was cooly rejected by Pakenham. A nineteen-century historian concluded that Polk "could not possibly have considered this offer as made in earnest." But Polk was earnest. He was offended by Pakenham's rebuff and made no further attempts to negotiate with the British for months.

By February 1846, however, it was clear that Polk's hard line could not be held. In a February 3 dispatch from London, McLane reported a conversation in which Aberdeen said that Britain was preparing for "offensive operations" against the United States, including the immediate deployment of thirty warships. Polk and his Cabinet quickly agreed that McLane should tell Aberdeen "that the door was not closed" to further discussion and that Polk was prepared to send to the Senate a proposal that ceded British control of the whole of Vancouver Island and access to the Columbia River— that is, terms very much like those discussed by Aberdeen and Everett in November 1843. Within weeks, the Oregon question was resolved. The British plan to settle the dispute on these terms was received by the Polk Cabinet on June 6, 1846; ratified by the Senate without any modification four days later; and signed by the president on June 15. The threat of war instantly dissipated.

The Oregon dispute provided hard proof of the extent to which national ambitions had to be trimmed to accommodate economic and military realities. Perhaps the fact that a Whig administration was prepared to negotiate with the British did not prove much: the Whigs were closer to the country's commercial interests and more susceptible to Anglophilia. The same could not be said of Polk and his Democratic base. They distrusted the British and were temperamentally indisposed to negotiate with them. Once the British threatened war, however, there was no choice but negotiation.

Negotiation implied compromise, and compromise implied the disappointment of many of Polk's supporters. The White House directed party leaders to suppress demonstrations against the treaty, while the administration press attempted to argue that the president's hard bargaining had won unprecedented concessions. Even so, Polk paid a heavy price for giving up the American claim to the whole of the Oregon Territory. The Cleveland *Plain Dealer* complained that its readers had been duped by the president and "despoiled . . . by a traitorous alliance of Southern Democrats with Tory Whigs." Ohio Senator William Allen resigned as chair of the Foreign Relations committee so that he could "take the stump and denounce" the treaty. By the summer of 1846, Democrats in both the House of Representatives and Senate were in disarray, complicating Polk's ability to pursue other policies. In the House, the party was about to lose the majority it had won just three years earlier. Transatlantic commerce and finance had been protected, but at the price of political disorder at home.

CHAPTER 4

Law and Order

The First Great Depression began as a crisis among financial institutions and then effloresced into something larger and more complicated. Economic troubles led to political turmoil. The machinery of state and federal government strained to manage a welter of old and new antagonisms—between sections, between parties, between debtors and creditors, between Americans and Britons. Voting rates surged, the duration of incumbency for officeholders became more uncertain, tempers frayed, and the capacity for conciliation declined. The country's nascent democratic institutions were like the boiler on a steamboat. Could the pressures within those institutions be regulated and contained, or would the whole system blow apart, as did steamboats on the Hudson and Mississippi with lamentable regularity?

The fear that political troubles might end in violence was real and well-justified. In cities and on farms across the country, economic decline awakened old grievances about inequities in the distribution of economic and political power. In good times, when farmers and workers were doing well, these complaints might be put aside. In bad times they acquired new force, and disgruntled Americans were organized more easily to push for change. These early protests were often garbed in the language and symbolism of the Revolutionary War. Many took the idea of revolution seriously, offering violent resistance to the status quo. This was most clearly the case in the northeastern United States, where agrarian and industrial laborers, not shackled by the institution of slavery, had the capacity to organize and articulate their grievances.

At the time, these uprisings were widely regarded as symptoms of a sickness within the American polity. The violence raised questions about the capacity of citizens to regulate themselves, and also about the ability of a nation organized on democratic principles to maintain civil peace. Here was the basic problem of the crisis—the balancing of liberty and order—presented in its barest form. And once again domestic and international affairs became entangled, as creditors in Europe wondered whether they could trust their investments to a land in which peace could not be maintained. Authorities in three states that experienced severe outbreaks of violence responded to this challenge in similar ways. Tentative attempts to maintain order eventually gave way to the ruthless suppression of resistance against established authority. Law and order had to be preserved, and if the governmental capability to maintain order did not exist, it had to be created. One of the essential requirements for the survival of a fragile, open economy proved to be the availability of an effective domestic police power.

☙ Rebellion in Rhode Island

> It was a state of war, and the established Government resorted to the rights and usages of war to maintain itself, and to overcome the unlawful opposition.
>
> —Chief Justice Roger Taney, *Luther v. Borden*, 1849

Thomas Dorr was an unlikely rebel. The son of a wealthy Providence merchant, Dorr was a graduate of Phillips Exeter Academy and second in his class at Harvard College. He apprenticed as a clerk to one of the country's most prominent jurists and then began to practice law in Rhode Island. Short, balding, and overweight, with a chin "lost in the flesh that underlaid it," Dorr always appeared in public with a silk hat, cloak, and cane. He was one of Rhode Island's gentry. In June 1844, though, Dorr was convicted of treason by the Rhode Island Supreme Court and sentenced to hard labor, in solitary confinement, for the rest of his natural life. That was the end of the Dorr Rebellion.

For two months in 1842, two governments—one led by Dorr—claimed to lead the state of Rhode Island and command its militia. The rebellion was an extraordinary moment that arose when a longstanding grievance about voting rights was combined with economic distress. It ultimately provoked long-needed constitutional reform, but also tested the country's tolerance of open challenges to established authority. As President John Tyler said before sending troops to help crush the rebellion in the summer of 1842, insurgency could not be tolerated, whatever the merits of the rebels' complaints. Dissidents could pursue their goals only through "regular and, if necessary, repeated appeals to the constituted authorities," and would be forcibly suppressed otherwise.

The ostensible cause of the Dorr rebellion were the defects of the Rhode Island constitution, a relic of the colonial era. Unlike other states, Rhode Island did not adopt a new constitution at the time of the American Revolution. Instead, it continued to organize its government on the basis of the royal charter granted to colonists by Charles II in 1663. The charter had three major difficulties: it limited the right to vote to citizens who owned land worth at least $134 (in 1840, per capita income in the state was probably about $100); it gave an equal number of representatives to each town incorporated after 1663; and it lacked any mechanism for amending its terms.

As the economy of the state developed, the language of the state charter became increasingly problematic. Rhode Island was an important center of manufacturing in the first decades of the nineteen century. The shift from an agrarian to industrial economy meant that there were a growing number of landless mill workers, many Irish or French Canadian immigrants, who were disqualified from voting. Meanwhile, towns that were expanding because of industrialization at the northern reach of Narragansett Bay saw no similar growth in representation in the state assembly. Industrial communities in the Blackstone-Pawtuxet region had two-thirds of the state's population in 1840, but elected only one-third of the state's representatives.

Between 1820 and 1840 there were many unsuccessful attempts to reform the state constitution by extending voting rights and redistributing seats in the assembly. Thomas Dorr was one of several moderate liberals who campaigned fruitlessly for change. The unwillingness of landed voters to give up their political monopoly was predictable, but the reformers were also compromised by ineffectual leadership and the lack of broad popular anger about the status quo. A Constitutional Party organized by Dorr and others in 1834 was dead by 1838.

The Reverend Francis Wayland, president of Brown University and a diehard opponent of broader voting rights, said in 1842 that demands for reform before the economic crisis "never seemed to arise from any strong feeling, nor to assume a form that called for immediate action." "Before

1840," a sympathetic historian concedes, "[t]here was no definite general demand for a change." In other words, Rhode Island resisted voting reform even at the zenith of the Jacksonian era. While nearby states abandoned property requirements for voting, Rhode Island held firm. The result was evident in the presidential election of 1840. In the adjacent state of Connecticut, 75 percent of adult white males voted in 1840. In Massachusetts 66 percent of adult white males voted, in New York State 78 percent, and in New Hampshire nearly 90 percent. But in Rhode Island, only one in three white adult males voted. This was the lowest participation rate of any state in the union. In a state with a population of 109,000 people, only 8,622 cast a ballot in 1840.

Things finally began to change in Rhode Island in 1840. In February, a small group met in Providence to revive the suffrage question. They were not the leaders of the earlier reform efforts—only "a few men without wealth, with little or no popular influence"—but they quickly gained adherents. The momentum of the new suffrage movement surprised observers: "The meetings were continued from week to week, and the attendants rapidly increased in numbers. Still, leading politicians . . . stood aloof, and for a long time the party consisted almost entirely of mechanics and working men, in the humbler walks of life."

The Rhode Island Suffrage Association was organized in Providence in March 1840, declaring that "the time has gone by for submission to most unjust outrages upon social and political rights." Within a few months, nearly every major town in the state had its own suffrage society. "There were vital questions abroad," a contemporary writer said, "and nothing could quell them." Many of the moderate liberals who had championed earlier reform efforts, like Dorr, were eventually drawn to the new suffrage movement. But so were more radical elements. One of the militants was Seth Luther, already notorious as a labor agitator across the northeast. His 1833 *Address to the Working Men of New England* condemned the cruelty of the system of manufacturing and the growing divide between rich manufacturers and factory workers. ("So much for equality in a republican country," said Luther.) His campaign for suffrage was cast in the same terms. "Peaceably if we can, forcibly if we must!" Luther told suffragist rallies in early 1841.

The New Age, a suffragist newspaper, began publication in November 1840, and the suffragists' meetings continued to draw larger crowds. A rally in Providence on April 17, 1841, that was expected to attract a few hundred people, instead drew three thousand. It began with the peal of church bells across the city and a parade almost a mile long, with banners and bands playing the specially commissioned *Free Suffrage Quickstep*. Another mass meeting was held in Newport on May 5, and a third in Providence on July 5. At the July meeting the Universalist minister William Stevens Balch urged the crowd on:

> It may be said that these views are revolutionary. Allow it. . . . But is a revolution to be dreaded when *right*, and *justice*, and *virtue*, and *equality* are to be gained to the whole community? . . . Call it a revolution, that we level every false distinction, every grade not based on talent or moral worth, and proclaim liberty and equal rights to the people? Then are we revolutionists, and we glory in it, and we will rejoice when such a revolution is consummated, and its blessings are revealed!

Why did the campaign for constitutional reform suddenly revive and acquire such energy? The economic crisis was undoubtedly an important factor. Evidence of the state's quick decline is found in trade statistics. The value of Rhode Island's exports and imports declined by roughly half between 1837 and 1840, and stayed at that depressed level for the next three years. Manufacturing in the state slumped as well. Many of the state's new cotton mills halted production. The nascent metalworking industry was hard hit. Finance stagnated too, with no new banks chartered at all in the decade after the panic. The disenfranchised workingmen of Rhode Island were vulnerable and quick to anger.

The presidential campaign of 1840 also encouraged radicalism in Rhode Island. That election was one of the most bitterly fought in early American history. In other parts of the country, voting rates surged to unprecedented levels, while most white adult males in Rhode Island were compelled to remain spectators to the contest. They could watch other states battle over the country's future, but could not translate their own preferences into votes. Even if they were disenfranchised, though, Rhode Islanders shared the frustrations that sank the candidacy of President Martin Van Buren.

A third factor also bolstered the strength of the campaign for constitutional reform. Unlike earlier efforts, the post-1840 suffragist movement gained national attention, as Democrats in other states and Washington realized that it could be used to maintain popular anger against their Whig opponents. Especially in the later stages of the conflict, Rhode Island's rebels were encouraged by the sense that they were at the center of the national stage. They were incited by party activists outside the state who believed they could turn the conflict to their own advantage.

The Rhode Island assembly attempted to conciliate the suffragists by promising to hold a constitutional convention in November 1841. However, the state assembly refused to allow landless citizens to participate in the election of delegates to the convention, or give towns the number of delegates proportionate to their population. Suffragists responded to the assembly's overture by insisting that they would not recognize any government established by its convention. The suffragists convened their own People's Convention in Providence in October 1841.

The landowners' convention, as the state assembly's meeting was called, proposed a slate of modest amendments to voting rights that satisfied neither conservatives nor liberals, and was rejected in a referendum in March 1842. Meanwhile, the suffragists drafted a People's Constitution that was ratified in an improvised election in December 1841, open to any male who affirmed he was a citizen and resident of the state. Next, the suffragists announced plans to hold state-wide elections under the People's Constitution, with Dorr standing as their candidate for governor. At the same time, suffragists solicited military aid. In Providence, the bulk of four companies of state militia—the Independent Volunteers, the United Train of Artillery, the National Cadets, the First Light Infantry—pledged support for the People's Constitution. Suffragists were able to exploit the amateurism and disregard for chain of command that typified the antebellum militia. In many wards of the city, volunteers also armed themselves "and almost nightly paraded the streets."

Rhode Island's social and political elite were alarmed by the power of the suffragist movement. "The controversy," said William Goddard, a philosophy professor at Brown University, "is mainly between the farmers of Rhode Island and the masses who congregate in the cities and factory villages of Rhode Island." The central question was whether the "floating masses of Providence, Woonsocket and Chepachet [would] rule the State" and cause "complete destruction of the political power of the agricultural interest, and of all other conservative interests." Francis Wayland—the same man who was recruited by a Barings Bank agent to inveigh against repudiation of state debts—told his Rhode Island parishioners that the problem posed by the suffragists was one "affecting the very existence of society. . . . Whether law or anarchy shall bear sway; not at the ballot boxes, to express our peaceful wishes, but, at the cannon's mouth, to determine whether we shall be governed by constitutional law, or trampled underfoot by a lawless soldiery."

Many of the state's elite, both Whigs and Democrats, met in Providence to establish the new Law and Order Party while the suffragists prepared for their elections in March 1842. They resolved to support the state assembly "should any crisis occur to demand our aid." Prompted by an informal query from Law and Order supporters, Rhode Island's supreme court announced that the People's Constitution was "without law. Any attempt to carry it into effect would be treason against the State." The federal judge for Rhode Island, John Pitman, agreed on the need to resist the suffragists' challenge. "The first duty of government," Pitman said, "is to protect itself."

A few days later, the state assembly adopted legislation that threatened individuals accepting office under the People's Constitution with arrest for treason. (This became known as the Algerine Law, because it was alleged to give Governor Samuel King the same despotic powers wielded by the Bey of Algiers.) At the same time, it authorized Governor King to bolster the loyal part of the state militia. Over the following six months, the Rhode Island government spent $102,000 to suppress the suffragists—more than the state government ordinarily disbursed for all purposes in a year. Governor King also sent a deputation to Washington to ask for aid from President Tyler, carrying a letter in which King warned that Rhode Island was "agitated by revolutionary movements, and is now threatened with domestic violence." In some parts of the state, and particularly in Providence, the rebels appeared to "constitute a majority of the physical force." King asked Tyler to issue a proclamation supporting the state government and send a military commander to Providence to show the federal government's resolve. Tyler temporized. On April 11, 1842, he told King that he would provide aid in the case of an actual insurrection, "manifested by lawless assemblages of the people or otherwise," but that he lacked any authority to "anticipate insurrectionary movements." In the meantime, he hoped that "a spirit of conciliation will prevail . . . [and] all actual grievances will be promptly redressed" by the Charter government.

This reply, which conceded the president's ultimate obligation to support the established state government, inflamed many suffragists. His letter, said one, "was a virtual declaration of war against a majority of the People of Rhode Island." On April 18, six thousand citizens voted in the "People's election," ratifying Dorr as their governor, and choosing a full slate of senators and representatives as well. The following day, April 19, the state assembly held its own election, in which Governor King trounced a moderate opponent among landowning voters.

The state now had two rival governments. On May 3, Dorr led a procession of two thousand people, escorted by two military companies, past the barricaded statehouse to an unused Providence foundry, where he convened the People's Assembly. It repealed the Algerine Law, selected a supreme court, demanded the surrender of public property to the People's

BY HIS EXCELLENCY,
SAMUEL WARD KING,
GOVERNOR, CAPTAIN-GENERAL, AND COMMANDER-IN-CHIEF OF THE STATE OF
RHODE-ISLAND AND PROVIDENCE PLANTATIONS.

A PROCLAMATION.

WHEREAS on the eighth day of June instant, I issued a Proclamation, offering a reward of one thousand dollars for the delivery of the fugitive Traitor, THOMAS WILSON DORR, to the proper civil authority: and whereas the said Thomas Wilson Dorr having returned to this State and assumed the command of a numerous body of armed men, in open rebellion against the Government thereof, has again *fled* the summary justice which awaited him; I do therefore, by virtue of authority in me vested, and by advice of the Council, hereby offer an additional reward of four thousand dollars for the apprehension and delivery of the said Thomas Wilson Dorr to the Sheriff of the County of Newport or Providence, within three months from the date hereof.

GIVEN under my hand and the seal of said State, at the City of Providence, this twenty-ninth day of June, in the year of our Lord one thousand eight hundred and forty-two, and of the Independence of the United States of America the sixty-sixth.

SAMUEL WARD KING.

BY HIS EXCELLENCY'S COMMAND:
HENRY BOWEN, Secretary of State.

FIGURE 10. Reward for the Arrest of the Rebel Thomas Dorr, 1842. Source: A. Mowry, *The Dorr War* (Providence, RI: Preston & Rounds, 1901).

officers, and passed resolutions notifying President Tyler, Congress, and other states that it was now the legitimate authority in Rhode Island. The next day, King and the state assembly convened in Newport. It declared the existence of an insurrection, ordered the arrest of rebel leaders, and sent commissioners to Washington to demand assistance from the federal government. Meanwhile, it continued its military preparations. Five hundred artillery pieces and over two thousand muskets were collected in the arsenal at Providence. Friendly militia companies were drilled and arms were distributed to volunteers.

Both sides believed that the attitude of the federal government might be critical in resolving the conflict. Dorr quickly followed the state assembly's commissioners to Washington and lobbied Tyler's cabinet and Congress for support. But law and order got the upper hand. On May 7, Tyler wrote to King promising that the federal government "will stand ready to succor the authorities of the state in their efforts to maintain a due respect for the laws." The insurgents, he said, had no right to impose changes "by violence and bloodshed." Many suffragists thought Tyler had thrown the fight. In Rhode Island, some who had been elected to posts under the People's Constitution quickly resigned, announcing that that they had no intention of "carrying the Constitution into effect against the power of the General Government of the United States, which has been called upon to act against us."

Dorr had a friendlier reception in New York City on his return from Washington. Democratic leaders hoisted a flag in his honor over Tammany Hall. He left the city in a procession of five hundred people, accompanied by a marching band and convinced that he had New Yorkers solidly behind him. Several companies of New York state militia offered to travel with Dorr to Rhode Island. Dorr declined for the moment, but warned that "the time may not be far distant when I may be obliged to call upon you for your services in that cause to which you will so promptly render the most efficient aid—the cause of American citizens contending for their sovereign right to make and maintain a republican constitution and opposed by the hired soldiers of the General Government."

Dorr arrived back in Providence on May 16, met by a parade of several thousand and an escort of hundreds of armed men. Brandishing a sword given to him in New York City by a veteran of the Seminole wars, Dorr called on friendly militia to prepare for immediate service, and warned that if federal troops came to support the established state government, he would have the help of five thousand volunteers from New York as well. "The contest will then become national," Dorr said, "and our State the battle ground of American freedom." The following night, Dorr and a group of two hundred supporters attempted an attack on Providence's arsenal. Dorr was an incompetent commander, and the assault was a fiasco. The garrison within the fog-bound arsenal would not surrender, as Dorr had expected; Dorr's two field guns, seized from the state militia, misfired; and many of his own band deserted. Dorr fled from Providence the next morning before the arrival of troops in support of the Law and Order government. King issued a warrant for the arrest of Dorr for treason and won promises from the governors of New York and Massachusetts that they would detain and return Dorr. (The governor of Connecticut refused.) But Dorr could not be found.

In late May 1842, King appealed to Tyler for help for a third time, conveying rumors that Dorr was recruiting men in neighboring states to wage open war against his government. This time, Tyler was more responsive, if still skeptical about the threat posed by Dorr and his allies. He issued private orders to military commanders in Rhode Island, New York, and Massachusetts to deploy spies to follow Dorr's activities. Two companies of federal troops were moved from New York to Rhode Island.

Meanwhile, Dorr was attempting to regroup his friends at Chepachet, a hamlet fifteen miles northwest of Providence. On June 22, the federal commander in Providence reported to the secretary of war that

> several large boxes of muskets, supposed to contain about eighty, were received the evening before last at Woonsocket from New York; that several mounted cannon had been also received there and forwarded on to Chepachet; that a number of men, not citizens of the State, with arms, were in and about Woonsocket and Chepachet; that forty-eight kegs of powder were stolen on Sunday night last from a powder house in this neighborhood, and that Dorr, with about twenty men, landed last evening at Norwich. An unsuccessful attempt was made two nights ago to steal the guns of the artillery company at Warren, and at several other places where guns had been deposited by the State, by some of Dorr's men, one of whom has been identified and arrested. It has been observed for several days past that many of the suffrage party and residents of this city have been sending off their families and effects. The inhabitants of the city are seriously alarmed and in a state of much excitement.

The next day the mayor of Providence, writing to Tyler at Governor King's request, warned that bodies of men had been seen marching toward Chepachet, and that many in Providence were "ready to join in any mischief" if Dorr's forces came near the city. King himself told Tyler that the rebels, perhaps as many as one thousand men, had "established a kind of martial law" at Chepachet. Tyler finally took action. On June 29, he sent Secretary of War John Spencer to Rhode Island with instructions to prepare federal forces to put down the insurrection.

King had already declared martial law in Rhode Island on June 25, warning citizens against providing aid to "the traitor Thomas Wilson Dorr, or his deluded adherents, now assembled in arms against the laws and authorities of this State." The Law and Order government mustered three thousand militiamen in Providence, and five hundred were dispatched to Chepachet. Rumors had exaggerated the size of Dorr's force. He had about two hundred men, and a few cannon, protected behind primitive earthworks on a hill overlooking the Providence turnpike near Chepachet. Hearing that troops were on their way, and seeing the condition of his own supporters, Dorr ordered his forces to disperse. He again fled Rhode Island—this time to New Hampshire, whose legislature eventually passed a resolution promising him freedom of the state. There was no conflict at Chepachet, although about one hundred sympathizers were arrested by the militia. At Pawtucket, however, militiamen fired on a crowd of three hundred suffragists, killing one man and wounding several others.

"Dorr was politically dead," a sympathetic biographer said. "The People's Constitution was also a corpse." In August 1842, Dorr, Seth Luther, and five others were indicted for high treason. Martial law was maintained for another two months.

With the insurrection suppressed, the state government did proceed with constitutional reform. Its constitutional convention reconvened in November 1842, this time with delegates elected by all native-born adult males. The new state constitution went into effect the following May. It eliminated the property requirement for native-born taxpayers. In the next election, a Law and Order candidate, James Fenner, was elected governor, although the voting was marred by unprecedented corruption as landlords and mill owners sought to influence newly enfranchised citizens. Law and Order candidates also won elections for two open seats in the House of Representatives, while a third, the chancellor of Brown University, took a vacant Senate seat.

Dorr and the suffragists might have moved the established authorities to action, but the essential fact was that they were, at the same time, destroyed as players in Rhode Island's political theater. The principal aim of the authorities had been to preserve order, and the full resources of the government were mobilized to that end. The only path to political transformation that was tolerable was through peaceful renovation of existing structures. That the insurgents had a well-founded complaint about the illegitimacy of those structures was beside the point. When Dorr eventually returned to Providence in October 1843, he was immediately arrested and put on trial before the state supreme court in Newport for "wickedly and traitorously devising to disturb and to stir up, move and excite, insurrection, rebellion and war." He was convicted and sentenced to hard labor the following year.

During the rebellion, President Tyler had also come down on the side of law and order. He rebuffed the suffragists' complaints that they had been denied the "republican form of government" guaranteed by the Constitution. Tyler could have pressed harder for constitutional reform as a condition for federal intervention, but refused to do so. This would be a power "of the most dangerous character," Tyler later said.

> Under such assumptions the States of this Union would have no security for peace or tranquility. . . . [The President] might become the great agitator, fomenting assaults upon the State constitutions and declaring the majority of to-day to be the minority of to-morrow, and the minority, in its turn, the majority, before whose decrees the established order of things in the State should be subverted. Revolution, civil commotion, and bloodshed would be the inevitable consequences.

The final word was left to the U.S. Supreme Court. In January 1848 it heard arguments in a case brought by Martin Luther, a suffragist organizer who was arrested in his home by militiamen immediately after the declaration of martial law in June 1842. Luther sued his captors, denying that the state government had any right to exercise authority because it was not the "republican form of government" promised by the Constitution. The Court's judgment was written by Chief Justice Roger Taney, a Democrat who served as Andrew Jackson's attorney general before joining the court in 1835. In 1829 Taney declared that Jacksonianism was "the only -*ism* about which I now feel any concern." Of course, Jacksonianism was a conflicted doctrine. On the one hand, concern for popular sovereignty might have implied sympathy for the Rhode Island rebels. On the other hand, southern states that worried about slave rebellion would be alarmed by any decision that appeared to circumscribe the right of state governments to maintain internal order through the use of force. In 1849, Taney came down squarely on the side of the established authorities, defending the state government's prerogative to invoke martial law: "to meet the peril in which the existing Government was placed by the armed resistance to its authority. . . . Unquestionably, a State may use its military power to put down an armed insurrection. The power is essential to the existence of every Government, essential to the preservation of order and free institutions. . . . The State itself must determine what degree of force the crisis demands."

✦The Anti-Rent War

> [Anti-Renters are] the most violent faction which has
> disgraced the State since laws were heard of in this
> hemisphere—a faction which assumed the exterior
> of Indians, shot down the officers and defied the
> government of the State, till superior force brought it
> to a *temporary* submission. Let the people of the State
> themselves judge whether these Indians shall raise
> again their fiendish cries, their fires blaze forth anew,
> and the blood of legal functionaires again be shed.
>
> —Walt Whitman, 1846

In New York State, as in Rhode Island, economic crisis provoked a violent challenge against archaic institutions. The object of protest in New York State was a system of landowning that had been established long before U.S. independence and persisted in spite of it. In the early seventeenth century, the Dutch West Indies Company sought to establish control of the upper Hudson River Valley by giving a vast grant of land, spanning both sides of the Hudson near what is now Albany, to Kiliaen Van Rensselaer, a diamond merchant in Amsterdam. The Manor of Rensselaerwyck spanned more than four hundred thousand acres of land and Van Rensselaer became known as its first patroon.

Van Rensselaer and his heirs adopted a feudal model for settlement on their lands. Settlers acquired a form of property which fell between outright ownership, as we know it today, and tenancy. They were considered owners of the land and could pass on their interest in the land to their heirs; however, the patroon reserved the right to build roads, dams, and mills on the property, and also the right to dig mines and cut timber. Tenants (as they were known) owed an annual rent to the patroon, payable in perpetuity, usually in the form of a set amount of wheat or fowl and a day of labor with the tenant's wagon and horses. And while the tenant could sell his interest in the land, along with these encumbrances, a certain share of proceeds—usually a quarter—had to be paid to the patroon.

This model of settlement survived the transition to British rule in the late seventeenth century. Indeed, British colonial governments used Rensselaerwyck as a model, creating several other manors and patents with similar forms of tenancy. The largest was the Hardenbergh Patent, created in 1716, which spanned a large part of the Catskill Mountains. Much of this system was untouched by the Revolutionary War and survived intact throughout the early years of American independence. On the eve of the First Great Depression there were still more than ten thousand tenant families living on

almost two million acres of land, and owing rents to a small handful of landowners, including most prominently the ninth patroon of Rensselaerwyck,
Stephen Van Rensselaer III. The ninth patroon had a reputation for benev-
olence, often allowing tenants to defer rents in times of hardship.

In 1839, chance and economic distress combined to produce open conflict between landowners and tenant farmers. Stephen Van Rensselaer III
died in January 1839. Most tenants expected that in his will Van Rensselaer,
widely accounted as one of the richest men in the United States, would
forgive back rents, by then totaling more than four hundred thousand dollars. But the apparent worth of Van Rensselaer's vast holdings was misleading. His estate had a liquidity problem. Van Rensselaer owed more than
three hundred thousand dollars to various creditors at the time of his death.
He also had a wife and ten children, all of whom expected to be supported
in the manner appropriate for one of the country's most prominent families. One of his sons, William, "a scholarly man with intellectual tastes," was
completing a Greek Revival mansion in Albany for his new wife, modeled
on the home of the Baronet of Sheffield: "He furnished the interior with
objects of art gathered abroad, and his library was a notable feature of his
home. The winding staircase of selected Italian marble was greatly admired
by critics of architecture. On the southern side, as a wing, he built a mammoth conservatory. The stables were at the further end of the lawn extending nearly half a mile eastward." And so Van Rensselaer chose not to forgive
his tenants' debts. On the contrary, his estate was instructed to collect back
rents and use the proceeds to extinguish his own liabilities.

Unfortunately, Van Rensselaer's tenants were even more painfully distressed.
The farm economy of eastern New York was collapsing. In the highlands
especially, farmers suffered from the lack of easy access to markets. The land
was uneven and rocky, and the soil exhausted. Worse, the Erie Canal—a project which Van Rensselaer had actively promoted—had introduced fierce
competition from better farmland in western New York and the new western states. Competition put tremendous downward pressure on agricultural
prices, and this was aggravated by the collapse in commodity prices after 1837.

When it became clear that the inheritor of most of Rensselaerwyck,
Stephen Van Rensselaer IV, was unwilling to compromise over the collection of back rents, opposition among tenants quickly crystallized. On July
4, 1839, mass meetings were organized all over the manor on the west side
of the Hudson. At Berne, one of most virulently anti-rent of the manor's
hill towns, farmers adopted a new declaration of independence, promising
to resist attempts to seize their property "even to the last extremity." "We

will take up the ball of the Revolution where our fathers stopped it," the declaration said, "and roll it to the final consummation of freedom and independence of the masses." The invocation of the language and symbols of the Revolution was not surprising—Rhode Island's rebels had done it as well—and in the New York highlands it would soon be extended in a more flamboyant form.

In August, Van Rensselaer demanded that the sheriff of Albany county, Michael Artcher, execute writs to evict the ringleaders of the anti-rent movement. A deputy sent into the mountains to deliver papers returned the next day, his wagon and harness wrecked by farmers. Another agent, sent a few days later, was seized by a mob, which burned all of his papers. "They took [him] to Lawrence's tavern and burned a tar barrel there; a person named Witbeck . . . threatened to put him into the fire. . . . [T]hey then cut off a portion of his hair, called him their prisoner, and with continued demonstrations of anger and violence detained him" for the whole of a day. Finally, Sheriff Artcher issued a summons for a *posse committatus* to be organized in Albany. Five hundred men massed in the city, "some on horseback, others in carriages, others on foot, and all unarmed," and together they began an advance into the Helderberg mountains west of Albany. One of the posse recalled:

> When we got to the Helderbergs . . . we met four or five hundred men on horseback. . . . The crowd closed in upon us and prevented our moving for half an hour but finally let us pass and we pushed on to Reidsville where we found fully eighteen hundred people assembled who entirely filled up the highway and would not let us pass. The sheriff went quietly among us and told us to move at a signal from him but when it was given and we tried to force our way the mob made a rush upon us, crying "stop them," and it was impossible for us to move. The men were very much excited and nearly all carried clubs. The sheriff saw it would be useless to try and go any further and so he commanded us to turn about. . . . It was long after dark before we reached Albany.

These three failed forays demonstrated a truth that would be evident throughout the anti-rent war: even if local officials wanted to enforce the law—and sometimes sheriffs, counting votes, were reluctant to do so—they simply did not have the capacity to exercise authority in the highlands that compromised much of Rensselaerwyck and the other manors and patents. Each county's sheriff was located in the county seat, usually a town on the shores of the Hudson River. The rebellious farmers were hours away, dispersed across a terrain that was difficult and unfamiliar to the sheriff and his agents from the lowlands. Farmers became adept at using tin horns to give warnings about the arrival of the sheriff's agents. Civil authorities never had the advantage of surprise or numbers.

Finally, in December 1839, New York Governor William Seward acceded to demands that the state militia be called out to enforce law in the Helderberg Mountains. Hundreds of troops in the state's southern counties were warned to prepare for action. In Manhattan, the diarist Philip Hone observed:

> The Governor has ordered a body of fifteen hundred of the infantry of this city to hold themselves in readiness to repair to Albany at a moment's warning, and has provided them two steamboats to transport them to the seat of war. Division and brigade orders fill a column in the morning papers, and names of major-generals, A.D.C.'s, and brigade-majors are blazoned in staring capitals. Young men with muskets, unconscious yet of murderous lead, parade the street, panting for the fray. . . . [T]his is a serious business. Conduct so disorganizing must be resisted, and the laws be maintained at all events.

Seward himself was ambivalent about the resort to force. He was a Whig, but with progressive instincts, and he had been elected only a year before as part of a great surge against Democratic incumbents in the wake of the 1837 panic. He knew that attempts by wealthy landowners like the Van Rensselaers to extract money from distressed farmers were regarded with disgust by much of the public. Banks had been treated leniently when they suspended in May 1837, and it seemed incongruous to treat small tenant farmers more roughly. "For the ignorant big-breeched Dutchmen of the hills to suspend paying their rents is a big crime," joked James Gordon Bennett, publisher of the *New York Herald*. "None but the educated, the refined, the financial, the brokers, the great commercial interests of society have the right to suspend their just debts."

It was good politics, as well as good policy, to temper the application of force. As the militia prepared for deployment to the Helderbergs, Seward issued a proclamation that contained a warning and a promise. Organized resistance by anti-renters to sheriffs and the militia would be treated as insurrection and treason against the state. The only legitimate method of obtaining relief against the landowners was through the courts and the legislature. But if the farmers ceased resistance, Seward would use his own office to advocate for relief. The governor sent close advisors to negotiate with anti-rent leaders and soon announced that his "pacific offers . . . had been cordially embraced."

The farmers would cease resistance and allow the institutions of government to do their work. Three weeks later, Seward sent a message to the legislature urging reforms that would produce a system of land ownership "more accordant with the principles of republican government, and more conducive to . . . the peace and harmony of society."

The task that Seward gave to state legislators was not an easy one. Legislation that tinkered directly with relations between the patroon and his tenants threatened to run afoul of the contracts clause of the federal Constitution, which explicitly bars state governments from passing laws "impairing the obligations of contracts." One technique for evading the contracts clause was to establish preconditions or restrictions on the enforcement of a contract, for example, by compelling landowners to prove the legitimacy of their own title to the land before permitting action against delinquent tenants, but there was a risk that federal courts would find the restrictions so onerous that they constituted a de facto overturning of the entire contract.

In 1843, the Supreme Court made clear its hostility toward state laws that changed contracts retroactively. *Bronson v. Kinzie* arose out of an Illinois law designed to protect defaulting homeowners from foreclosure. The Court found the Illinois law to be unconstitutional because the burdens imposed by the legislature had fundamentally altered rights established by the contract. Chief Justice Roger Taney—the same judge who upheld Rhode Island's right to impose martial law—wrote for the majority that Illinois' attempt to discourage foreclosures "was injurious and unjust."

Other approaches to reform were equally difficult. It was conceivable, for example, that the state government could use its power of eminent domain to restructure the existing contracts, essentially acknowledging that the state was expropriating property from landowners and giving it to the tenants. Unfortunately, the state constitution only permitted the taking of private property "for public use," and New York state courts interpreted this term strictly. Reform of manorial tenancies might serve the public interest, but it could not be said that the property taken from landowners and given to tenants would be available for public use. Moreover the constitution also required "just compensation" for expropriated property, a liability that the straitened state government could not easily assume.

Politics complicated the task of responding to the tenants' complaints. The landowners were less numerous but they were wealthier and more closely connected to the centers of financial and political power than the tenants. In addition, there was a mass of disinterested voters who might be persuaded by the argument that tenants had willingly accepted the terms of their contracts and should therefore be bound by them. Landowners could also hope that land reform would simply be lost in the confusion of legislative debate. The New York state legislature only met for four or five months of the year—convening in January and typically adjourning in early May—and there were larger issues seizing its attention. The dominant concerns, by far, were whether the state should abandon its ambitious program of canal and rail development, and if it should adopt constitutional restrictions on government borrowing.

The state legislature's capacity to sort through these complicated matters of policy and politics was not limited just by the brevity of the legislative calendar. The lower house of the New York state legislature consisted of more than one hundred assemblymen elected annually. Turnover within the assembly increased after the extension of the franchise in 1821, and rose even more after the Panic of 1837. On average, three-quarters of the assembly was newly elected in the sessions held between 1838 and 1848, and less than 2 percent served for more than three years. Within that same decade, the assembly was ruled by nine different speakers. Party solidarity was also weak. The economic crisis aggravated fissures within both the Whig and Democratic camps, and this corroded the capacity of either party to pursue a coherent agenda. Seward himself narrowly escaped defeat in the election of 1840. He announced two months later that he would not seek another term.

Seward lacked the power to make good on his promise to the Helderberg farmers. On the last day of the legislature's 1840 session, the governor signed a bill that offered a much weaker remedy—a commission to mediate between Van Rensselaer and his tenants. Mediation failed, and the commission did not make its final report until April 1841—too late to allow further legislative action before the end of that session. When the legislature reconvened in the winter of 1842, it approved a law that gave limited relief to tenants and other debtors by protecting a substantial amount of their personal property from seizure for nonpayment of debts. The law would have gutted the ability of landowners to move against delinquent tenants, but the New York Supreme Court, following the logic of *Bronson v. Kinzie*, ruled that the law would be unconstitutional if it were interpreted to apply to contracts executed before its adoption. The legislature "cannot legislate backwards," the court said, "and annul the force of prior obligations."

Frustrated tenants became increasingly well organized. Anti-rent associations were established in all the major manors and patents. Active resistance against landowners' agents and sheriffs was spreading and becoming better coordinated. Five thousand tenants attended a meeting of anti-renters in

Ulster County in June 1844. Farmers had also begun disguising themselves during confrontations—painting their faces black or red or hiding behind masks, and wearing costumes of calico and animal skin decorated with horns, feathers, and tin ornaments. They became known as Calico Indians. The anti-renters were consciously drawing on the symbolism of the Boston Tea Party of 1773, in which "a number of brave and resolute men, dressed in the Indian manner . . . gave the war whoop" and destroyed a shipload of tea in Boston harbor.

By 1844, thousands of farmers were organized into a covert network that was integrated with, but formally disavowed by, the anti-rent associations. The Calico Indians were organized in a "cell structure" to avoid disruption by civil or military authority: "The identity of the ten or fifteen members of a unit was to be known only to the unit chief, who in turn was only to be known as 'Red Jacket,' 'Yellow Jacket,' 'Black Hawk,' 'the Prophet,' or a similar designation. . . . [T]hey were bound by oath, secretly administered." A disproportionate number of the Calico Indians were restless young men from the tenant farms, and they were becoming increasingly belligerent. In July 1844, one hundred Calico Indians armed with pistols, knives, and tomahawks surrounded a posse of thirty that had been sent to serve legal papers on delinquent tenants in Rensselaer County east of Albany. A deputy sheriff was tarred and feathered and "compelled to run around the town pump and up and down the streets for the amusement of his persecutors." A few days later, Calico Indians ransacked the home of another deputy sheriff in Rensselaer County, tarring and feathering him and burning his papers. In August, the sheriff of Albany County was assaulted in the Helderberg hills by sixty Calico Indians. "He was carried to the ground. . . . Pistols and rifles were held to his head, and he was ordered to give up his papers." The sheriff was bound, tarred, and feathered, and then sent back to Albany with his deputies.

Radicalism among tenants in upstate New York was encouraged by activists in New York City who saw the anti-rent movement, as well as the rebellion in Rhode Island, as the raw material from which a broader campaign for economic and social reform could be constructed. Thomas Devyr, an Irishman who fled England after the failure of Chartist protests in 1840, steamed north from New York City to propagandize on behalf of the anti-renters. He gave advice on how to organize the Calico Indians and urged anti-renters to "carry on a *guerrilla warfare*" against landowners. Another veteran of the English radical movement, New York City publisher George Henry Evans, also egged the anti-renters on. "The Anti-Rent organization is so powerful and so widely extended," Evans' *Working Man's Advocate* proclaimed in

October 1844, "that any attempt to put it down by military force would cost an immense sum to the state, and would after all be unsuccessful. Of this there can be no doubt in the minds of those who understand the 'Indian' plan of operations."

In early December 1844, five hundred Calico Indians confronted the sheriff of Columbia County, Henry Miller, and stole papers that he intended to serve on tenants who had refused to pay their rent. A week later, at a rally of three thousand tenants in Columbia County, a young farmhand was killed by stray gunfire. Two days later, in Rensselaer County, fifty Calico Indians assaulted lumbermen who had broken ranks and purchased a woodlot from the Van Rensselaers, and in the scuffle one of the lumbermen was shot and killed.

This concentrated bout of violence marked a turning point in the anti-rent protests. One of the anti-rent movement's leaders, Smith Boughton—widely and correctly suspected to be the head of the Calico Indians—was arrested in Columbia County and taken to Hudson, the county seat. The valley town quickly took on a siege mentality, fearing that its population of five thousand would be overrun by farmers massed to rescue Boughton. "A patrol for each night of twenty citizens in each ward was established . . . and the Hudson Light Guard [the town's volunteer militia] were ordered to rendezvous with loaded muskets at the Court House in case of an alarm." Artillery loaded with grapeshot were placed at every road into the town, and a Committee of Safety was organized to solicit aid from the state government. Reinforcements soon arrived at the town's wharves—riflemen and artillery from Albany, and a troop of German-American cavalry from New York City. The town "presented the appearance of a military encampment. . . . [T]he streets resounded with martial music and the tramp of soldiery."

The mayor of Hudson issued a proclamation lamenting the presence of a standing armed force in the town. "But no alternative is left. The Supremacy of Law must be maintained, or the tyranny of Anarchy reigns triumphant!" A few days later the troops gathered for services at the Episcopal Church, where the minister warned: "Power comes from God. It was delegated by Providence to our Governor and other ministers of the law. Resistance to the powers that be is rebellion against the Almighty." However, the jury at Boughton's trial was not so easily persuaded. In March 1845 it proved unable to reach a verdict on any of the charges against him, and four months later the sheriff of Columbia County reluctantly set Boughton free.

But the violence of December 1844 had definitely caused public opinion to swing against the anti-renters. James Gordon Bennett, the New York City publisher who had ridiculed landowners in 1837, now condemned anti-renters for subverting the ability of "constituted authorities . . . to carry the laws into execution." Whig congressman Daniel Barnard complained that "the boldest acts of violence are perpetrated, and treason itself is committed. . . . We have claims openly presented and doctrines advocated . . . tending, essentially and necessarily, to the utter overthrow of the whole social fabric." In his contemporaneous novel *The Redskins*, James Fenimore Cooper condemned "[a]rson, anti-rentism, attempts at murder, and all sorts of enormities, going hand in hand . . . and the laws as profoundly asleep the whole time, as if such gentle acts were considered meritorious. This out-does repudiation twenty-fold." Barnard, too, equated the anti-rent protests with the lapses of the defaulting states. The tenants, he said, were engaged in a "CONCERTED, PRACTICAL REPUDIATION" of contractual obligations freely undertaken.

In 1845 the authority of the New York government was brought down firmly against radical elements of the anti-rent movement. The newly elected Democratic governor, Silas Wright, had already authorized the sending of troops to Hudson. In his message to the state legislature in January 1845, Wright said that the events of 1844 had given the public "a shock, which nothing but the prompt and effectual restoration of the reign of law and order can calm." It was impossible, he said, to contemplate relief for tenants until "open and criminal resistance to the laws and authorities of State" had been broken. Wright asked the state legislature for legislation imposing a criminal penalty for appearing in disguise, as the Calico Indians did. The legislature, which had grappled fruitlessly with tenancy reform for four years, delivered this new law within three weeks. In April the legislature also gave Wright the power to declare counties in a state of insurrection, deploy state militia to restore order, and arrest citizens who failed to cooperate with suppression of the insurrection.

The counterreaction intensified in August 1845, after a deputy sheriff in Delaware County, Osman Steele, was shot and killed in a confrontation with Calico Indians while attempting to sell the cattle of a delinquent farmer. Sheriff Green More rousted a posse of five hundred men and began scouring the hills for anti-rent militants. Soon Delhi, the county seat, was seized with the same alarm as Hudson, fearing an assault by Calico Indians. Governor Wright declared a state of insurrection and sent a battalion of light infantry to protect Delhi. Troops began "scouring the infected districts" for suspects and building log pens to hold the dozens of prisoners who could not be contained in the Delhi's jail or courthouse. By September, when trials began, one hundred anti-renters had been indicted for complicity in Steele's murder, and another hundred charged with other offences.

These trials, unlike the trial of Boughton six months earlier, were designed to produce quick and hard results. The first prisoner brought before the court, John Van Steenburgh, had been disguised at the farm sale at which Steele was killed, but there was no evidence that he had attempted to shoot Steele himself. Judge Amos Parker warned the jury that no direct evidence was needed. Van Steenburgh had broken the January anti-disguise law at a riot during which Steele had been killed, and that was enough. On this formulation of the law, the jury could not avoid a finding of guilt. Van Steenburgh was convicted of murder and sentenced to death by hanging. A second man, Edward O'Connor, was also condemned to death. "The convictions were in a measure political ones," an early chronicler observed. Judge Parker had admonished the Van Steenburgh jury to take firm action against "open rebellion. . . . There can never be in a free government, a government of the people, either necessity or excuse for treason."

The two convictions had a sobering effect on the other defendants. Within three weeks, Parker disposed of two hundred fifty cases. Seventeen men were sent to state prison, four for life. Most of the others were fined or given suspended sentences. Judge Parker, the *New York Herald* reported, "has done more by this one act to restore peace, quiet and order to the county than all the bayonets this side of Texas." In Columbia County, meanwhile, Smith Boughton and other anti-rent leaders were taken back into custody and retried for the violence of 1844. Judge John Edmonds, appointed to the court by Governor Wright only a few months before, began the trial by excluding any prospective juror who expressed discontent about tenancies. Edmonds warned the jury that the state legislature would never provide relief to tenants until "the base and guilty were denounced and punished." When the jury deadlocked, Edmonds refused to dismiss it. Eventually the jury found Boughton guilty on a charge of highway robbery. This was enough for Edmonds.

> Your [Broughton's] offence, though in form it is presented to us as robbery, is high treason, rebellion against your government, and armed insurrection against the supremacy of the laws. . . . You have made yourself an example of disorder and violence, and you have caused many erring and misguided men to follow it, to their ruin and the disturbance of the public peace. You have, therefore, rendered it necessary that the court should cause you to be a warning example of the certain consequences

of such conduct. . . . The sentence of the court is that you be confined
in the state prison, at hard labor, for the term of your natural life.

The crackdown of 1845 brought a decisive end to radicalism within the
anti-rent movement. Many leaders of the Calico Indians remained in hiding, and thousands of others abandoned their costumes. Anti-rent associations renounced the Calico Indians and the idea of active resistance to civil
authorities. "This Association disapprove[s] of using any other means of
redress," said the Rensselaer County association, "except those which the
existing laws and the legislative power can furnish us."

Still, the anti-renters constituted an important voting bloc, and in the
year preceding the elections of 1846, both Whigs and Democrats jostled for
their favor. With the Calico Indians decisively crushed, Governor Wright
commuted the death sentences of Steenburgh and O'Connor. In January
1846, Wright reported that the "mad spirit of insubordination" had been
suppressed and urged the legislature to respond to the tenants' demands for
relief. However the reforms produced in the session of 1846 were not substantial. The landowners' income from rents would now be taxed, and their
ability to seize property for nonpayment would be restricted; however, the
second reform was understood to be prospective only, to avoid a constitutional challenge on the precedent of *Bronson v. Kinzie.*

A third reform worked more clearly in the tenants' favor. In the summer
of 1846 a convention was convened to renovate the state constitution, and
the changes which it recommended were ratified in the November election.
The main aim was to restrict the state's capacity to borrow and undertake
public works, but the new constitution also abolished the system of manorial tenure—again, prospectively. Moreover, it provided that county and
supreme court judges would be popularly elected. There was evidence that
the state supreme court became more pliable in following years. Eventually,
the popularly-elected court ruled that the 1846 law protecting tenants,
drafted by legislators with the expectation that it would have only prospective application, was a constitutionally valid restriction on older landlord-
tenant contracts as well.

More significantly, landowners were giving up the fight and offering to
settle with tenants on more favorable terms. By the late 1850s, the Van Rensselaers had abandoned the manor of Rensselaerwyck to other investors.
More than 40 percent of the manorial contracts in force in Albany County,
on the west side of the manor, had already been converted to conventional
freehold properties. In 1852 William Van Rensselaer left his ornate Greek
Revival mansion, scarcely a decade old, and moved to the shores of Long

Island Sound. Exhaustion with the conflict played an important part in motivating the landholders, but a more fundamental reality also shaped their behavior. Agricultural production on the great estates was in a precipitous decline. By 1865 many towns that had been centers of anti-rent resistance were smaller than they had been a quarter-century earlier. John A. King, owner of the seventeen thousand-acre Blenheim Patent, settled with his tenants in 1847, and invested the proceeds in railroads.

✒Cannon Fire in Philadelphia

> Order must be restored, life and property rendered secure. The idle, the vicious, the disorderly must be curbed and taught to understand and respect the supremacy of the law.
>
> —Major General Robert Patterson, First Division,
> Pennsylvania Militia, May 1844

In Philadelphia, the nation's manufacturing center, the First Great Depression was the trigger for an outbreak of extraordinary ethnic and racial violence. Animosities that were contained in better times became the defining features of urban politics and were expressed in mayhem unlike anything the city had seen before. By July 1844, rioters were assaulting militiamen with cannon on the streets of south Philadelphia. The result was the radical reconstruction of the city's police functions. Philadelphia, like other major U.S. cities, would build a "civic army" to suppress the tensions that had been aggravated by economic decline.

In 1840, Philadelphia was the country's second largest urban center, closely following New York. The city itself comprised only two square miles of land on the peninsula bounded by the Schuylkill and Delaware rivers, and had a population of about ninety thousand. Twice as many people lived in districts that abutted the city on the north and south, and which combined with the city to constitute the county of Philadelphia. Philadelphia was the most important manufacturing center in the United States. At that point, its economy was in the midst of a transition from artisanal to industrial production. Employment in factories was growing rapidly, but many Philadelphians still worked in small shops run by master craftsmen. Still others worked in a middle ground, as laborers in subcontractors' sweatshops. The city also had a substantial weaving industry organized under "putting out" arrangements, by which weavers worked on handlooms in their own homes.

The promise of employment made Philadelphia a magnet for immigration, either from the rural interior or overseas. The county's population almost doubled between 1820 and 1840. In the late 1830s and early 1840s, a relatively constant flow of immigrants—three thousand per year—landed in the city. Roughly half were Irish; another quarter were German. (The great wave of immigration triggered by the Irish potato famine would not be felt until 1846–1850. In those years, roughly ten thousand immigrants arrived annually in Philadelphia.) By the early 1840s, Irish immigrants accounted for one-fifth of the county's population. Blacks, who competed directly against unskilled immigrants for jobs, accounted for another tenth.

Even before the depression, the city was plagued with ethnic and racial divisions. Many Irish immigrants despised the black minority, and the native-born majority shared a casual bigotry toward both immigrants and blacks. Many native-born Americans viewed the Irish Catholic population with a disdain inherited from their own English Protestant forebears. The Irish, it was said, were filthy, indolent, untrustworthy, and disrespectful of the laws.

Despite this pervasive bigotry it was possible, in the years before the depression, for emigrant Irish and native-born Americans to work together when it appeared in their interest to do so. Philadelphia was fraught with labor unrest in the decade before the Panic of 1837, as workers responded to the pressure of industrial transformation and rapid inflation. By one estimate, there were more than sixty strikes in the city between 1827 and 1837. In 1834, many of the city's labor associations combined to form the General Trades Union. The Trades Union grew rapidly and in 1835 coordinated a general strike (the nation's first) which succeeded in winning a ten-hour day for Philadelphia's workers. By 1836, the Trades Union was supported by fifty separate trade organizations with more than ten thousand members. The proportion of Philadelphia's population enrolled in a labor organization reached a peak that would not be exceeded for the remainder of the century.

The Trades Union was distinguished by its determination to keep ethnic and religious divisions out of its business. "We preach no religion in the Union," said one of its 1836 declarations. "The Union was founded for other purposes, and therefore it is no place for discussion about theology." One of its leaders was the Irish-born John Ferrall, while another was Benjamin Sewell, a native-born American who later became a charter member of the anti-Irish American Republican party. The 1835 general strike was triggered by a protest of coal heavers who were mainly Irish immigrants; but other trades struck in solidarity. The Trades Union included handloom weavers, a predominantly Irish occupation, but also shoemakers, a trade that would be later distinguished by the virulence of its anti-Irish sentiment.

When weavers and shoemakers struck again in 1836 for higher wages, the union gave money to support the workers of each trade.

The ecumenism of the city's labor movement was real but fragile. Like the Trades Union itself, it was destroyed by the economic crisis. "With the first descent of the panic in 1837," the labor historian John Commons has written, the American labor movement "was crushed out of existence." While there were dozens of strikes in Philadelphia in the years before the panic, there were only three between March 1837 and the end of 1840. The General Trades Union collapsed, starved of dues from its member associations and deprived of its most potent unifying tool, the strike. The city was cloaked in despair, especially after the shuttering of United States Bank's headquarters on Chestnut Street in February 1841: "The bankruptcy of that great institution . . . was as sudden as the descent of an avalanche. Other financial disasters followed it, in quick succession. . . . Where ruddy health had appeared, all was paleness and dejection, wan extenuation, and prostrate syncope. If a volcano had opened its fiery jaws in our midst, or an earthquake had shaken the firmest edifices to their foundations, the popular terror could not have been more complete."

The city began to experience violent outbreaks of unprecedented intensity. In August 1842, many weavers struck against reductions in piecework rates and began a campaign of intimidation against workers who continued to accept work at lower rates, invading their homes and destroying their handlooms. In September, a mob of weavers attempted to burn down a cotton mill near the city; they were turned back, but only after two constables were shot. When aldermen attempted to stop violence between striking and non-striking weavers in the district of Kensington in January 1843, they were beaten by the mob. The sheriff of Pennsylvania County then recruited a posse which, on arrival, was charged by four hundred weavers armed with muskets and brickbats. Most of the posse fled. The next day, eight companies of state militia occupied Kensington and imposed a settlement between weavers and employers. "God knows, some of the poor fellows have great cause to feel rebellious," a newspaper wrote after the conflict. "Empty stomachs and empty purses are not the best advocates of good order."

As these conflicts revealed, the capacity of local officials to maintain civic peace was limited. In the city of Philadelphia itself, each of the twenty-four wards had one elected constable and five night watchmen. This was roughly one constable for every four thousand people. Constables worked during daylight hours and were, according to an 1837 report, "generally more occupied with other business than with the maintenance of public order."

Night watchmen were responsible for announcing the hours as they made their rounds, and also for assuring that lamps were lit. Each of the neighboring districts maintained comparable systems. However, constables and night watchmen had no authority beyond their jurisdiction, and so offenders could easily evade justice by stepping over a municipal border. "A boundary street . . . was as effectual a barrier to the passage of a constable . . . as the Chinese wall." In a sense, these boundary lines performed the same function as the highlands of upstate New York: they constrained the effective exercise of civil authority over the whole municipal area. Many parts of the county were effectively controlled by gangs who marked the walls and fences of their territory with their titles—Killers, Rats, Blood-Tubs—in paint and chalk.

The sheriff, a county official, was not limited by municipal boundaries, and constables could call on him for help. But in serious cases of disorder the sheriff himself had to summon a posse of able-bodied men, and this took time. Citizens were required by law to respond to the sheriff's summons, but they were unpaid and untrained, and in the face of violence they could not be relied on to stand their ground. The sheriff, in turn, could appeal to the state militia, but this required even more time for mobilization. There was also uncertainty about whether militia commanders could respond to the sheriff's appeal without authorization from the governor. To further complicate matters, county officials were cautious about calling for state aid because they became liable for the militia's salaries and expenses.

Economic distress also led to violence between Irish and black workers. In August 1842 an Irish mob attacked a parade of the Negro Temperance Society in the district of Moyamensing, south of the city, and laid waste to three blocks in the black community, ransacking homes and dragging residents into the streets to be beaten. When constables attempted to make arrests, they were assaulted as well. The riot petered out at midnight, but only after the mob had razed a black church and community hall. The next day, Irish laborers working in a coalyard on the west side of Philadelphia assaulted a gang of black labors so viciously that Sheriff Henry Morris sent a posse of sixty men to restore order. The posse itself was attacked and retreated. Sheriff Morris appealed to the county commissioners for approval to call out the militia, a measure that would have to be paid out of county funds. The commissioners convened a special meeting to approve the expenditure and the militia arrived in strength, supported by artillery. Washington Square in southeast Philadelphia "took for the time the appearance of a military cantonment," and peace was restored.

W.E.B. Du Bois later explained the escalating violence between blacks and Irish in the 1830s and 1840s as the result of "social and economic competition" between "a mass of poverty-stricken, ignorant fugitives . . . [and] equally ignorant but more vigorous foreigners [who] outbid them at work and beat them on the streets." At the time, though, one Philadelphia Irish attributed the special fury of the 1842 riot to the depression:

Philadelphia . . . is now in a state of almost complete paralysis; and as a large portion of the laboring population of Moyamensing and the banks of the Schuykill are Irish, the consequence is, there is among them a great deal of distress, arising from an inability to find work. . . . Suffice it to say, that the Irish in this city seem to have imbibed the idea, that the blacks, not being citizens, have no right to stay in the city, and that if they can drive them out of the city, they will have their places, and have work enough to do. . . . "There's a house," said an Irish woman to the mob in Gaskill street, "that I want to have mobbed—there's some negroes living there, who are living just like white folks." I could fill a sheet with cases of this kind, showing that what was once contempt is now envy, and the most ferocious hatred, arising from the fact that a large portion of the blacks can find work, and they cannot.

Another fissure in Philadelphia society was aggravated by the economic crisis, and in this conflict the Irish minority were in the weaker position. As the depression ground on, antagonism among native-born Americans and Irish immigrants was expressed more coherently and forcefully. Irish Catholics were alleged to be subverting American culture; for example, by protesting the use of the King James version of the Bible, rather than the Douay version, in Philadelphia schools. In addition, they were said to be ill-prepared to participate in American political institutions: poorly educated, easily manipulated, and loyal to a foreign power—the Pope. The American Republican Party, which established its first ward association in Philadelphia in December 1843, became the main voice of anti-Irish feeling. Philadelphia's political class was stunned by the speed with which the new party took root. Within four months there was a similar association in almost every ward and township of the county.

The nativist movement drew on a bigotry toward the Irish that was long established in the United States. But bigotry alone cannot explain the movement's sudden efflorescence. The first attempt at organizing a native American political party in Pennsylvania was actually made in 1837, and quickly abandoned for lack of popular support. Prolonged economic distress was the essential catalyst. The necessary combination was described 1845 by Orestes Brownson, a native-born Protestant intellectual who had converted to Catholicism the previous year:

> The great mass of what may be called the common people in this country are of English descent . . . and they have inherited from their ancestors, and still retain, two strong prejudices—contempt of the Irish and hatred of the French. . . . Add to this that the influx of foreign laborers, chiefly Irish, increases the supply of labor, and therefore apparently lessens relatively the demand, and consequently the wages of labor, and you have the elements of a wide, deep, and inveterate hostility on the part of your Yankee laborer against your Irish laborer, which manifests itself naturally in your Native American party.

A propagandist for the American Republicans expressed the native-born citizen's anxiety in this way: "What northern man is so stupid as not to perceive that the immense immigration of the lowest classes of Europeans is calculated to reduce the price of labour, and bring to a level with serfs, peons, and slaves, the free labouring men of America? . . . [T]he yearly immigration of thousands of hungry and naked free labourers must constantly decrease the demand for and price of free labour, and produce a corresponding decrease of their means of comfort and enjoyment."

There was a second sense in which economic anxieties encouraged the rise of nativism. Before the crisis, many Irish were allied with native-born workers in their support of the Democratic Party. Whigs in Philadelphia initially exploited the emerging rift in the Democratic Party that was caused by the rise of nativist sentiment by running Irish candidates on the Whig ticket. The defection of Irish voters to the Whigs accelerated the collapse of the Democratic Party and intensified the turbulence that plagued politics at all levels of government. "The foreign population," an American Republican manifesto complained in 1845, was "aggravating the virulence of partizan warfare within our own borders. . . . It has acquired a control of our elections . . . [and] swayed the course of national legislation." For native-born Americans with Jacksonian sympathies this was another reason to hate the immigrants: the Irish were blocking the adoption of policies which they believed would bring an end to the depression. At the same time, the fragmentation of the Democratic Party made the nativists' own defection to the American Republicans seem defensible.

In early May 1844, leaders of the American Republican Party attempted to hold a rally in a predominantly Irish part of Kensington, only a block from the hub of the Irish community, St. Michael's Church. The meeting was quickly disrupted and the nativist speakers retreated to a neighboring district. Three days later, on May 6, they returned to Kensington, and this time found a crowd of three thousand, both nativist and Irish. When rain disrupted the gathering, the nativist leaders moved to a nearby market house and resumed their tirade against Popish interference in American politics. Heckling soon escalated into open warfare around the marketplace. Both nativists and Irish were armed and ready to fight. The Irish, sniping from windows of their homes and businesses, initially had the advantage, and within an hour one nativist had been killed and three others wounded by gunfire. Nativists brought reinforcements and the battle continued for another hour, before Sheriff Morton McMichael arrived with deputies and established an uneasy peace.

That evening, McMichael appealed to General George Cadwalader, a brigade commander in the state militia, for help in maintaining order. Cadwalader declined, doubting his authority to act without direction from the governor. This proved to be a fatal error. Late in the evening, a nativist mob marched into Kensington, destroying homes and attacking a Catholic seminary. Two more nativists were killed by the reply of musket fire. The next afternoon, three thousand people gathered for an American Republican rally in the city and marched north into Kensington. Four more people were fatally shot, and many homes torched, before Cadwalader finally arrived with troops.

FIGURE 11. *Riot in Philadelphia, July 1844.* Lithograph by H. Bucholzer. Source: Library of Congress.

The third day, May 8, began with Kensington under an uneasy military occupation. Nativists exploited the peace to search and fire abandoned Irish homes. Military patrols, either out of reluctance or sympathy, failed to intervene forcefully. In the early afternoon, nativists set fire to St. Michael's Church itself, as well as the seminary, and assaulted the fire companies that attempted to intervene. Peace was not regained until Cadwalader summoned more troops late in the day. However, the nativists had already found a new target: St. Augustine's Church in the City of Philadelphia. An attempt by the mayor to deter the massive crowd failed, and St. Augustine's was completely destroyed by fire. This was the end of the riot. Cadwalader's superior, General Robert Patterson, called out the entire First Division of the Pennsylvania Militia—three thousand troops—and declared martial law in the county.

News of the Kensington riot spread rapidly and created embarrassment for Philadelphia's elite, already humiliated by the default on Pennsylvania bonds. "Is it safe to go to Philadelphia?" travelers asked. "Is there no danger at all?" Details of the unrest arrived in Liverpool by the steamer *Hibernia* shortly after noon on May 29. Five hours later, London's *Morning Chronicle* wrote: "The alarming occurrences in Pennsylvania have naturally created serious apprehensions among the holders of the state's securities. The utter inefficiency of the city authorities of Philadelphia—the insecurity of life and property there . . . all tend to rouse the most serious apprehensions for the honor and integrity of the people of Pennsylvania. . . . [I]t is evident that the occurrences of this week will tend to the withdrawal of capital from that city." Instantly, the riots became a matter of international creditworthiness, with implications for every other American government that was tainted with collective guilt for default. The next day, the *Times of London* also chastised the Quaker city: "[A] more outrageous and bloody disturbance of the public peace, unchecked for a very considerable time by the intervention of any civil or military authority, has seldom disgraced a civilized community. . . . If such elements of discord were known to exist between two elements of the population, it seems inconceivable that no attempt should have been made to suspend their hostile meetings, and to interpose the force of arms to check their rash proceedings."

City leaders in Philadelphia were already taking steps to discourage further violence. At a law and order rally held in the statehouse yard, authorities were urged to use "*whatever force is necessary* . . . to prevent the lives and property of citizens from being destroyed." The governor assured the sheriff that he had the right to call on the state militia, while the state's attorney general urged the mayor and sheriff to use force without hesitation. If rioters made credible threats to take life, their own lives could "unquestionably be taken in the same manner as if they were open enemies or pirates."

Sheriff McMichael was admonished for his timidity in handling rioters. A county judge charged with investigating the riots warned on July 1 that "men who array themselves forcibly against the laws . . . may be killed as legitimately as the foreign invader, and ought to be killed as a duty if they cannot otherwise be overcome. The sheriff who will not act out this principle, is afraid to look his official responsibilities in the face." General Cadwalader was criticized as well. In the final hours of the May 8 riot, Cadwalader had saved a third church by placing artillery in front of it and threatening to rake the street with cannon fire. The mob dispersed, but critics wondered why other buildings could not have been protected in the same way. The *Philadelphia Public Ledger* reminded readers that Napoleon once subdued a Parisian mob with a "whiff of grapeshot" and that this act had been "humanity, mercy; it saved bloodshed."

Unfortunately, the Kensington riot was a boon for nativists. While city elders prayed for civic peace, thousands of Philadelphians, convinced that Irish Catholics had provoked the violence, flocked to the American Republican camp. It did not help that most of the fatalities were nativists. The July 4 parade through the city and districts served as an aggressive display of the nativists' power. Five thousand marched in the procession, the largest the city had ever seen. "Four barouches [carried] the orphans of the martyrs, and the wounded in the assault at Kensington; the front barouche bearing a small banner trimmed with crepe, with letters painted on it, describing their position."

The next day, a Friday, an even more violent conflict commenced in Southwark, south of the city, triggered by a rumor that Irish Catholics were gathering weapons in St. Philip de Neri Church. (In fact, the priest's brother had obtained muskets from the state armory to protect the church, with the governor's approval.) A mob quickly gathered to demand the removal of the weapons. Sheriff McMichael negotiated for the return of most of the guns, but the crowd would not disperse, and militiamen were ordered to the church. By Saturday morning there were still a crowd of hundreds gathered before it. McMichael attempted and failed to gather a larger posse, and four more companies of militia were sent as reinforcement against the nativist mob.

On Saturday evening, General Cadwalader took the first of several actions which ratcheted up the conflict in Southwark. Frustrated by the refusal of the crowd to disperse peacefully, Cadwalader ordered his troops to clear the streets by advancing with fixed bayonets. When officers were hit with paving stones and rocks, Cadwalader ordered the soldiers to open fire. A Whig ex-congressman serving in McMichael's posse, Charles Naylor, stepped in front of the guns and implored the infantry not to fire. The troops complied, and an exasperated Cadwalader had Naylor detained in the church on the charge of incitement to mutiny. Still, the threat of action restored quiet for the remainder of Saturday night, and the posse and most of the militia were dismissed at dawn.

Naylor was kept in the church, which was defended by one remaining company of militia, the Hibernia Greens. On Sunday morning, nativists gathered to demand Naylor's release and the Greens' withdrawal. By noon there was a crowd of two thousand. Some nativists brought a small cannon up from the docks, loaded it with scrap metal, and began firing at the church. Soon a second cannon was brought up. Outnumbered, the Greens negotiated a retreat, but opened fire when they were assaulted on their march away from the church. There were no casualties, and moderates within the nativist camp protected the church from arsonists.

However, Cadwalader heard mistaken reports that the church was ablaze, and returned on Sunday evening with a larger force. He immediately began clearing the streets. When the troops were again pelted with paving stones, they opened fire and two civilians were instantly killed. Nativists hiding in nearby houses fired their own muskets, more rushed to provide support, and cannon were again rolled up from the docks. The first discharge of the nativists' cannon killed two militiamen, and Cadwalader ordered a reply with his own artillery. Throughout the evening there was "a continued discharge of cannon to be heard, followed by the regular roll and rattle of the muskets." The nativists' guns were finally silenced by a cavalry charge at midnight. A dozen soldiers and civilians were dead, and several dozen more were wounded.

When Monday morning dawned, the streets around St. Philip de Neri Church "presented a truly warlike appearance. Window shutters, doors, fronts of houses, trees, tree-boxes, awning posts, lamp posts, pumps, watch-boxes, and signs, are all pierced with balls and shot; and the pavements, gutters, streets, steps, and doorjambs stained with blood. In some places it flowed down the gutters." General Patterson appealed for reinforcements from across the state, and by Tuesday morning the city was occupied by more than four thousand troops. Philadelphia was again under martial law.

"We are in the midst of a civil war!" said a city newspaper on Tuesday morning. "Riot and anarchy are around us! Death and destruction stare us in the face; and for once we behold the strange anomaly in this country, of an open and regularly organized rebellion on the part of a certain faction against the constituted authorities of the law." "This is worse, much worse, than a foreign war," said another journal. "The State is . . . at war with treason. . . . [Th]e elements of mischief are among us, a part of ourselves." Overseas, the British press was aghast when the steamer *Britannia* brought news of the "dreadful massacre" in the streets of Philadelphia. The ongoing violence, said the *Bristol Mercury*, was "deeply injurious both to the reputation and property of Philadelphia."

Building Civic Armies

> What are the effects of feeble, discordant municipal governments? Insecurity of person and property to an illimitable extent, from a liability to riot, carrying murder and arson in its train.
>
> —*Philadelphia Public Ledger*, November 13, 1844

In the summer of 1844 the *Spectator*, a London magazine, explained the American predicament with regard to riot control. "The great problem in politics," the magazine said, "is to adjust the counteracting forces of control in the government and spontaneous action in the individual. Too much control paralyzes and renders imbecile the national mind; too much spontaneous action in the individual generates anarchy." The difficulty in the United States, the *Spectator* thought, was that local authorities had yielded too much to spontaneous action. Indeed, American riots were usually "a struggle of parties almost on an equality in point of means, personal strength, and discipline. The rioters of Philadelphia had cannon and ammunition; and the military were impromptu soldiers, with little if any more discipline than their opponents."

For the *Spectator*, the Philadelphia riots were not simply a matter of local concern. They raised a broader question about the American attitude toward liberty and order, and about the viability of its methods of self-governance. Since Jefferson, the magazine said, the country had been carried by a strong democratic impulse, which privileged individual freedom over the needs of government. Decades earlier, Hamilton and his allies had questioned the wisdom of Jefferson's philosophy. The *Spectator* alleged that the riots provided further evidence that the Jeffersonian experiment was reaching its breaking point.

In Philadelphia, too, the violence produced reflection about the limits of self-rule. For many, the riots were a sign of moral decay: they arose "from an impaired sense of the obligations which a good citizen owes to the law." If this was right, then the solution was education to change public sentiment toward the law. However, as one Philadelphian said, this remedy would be "slow and . . . extremely difficult. . . . [T]hese moral agents are less effective than a resort to physical force." The more efficient solution was the immediate improvement of law enforcement capabilities in the city and surrounding districts. On July 11, only three days after the riot, prominent businessmen and lawyers petitioned the city to create its own reserve army. The city council acted the same day, authorizing the recruitment of "a full regiment of Infantry, a full battalion of Artillery, and one or more full troops of Cavalry . . . ready and willing . . . to assist in maintaining the public peace." By September 1844, General Cadwalader had recruited the full force, consisting of volunteers already serving in the state militia. When necessary, the volunteers would be mobilized under city rather than state authority.

This was widely regarded as a quick but imperfect solution. It did little to help with prevention, rather than suppression, of riots, and threatened to turn Philadelphia into a garrison town "saddled and bridled . . . after the fashion of St. Petersburg." The deeper problem, said critics, was that "the conservators of the peace . . . *have no police*." In December 1844, Philadelphia Mayor Peter McCall asked for a more radical reform: the creation of a larger and more professional police force, unified in command and serving the entire county, comparable to the metropolitan police force established in London fifteen years earlier. "The great object," said McCall, "is to crush disorder in the bud. . . . [T]o attain this object, there ought to be at hand, and speedily disposable a force sufficiently numerous to strike terror into the evil-disposed."

The Pennsylvania legislature mandated some reforms in Pennsylvania County four months later. The law established a minimum size for police forces for the city and surrounding districts—at least one officer for every 150 taxable inhabitants—and gave the sheriff authority to requisition any of these forces to suppress riots. The police were authorized to use "all necessary force" to disperse rioters and absolved of liability for any injuries or deaths that might result. The law also affirmed the sheriff's power to requisition the state militia when the police were unable to establish order.

This was an improvement but still short of Mayor McCall's demands. There was no unified county force, and districts dragged their feet in hiring full-time officers. But other reform efforts soon followed. The City of Philadelphia established its own police department in 1848. In 1850, following another mismanaged riot, the state legislature created a county-wide police force to complement the city and district forces. In 1851, Philadelphia's civic leaders were still pushing for more reform, reminding state legislators how "the disastrous and destructive mobs of 1844" had demonstrated the need for a stronger police power. Three years later, all of the county's forces were integrated into the Philadelphia Police Department as part of a larger consolidation of city and district governments. Philadelphia had finally established the rudiments of a professional, metropolitan police force.

There was some irony that the correction to problems of domestic disorder in the United States—an excess of the Jeffersonian tendency, as the *Spectator* put it—was the deliberate importation of the policing model developed for the British metropolis. And this was done even though, in matters of finance and foreign policy, Anglo-American relations were so sour that the two countries were thought to be teetering on the brink of war. And Philadelphia was not the only American city to follow this path. The problem of riot control also came to a peak in New York City during the depression. At the time of the 1837 panic, a mob of five thousand assembled in City Hall Park to "inquire into the cause of the prevailing distress [and] the high price of flour," and then ransacked the warehouse of a prominent grain dealer a few blocks away. So long as the city was so sharply divided between the "rich and powerful . . . [and the] wretchedly poor and dependent," the *New York Tribune* said in 1844, there would be "the necessity (as in London) of a civic ARMY, a numerous Municipal Police." The city established its police department the following year. Baltimore, which followed news of the Philadelphia riots closely, eventually adopted the London model of policing in 1853.

Boston also struggled with riots and anguished about their implications for the ideal of self-rule. In 1838, following a massive riot in the heart of the city that was suppressed only by cavalry and eight hundred infantrymen, Mayor Samuel Eliot warned that the city needed "some more prompt means . . . to check or prevent the occurrence of riots than any now existing." Bostonians watched with alarm as violence struck other cities in the northeast in the early 1840s. The president of Boston city council, Peleg Whitman Chandler, made the uprisings in Rhode Island and Philadelphia the subject of his oration for the celebration of July 4, 1844.

The monarchies of Europe, Chandler said, maintained order with a strong "internal police." The United States had chosen instead to rely on the self-governing instincts of its people. But something had gone awry, Chandler said; the sense of "personal responsibility [and] manly self-denial" among Americans was manifestly in decline. The effusion of riots and rebellions was symptomatic of a moral decay. "The riots of our day differ in an important particular from those of an earlier date," Chandler said. "They are no longer the sudden ebullitions of passion and rage, rushing forward without aim or end, and rendered comparatively harmless by the want of system and skillful directors; but they have become organized bodies, with conspicuous leaders, and plans deliberately made." Chandler underlined the gravity of this challenge to the American system of self-government. "It is not from foreign aggression that our country is threatened," he warned. "It is ourselves that we need to fear."

The Southwark riot broke out in Philadelphia the next day. "This matter of riots in the large cities is becoming serious," Chandler wrote a few weeks later. He, too, was beginning to think that something more than moral regeneration would be necessary to "resist the shocks of anarchy." Chandler suggested that all of the big cities of the northeast needed "civic armies" like London's, with "numbers and discipline worthy of the name." Such a force would make government

> strong enough to overawe those, who cannot govern themselves. . . . [T]he tendency of events in our large cities has been such as must result in the creation of such a strong coercive power, as is not yet known among us, and which has heretofore been looked upon as foreign to the spirit of our institutions. It is to be hoped, that the indications and the necessity of such a change will be confined to our largest cities, but it is through them, if ever, that the American people are to learn, what a strong government is.

Boston had a system of day officers and night watchmen much like Philadelphia's, and it tinkered with that model for another eight years. Finally, in 1853, the City Council conceded that it was irreparable. The existing force, a report concluded, "even if concentrated upon one point, is not competent to cope with any riotous assemblage of more than four or five hundred in numbers, and it is notorious that there are many places in the city where a slight cause would bring together in a few minutes a much larger number of persons who are utterly lawless." The Boston Police Department was established in May 1854.

Within a decade, civic armies had been established to maintain order in the four largest cities in the United States. It may well be that American cities would have been compelled to create police forces eventually because of the pressures created by urbanization; but the fact that they were created at this time is undoubtedly attributable to the effects of the First Great

Depression. Economic decline induced unrest and violence. It forced municipal leaders to confront directly the question of whether it was prudent to rely on the moral sense of citizens—their consideration for the principles of personal responsibility and restraint—or whether it would be necessary to rely on governmental authority as the main guarantee of civil order. The depression led municipal leaders to a common answer. The large cities would, as Chandler proposed, make their governments "strong enough to overawe those, who could not govern themselves."

☙CHAPTER 5

The End of the Crisis

The Mexican War was a product of the First Great Depression, and also marked its end. Many Americans took the view that Texas, the territory at the center of the struggle, would eventually be joined to the United States. That Texas was annexed in 1845, rather than some later year, and that the United States fought a war to confirm its sovereignty over it, can be explained substantially by the bleak circumstances in which Americans found themselves in the trough of the depression.

The war was encouraged by American anxiety about British territorial and commercial ambitions. British leaders were surprised by the intensity of American feeling about Texas, which seemed to rest on a misunderstanding of British policy. But Americans were not thinking only of Texas. They had been stung by British criticism over defaults, and frustrated by their inability to press other claims against the dominant power. Americans felt that their honor had been slighted, and this affected the way in which they viewed and responded to British actions. Even though the belligerents in the war of 1846–1848 were the United States and Mexico, many Americans regarded it as a proxy campaign against the British—a way of thwarting British designs and replying to British insults.

Here, then, was another illustration of the way in which a purely commercial crisis had grown into something more complex. Panic caused the depression, which caused default, which caused a war of words across the

Atlantic, which caused a dissipation of good feeling, which now affected American policy on Texas. The United States was finally moved to war. There was no inconsistency between its militancy over Texas and its more restrained handling of other territorial disputes. Even though Americans might talk as though they were fighting the British, in fact they were not: they were fighting a weaker power, Mexico, and the expectation was that it would be an inexpensive and quick campaign.

The U.S. victory in the Mexican War marked an end to the depression in two ways. First, it revived the nation's spirits. In the eyes of many Americans, military success restored national honor, redeemed the democratic way of governing, and gave proof to Europe of the nation's vitality. Second, the war was an unexpected tonic for the economy, and the mechanism by which the United States was fully reintegrated into international financial markets. Within weeks of the peace settlement, Americans—and also, critically, European investors—learned of a mining bonanza in the newly acquired territory of California. The unexpected cost of the war forced the Democratic administration of President James Polk to offer U.S. bonds in London for the first time since 1842. This time, though, they were taken up by European investors—an expression of renewed confidence in the American economy.

◖ A Proxy War in Mexico

For now we've crossed the Rio Grande
With General Taylor in command,
Our banners floating, on we'll go,
To conquer all of Mexico.
And should old England interfere,
To stop us in our bright career,
We'll teach her, as we did of yore,
This land is ours from shore to shore.

—A. M. Wright, *A Song for the Army*, 1846

Texas, a territory largely populated by Anglo settlers who migrated from the United States, formally declared its independence from Mexico in March 1836. As a practical matter, its autonomy was secured after Texans defeated a much larger force of Mexican troops at the battle of San Jacinto the following month, although Mexico continued to assert its sovereignty and threaten military action to regain control over the territory. The small

Texan population voted overwhelmingly for annexation to the United States in September 1836, and a formal request for annexation was sent to Washington by Texas' first president, Sam Houston, in August 1837.

Andrew Jackson and his successor Martin Van Buren were initially cool to Texas' overtures. Van Buren, in particular, was distracted by the economic crisis after the Panic of 1837. Both presidents also understood that annexation was an explosive topic that threatened to split the Democratic Party, and perhaps also the country. Texas' new constitution sanctioned slavery, and northern abolitionists quickly condemned annexation as a conspiracy by southern slaveholders to increase the power of slave states within the union. The U.S. Congress received more than 180,000 petitions against annexation in 1837–1838. The subject threatened to "give new violence and passion to the agitation of the question of slavery," one abolitionist warned in 1837. Free states would be entitled to view the act of annexation "as the dissolution of the union." With the question of annexation framed in such stark terms, Van Buren declined to act. Houston withdrew his proposal in 1838.

In Texas, as in Oregon, time was on the side of the United States. After independence, and partly because of the depression, migration from the United States to Texas increased markedly. By 1842, the Anglo population was triple what it had been in 1835. In addition, the republic's growing trade was overwhelmingly with the United States.

When Houston found, in 1838, that the United States was not ready for annexation, he turned his attention to Europe, seeking treaties with the British and French governments that would bolster the new republic's autonomy, as well as a five million dollar loan to support the government's operations. Texas' agents failed to raise the loan but won recognition of its independence from France in 1839 and eventually from Britain in 1842.

There were some Britons who thought that their government should seize the opportunity to use Texas as a foil against the United States. A former Royal Navy officer and novelist, Frederick Marryat, became infamous in the United States for an 1839 book suggesting that Texas be "raise[d] up as a barrier against the profligate ambition of America." Another former British diplomat, William Kennedy, argued in 1841 that a free trade agreement with Texas would put pressure on the United States to reverse its own high-tariff policy, and that an independent Texas would limit American maritime influence in the Gulf of Mexico and, by checking westward expansion, on the Pacific as well. Charles Elliot, the British chargé d'affaires in Texas after 1842, thought that Texas could be induced to abandon slavery, and that this would undermine the institution within the southern states. A loan to Texas from the British government that was conditioned on the abolition of slavery, Elliot wrote, would promote a "just balance of power on this continent . . . [and] render as profitable returns as money spent in fortresses and military works on the Northern frontier of the United States."

However, the British government's official policy toward Texas was more cautiously crafted, especially after Lord Aberdeen returned to the post of foreign secretary in 1841. Its foremost concern was not with Texas itself, but with preserving good commercial relations with Mexico and the United States, two larger and better established markets. (In 1840, Texas had a population of seventy thousand people; Mexico had seven million; and the United States had seventeen million.) It had to accommodate opposition to slavery within Britain itself; but to avoid antagonizing the United States, Britain had to steer clear of a hard line against slavery in Texas. To maintain this delicate balance, British diplomats initially prepared to take a less forceful position against slavery, and also against annexation, in the hope that this would reconcile Mexico to the fact of Texas' secession and also appease British abolitionists.

British trade relations with the Texan republic were also handled gingerly. Britain's finance minister captured the British predicament in a letter to Aberdeen in October 1841. Discussing a Texan proposal for a new trade agreement that would give British businesses an advantage over American competitors, the Chancellor of the Exchequer asked:

> If this [trade agreement with Texas] can be done what will be the feeling of the United States at being excluded from the supply of a Country peopled mostly by her own subjects and governed by a constitution framed on the model of that of the U.S.[?] Will it not engender a feeling of animosity towards us and strengthen that party who are labouring to exclude our manufactures from the markets of the United States who are now without doubt our best customers[?]

In the final analysis it was the preservation of commercial relations with the United States that mattered most to the United Kingdom. Aberdeen explained this in a confidential note in July 1845 to Elliot, who had made a last-minute effort to forestall annexation by obtaining formal Mexican recognition of Texas' independence. Aberdeen criticized Elliot for the subterfuges involved in this failed gamble. There were limits to what Britain was prepared to do to prevent annexation. "We do not conceive that any material or direct British interest is involved in the independence of Texas," he explained. The recognition of Texan autonomy had been done mainly to support Mexico by buffering it from the United States. If a clash between the United States and Mexico was imminent, Aberdeen knew where his primary obligations lay: to "the vast amount of British Capital which is engaged in commerce with the United States."

John Tyler, always a supporter of annexation, was nevertheless cautious about promoting it during his first two years in office. Twice in 1842 the Texan government made overtures about annexation; both were rebuffed. This was not surprising to Sam Houston. For years, Houston later said, Washington treated Texas with "coldness, reserve, or palpable discouragement." The Tyler administration's rebuffs seemed only to demonstrate the "habitual apathy" of the United States toward annexation. In truth, the Tyler cabinet was wary about antagonizing northern abolitionists, who still insisted that annexation was part of a "slave-breeding conspiracy against the freedom of the North." In July 1843, Houston instructed Texas' chargé d'affaires in Washington, Isaac Van Zandt, to once again suspend any further discussion of the subject.

It was just at this moment that the policy of the Tyler administration took a surprising turn. In the fall of 1843 it secretly approached Van Zandt with an offer to make a treaty of annexation. Houston responded coolly at first, but by January 1844 the two governments were deep in negotiation. The treaty was concluded and publicly announced in April 1844. The Tyler administration also began a public campaign in favor of annexation, waged primarily through the *Madisonian*, a friendly Washington newspaper. The campaign played on the theme that annexation was not simply matter of new territory—the United States had enough of that already, the newspaper said in November 1843—but a question "touching both the welfare and honor of the nation." It had become clear, the *Madisonian* claimed, that Great Britain had designs on Texas and intended to bring the republic under its control, and that it would abolish slavery within it with the aim of undermining slavery in the southern states and eventually destroying the whole union:

> Her object is to attack the existence of our Government, and our Union, through the institution of slavery in the Southern States. . . . The existence of our Union under a Republican government is no longer compatible with the safety of her Oligarchy. The constant intercourse between the two nations . . . the effects of steam navigation in shortening the time of transit . . . has placed us in dangerous proximity with Great Britain, and she has not been slow in perceiving and taking measures to remedy the dangers of it. She has been steadily and cautiously preparing the means of attack upon our weakest point.

Suspicion of British motives regarding Texas was not new. Months earlier, for example, President Jackson had warned in a private letter to Tennessee congressman Aaron Brown that Britain could use Texas as a base from which to send troops into the south and up the Mississippi, while a second force spread "ruin and havoc" along the Canadian border. The United States would be caught in an "iron hoop," Jackson said. What distinguished this new campaign was its virulence and its source: the *Madisonian* was clearly a platform for the Tyler administration. Many suspected Secretary of State Abel Upshur as the author of some of its most stridently anti-British columns.

Upshur had replaced Daniel Webster as secretary of state in July 1843, and some thought this change alone could account for the shift in policy on annexation. But there was more at work than this. The Tyler administration had become extraordinarily sensitive to evidence suggesting that the British had designs on Texas. It assumed the worst as it watched the diplomatic shuttling between Austin, London, and Mexico City. Rumors reached Washington that the British government was giving aid to Mexico to support an attack on Texas. (This was unfounded, but Mexico was buying weapons from British suppliers. Some cannon forged in England in 1842 were taken as trophies during the Mexican War and are now displayed on the grounds of West Point.) In July 1843, Tyler and Upshur received more alarming news from Duff Green, an old ally whom Tyler had sent to London as a check on the American ambassador, Edward Everett, whose loyalties to the Tyler administration were in doubt. Green reported that a group of British and American abolitionists had met with Aberdeen, and that Aberdeen had endorsed a plan by which the British government would guarantee a loan that would be used to emancipate slaves in Texas.

Green was relying on hearsay, and he had his facts wrong, While Aberdeen did meet with the abolitionists, and did express the British position against slavery, he had also told the abolitionists flatly that Britain would not give any financial inducement to Texas to abolish slavery. But no one in Washington knew this. Instead, they had Green's admonition that annexation was the only way of "preventing Texas falling into the hands of English fanatics" who were determined to start a border war with the United States. In the fall of 1843 Green began writing directly to American newspapers with warnings about British scheming in Texas.

Historians have been divided about the motives of Tyler and Upshur in the summer and fall of 1843. Some argue that the Tyler administration was acting in good faith but on flawed intelligence from Green about British policy. Others are more skeptical. Tyler and Upshur, the skeptics say, deliberately exaggerated fears of British interference in Texas because they realized it was a way of undercutting abolitionist opposition to annexation in the North. Voters who hesitated about admitting another slave state might be won over by "exciting the prevalent distrust of that old enemy, England." Annexation would become feasible, the *Democratic Review* said in early 1844, when "jealousy of English power and English ambition on our Continent . . . should become sufficiently alarmed, to counterbalance the repugnance with which the first suggestion of [annexation] would be received by the North." Indeed, there was evidence by early 1844 that the Tyler administration's anti-British campaign was shifting northern opinion in just this way. In January, the Texan chargé d'affaires, Isaac Van Zandt, provided a confidential assessment to Houston of the likelihood that a treaty negotiated with the Tyler administration would be ratified by the Senate. He was now certain of ratification, because Washington had been seized by the opinion that "Texas must either be annexed to this Union, or become in some form a dependency of Great Britain. . . . It is also believed that Great Britain is now using every means to accomplish these purposes, and that the only security against her insidious policy is through annexation. . . . This view of the case has had an important influence upon many of the Senators of the non-slaveholding states. Were the question deprived of this feature I should despair of its success."

An administration that was susceptible to flawed intelligence, or one that was deliberately exploiting popular anxieties—which of the two explanations is more plausible? It may not be necessary to choose. The two explanations have something in common. By 1843 the Tyler administration, like much of the American public, had a sensitivity about British interference that was aggravated by the conflicts and humiliations of the preceding five years. The administration was, as a consequence, prepared to give credence to the worst rumors about British ambitions, just as the public at large was ready to accept the warnings of the *Madisonian* and other presses.

Consider the situation of Duff Green in London in 1843. Green, an old Jacksonian, bankrupted during the financial crisis, distrusted the British government even before his arrival in London in 1841. His experience while in London, fruitlessly attempting to raise personal loans that would save his own properties, or place the federal loan of 1842, or persuade the British government to amend their tariffs, would have done little to improve his opinion. Furthermore, by the fall of 1843, Green was engaged in a bitter squabble, played out in the pages of the *Times of London,* with Sydney Smith and other writers who had assaulted American honor. Green's persistence eventually produced a snub from the editors of the *Times of London.* In November 1843 they flatly refused to publish any more Green's correspondence and condemned his "impudence" for questioning the integrity of British leaders while defending a "confederation of public bankrupts." This was a deliberate humiliation of a man widely known in London as a friend of President Tyler. Undaunted, Greene took up his fight with Smith in American newspapers instead.

Green's frustration was also that of the country at large. Americans had been chastised for moral laxity because of default and repudiation. They had seen their state legislatures lobbied by agents in the pay of British bankers, while the agents of their own national government were rebuffed in London. They had seen their national ambitions repeatedly suppressed—in Maine, along the New York frontier, in Oregon, in the Sandwich Islands—because it seemed imprudent to confront British military power. In these circumstances, with this accumulation of grievances weighing on the nation's mind, it was natural that voters would be susceptible to warnings about the "ambitious designs of England."

Indeed, the *Democratic Review* warned in April 1844 that the rising acrimony between Britain and the United States might degenerate into violence. Registering its "just indignation" at the insults thrown at the United States by Dickens and other British travelers the previous year, the magazine's editors opined:

> Hostilities between nations are not alone produced by opposite interests or reciprocal injuries. To insult their pride or wound their feelings by sarcasm, sneering, and imputations of corruption, cowardice, or degeneracy, if it does not produce immediate war, will most assuredly lead to the adoption of an unfriendly policy, which is ever a source of strife and contention. Abuse or slander is also sure to provoke retaliation, and in this manner nations become insensibly alienated from each other, not so much by an opposition of interests . . . as from the fact of their having long been engaged in a war of words, which has at length resulted in a settled, inveterate antipathy, rankling in the hearts of an entire people.

The *Democratic Review* had provided a concise summary of the general predicament. The immediate issue was Texas, but the broader problem, which made the Texas question so awkward, was the collapse of good feeling between Americans and Britons, and this in turn was driven as much by the economic decline and repudiation of debt as by conflicting territorial aspirations. To look at it another way, the *Review* was describing the final stages of the transformation of the crisis that had begun with the Panic of 1837. A purely commercial phenomenon had transmuted into a literary conflict—a "war of words"—and this, in turn, was now infecting foreign policy.

Aberdeen, alerted to the Tyler administration's sudden aggressiveness on the Texas question, attempted to mollify it—first by meeting with Everett, the American ambassador in London, and then by sending a letter to the British ambassador in Washington, Richard Pakenham, intended for delivery to American authorities. Britain's aims in Texas, Aberdeen insisted, were "purely commercial," merely an expression of its general interest in the "extension of our commercial dealings with other countries." Britain was opposed to slavery, and would be pleased if it were abolished in Texas, but it would not "interfere unduly" to accomplish that goal, and it certainly had no intention of stirring up "disaffection or excitement of any kind" in the slaveholding states. Britain had no "occult design" in Texas, "no thought or intention of seeking to act directly or indirectly, in a political sense, on the United States through Texas."

Aberdeen was a diplomat but he was not diffident. He could make a clear and threatening statement of British ambitions when circumstances required it. Later, Aberdeen was direct in telling the United States that American intransigence on the Oregon question had raised the prospect of war. By contrast, diplomatic historians have concluded that Aberdeen's message of December 1843 was meant to be frank and conciliatory. While Britain might prefer an independent Texas, its main aim was to stabilize and promote commercial relations with all three of the parties to the dispute—Texas, Mexico, and especially the United States itself.

This is not how the letter was read by the Tyler administration and its allies. Aberdeen's missive, it was thought, was completely disingenuous—"a light gauze which covers the machinations and tactics of British diplomacy." John Calhoun, who became secretary of state after Upshur's death in February 1844, seized on Aberdeen's concession that it was British policy to encourage the abolition of slavery in Texas, as elsewhere. In two letters to the British ambassador made public in April 1844, Calhoun expressed alarm at Aberdeen's "avowal of a policy so hostile in its character and dangerous in its tendency, to the domestic institutions of so many States of this Union, and to the safety and prosperity of the whole." It was the "imperious duty" of the American government, Calhoun said, "to adopt, in self defence," measures to resist the extension of British influence in Texas. Calhoun clearly had in mind the annexation treaty that was concluded with Texas on April 12 and had been sent to the U.S. Senate for ratification. The agreement, Calhoun wrote to Duff Green on April 19, was "forced on the Government of the United States, in self-defence, in consequence of the policy adopted by Great Britain in reference to the abolition of slavery of Texas."

Pakenham and Aberdeen were taken aback by Calhoun's tone, and abolitionists were offended by the long defense of slavery which Calhoun included in his reply to Aberdeen's December letter. But, at the same time, many Americans were glad that an American statesman had stood up to the British. A Michigan Democrat wrote to Calhoun in May that the West was increasingly supportive of annexation, in large part out of "national pride . . . and hatred of British power and control." A Whig merchant in New York, Charles Augustus Davis, told Calhoun that his reply had impelled a second reading of Aberdeen's correspondence—and now Davis could see that it contained "dangerous sentiments . . . decorated with rose leaves." Calhoun's response, Davis predicted, would make the British recognize the danger of "meddling with other people's affairs."

The Whig-controlled Senate confounded Van Zandt's expectations and refused to ratify the annexation treaty before its adjournment in June. The question of annexation loomed large in the presidential campaigns of 1844. Expansionist Democrats were already advocating for annexation by playing on fears of British power, just as the Tyler administration had. One of the Democrats' strongest advocates was Senator Robert Walker. Walker, like Green, was a man whose circumstances might have caused him to take a sour view of the British. He helped to arrange the loans which the state of Mississippi repudiated in 1842, and was selected as a senator by the same state legislature that balked at honoring those loans. Walker was thus deeply implicated in an act that had drawn the most virulent criticism from British investors. *Niles' Register* called Walker "an open advocate of Mississippi repudiation."

Walker's long letter on annexation was published in February and reproduced by the millions over the next nine months. Three months after the election, the *Democratic Review* called it a "text-book of the Democratic Party" in the 1844 campaign, a document which had "a more powerful and decided effect upon the popular mind, than any publication of any American statesman of the present day." Calculated to woo undecided northern voters, Walker's letter appealed directly to American resentment of criticism from Britain in the preceding four years, and suspicion of its power:

> Look at her press in England and Canada, teeming with abuse of our people, government, and laws; look at her authors and tourists, from the more powerful and insidious assaults of Alison, descending in the scale to the falsehoods and arrogance of Hall and Hamilton, and down yet lower to the kennel jests and vulgar abuse of Marryatt and Dickens, industriously circulated throughout all Europe; and never was her hostility so deep and bitter, and never have her efforts been so great to

render us odious to all the world. The government of England is controlled by her aristocracy, the avowed enemies of republican government, wherever it may exist. And never was England endeavoring to advance more rapidly to almost universal empire, on the ocean and the land. Her steamers, commanded by naval officers, traverse nearly every coast and sea, whilst her empire extends upon the land. . . . Though saturated with blood, and gorged with power, she yet marches on her course to universal dominion; and here, upon our own borders, Texas is next to be her prey.

If Texas was not annexed, Walker warned, it would soon be "so completely within British influence as though already a British colony." In the event of war between Britain and the United States, Texas would take the British side, and easily take control of the lower Mississippi and Gulf of Mexico. Eventually the entire American southwest would be ruled under the "red cross of St. George."

Walker conveyed a second warning, directed at the distressed cities of the northeast. The plantation system was exhausting the soil of the southern states, Walker said, and thereby undermining the basis of the slave economy. Texas offered an outlet for the South's unemployed slaves. If Texas was not annexed, hundreds of thousands of slaves would eventually be freed and would migrate north, where they would compete for employment with white laborers. "Wages would be reduced until they fall to ten or twenty cents a day, and starvation and misery would be introduced among the white laboring population." For the voters of Philadelphia and other cities reeling from ethnic and racial violence in the summer of 1844, this was a frightening admonition.

James Polk, a diehard advocate of annexation, won the 1844 election with a slim lead in the popular vote but a clear majority in the Electoral College. The Democrats took most of the South and West and even New York and Pennsylvania, the two most populous northern states. After the election, but before the installation of the new president, Tyler made a last bid for glory by urging that Congress approve annexation by a joint resolution. Congress did so in March 1845. Texas agreed to annexation in July, and it was finally concluded by Congress in December 1845.

The U.S. government took these steps with full knowledge that it was creating a substantial threat of hostilities with Mexico. Twice in 1843 the Mexican foreign minister, Jose Maria de Bocanegra, warned the American ambassador that annexation would be "equivalent to a declaration of war against the Mexican Republic." In November 1843 the Mexican ambassador in Washington again cautioned Secretary of State Upshur that annexation would be viewed "as a direct aggression." By the end of 1843 these threats were widely publicized in the United States. So, too, was Upshur's dismissive reply: Mexico would not dictate American policy on annexation.

"Annexation and war with Mexico are identical," Henry Clay, the Whig candidate for president, concluded in April 1844. Clay was opposed to annexation, but he was right about its consequences. The United States was already moving warships and troops toward Mexico in anticipation of war. Mexican and U.S. troops met in combat for the first time on the banks of the Rio Grande in April 1846, and Congress issued a declaration of war against Mexico the following month.

Of all the territorial disputes in which the United States was engaged during the depression, the argument over Texas was unique. It alone ended in a clash of arms between nations. The Van Buren administration had avoided conflict along the Canadian border in 1837–1840; the Tyler administration had avoided conflict over the Sandwich Islands and Maine; even the belligerent Polk administration had avoided conflict over Oregon, despite the substantial cost borne by the president in terms of domestic political support. But the debate over annexation of Texas ended in war. Why was it not resolved peacefully, like the other disputes?

The Tyler and Polk administrations had been playing a similar and delicate game. Both presidents tried to build electoral support by indulging populist frustration about British commercial and military dominance. At the same time, however, neither Tyler nor Polk wanted an open break with Britain, precisely because of the country's commercial and financial dependence on the superpower, and its relative weakness in naval power. The Polk administration's calculations over the Oregon and Texas disputes were described by Truman Smith, a Connecticut Whig, in February 1846: "The Administration . . . have been mixing up 'foreign affairs' with 'domestic affairs.' We are trying to see how diplomacy and party politics will jump together. In the case of such an imbecile power as Mexico it may do, but when you are dealing with such a character as John Bull, it is quite another affair." Smith described the calculus well. In the case of Oregon, diplomacy triumphed over party politics because belligerence would inevitably lead to war with Britain. But this was not true of the Texas dispute. No claim was being made to British territory, and there was no British commitment to Texas or Mexico that raised a question of British honor.

There was no reason for Britain to fight over the annexation of Texas, and little evidence that it would. Aberdeen delivered no warning about

Texas as he did about Oregon. On the contrary, Aberdeen had cautioned the Mexican government as early as 1842 that it should not "count upon succour from Great Britain in their struggles with Texas, or with the United States." Briefly, in early 1844, Aberdeen considered offering a guarantee that the British would use force to maintain Texan independence as an inducement to Mexico to recognize Texas. (The French would have participated in the guarantee.) But Aberdeen never believed that the actual use of force would be necessary, and he hastily retreated from the idea when the British ambassador in Washington warned him about war fever in the United States.

Again, in March 1845, the Mexican government was told that it could count on nothing more than moral support from the British government: "whatever disposition may have at one time existed to go beyond that line, has now been withdrawn." Aberdeen wrote in April that his cabinet colleagues "do not conceive that they would be justified in exposing Great Britain to the serious risks of a war in seeking to establish [Texan] independence." The cardinal principle of British policy, wrote historian Ephraim Adams, was "to avoid war with the United States at all costs."

Why was the United States prepared to risk war over Texas, but not Oregon? Thomas Hart Benton, the Missouri Democrat, posed the question during the 1844 Senate debate on Tyler's annexation treaty. And he gave an answer: "Because Great Britain is powerful, and Mexico weak." A war with Mexico was widely expected to be fought and won quickly. "Only one bold, swift dash would be needed—no dull, plodding, grimy campaigning year after year." Precisely because it would be quick and inexpensive, there would be no need to seek foreign financing: the war could be funded either by existing taxes or domestic loans. Thus Sydney Smith's gibe of 1843— that Americans "cannot draw the sword, because they have not the money to buy it"—would be disproved.

There could be no doubt that Mexico was in terrible position to fight a war. Between 1843 and 1848 the presidency of Mexico changed hands fifteen times. This instability encouraged belligerence by Mexican leaders. Appeals to national honor were an efficient way of building political support, and attempts at conciliation with Texans or Americans were easily condemned as treachery. But the administrative apparatus of Mexican government was incapable of matching its leaders' blustering. The regime was in "a deplorable condition," as the Mexican correspondent for the *Times of London* explained in October 1845:

> There is literally not a shilling in the Treasury; the Minister of Finance
> has to borrow money from day to day with the greatest difficulty, for

the ordinary expenses of the government. . . . As for the army, its miserable destitution is so great, that except in the city of Mexico the soldiers are without rations. A detachment lately despatched toward California are dying of hunger on the road, and even the division of Paredes, the best in the country, has neither food nor clothing. . . . [The country] is already breaking up at the extremities. Tobasco and Yucatan furnish no supplies to the central Government; Texas has gone, California is meditating revolt, and New Mexico and other northern states are speaking also of annexation.

Indeed, some Americans thought Mexico would simply collapse once war became a reality. "Mexico . . . is unable to carry on a war," wrote William Tecumseh Sherman, a first lieutenant of artillery posted at Fort Moultrie, South Carolina, in June 1845. "Her government is hardly secure, [and] their provinces rebelling." This dim view of the adversary was widely shared among the Army's officer class. "The more we see of the Mexicans, the more improbable it seems that we can ever get into war with her," wrote Ulysses S. Grant, a second lieutenant of infantry serving under General Zachary Taylor, from Corpus Christi in October 1845. "We will have no fight," agreed Lieutenant Napoleon Dana, also serving under Taylor in Texas. "And even if Mexico were to declare war, we are too strong for her and are growing stronger and stronger every day. She cannot fight us, that is out of the question." (Dana almost died at the Battle of Cerro Gordo in April 1847. He was discovered by a burial party recovering bodies a day after the battle.)

In a sense, then, the United States was embarking in a sort of proxy war. It was widely understood as a conflict whose purpose was to check British interference and deliver a rebuff to its imperial pretensions. "The annexation is not, of course, palatable to John Bull," the *Richmond Enquirer* said in September 1845. "This is perhaps the best reason why it should be popular on the Western shores of the Atlantic." Indeed it was commonplace in the early phase of the war for Americans to rouse patriotic sentiments by talking as though the country was at risk of confronting British as well as Mexican soldiers. According to one song:

We're on our way to the Rio Grande,
John Bull may meddle if he please,
But he had better keep at ease,
For we are strong by sea and land—
If he don't mind we'll have old Ireland!

But the truth was that the British would not intervene at all. On the battlefield, the United States would meet only Mexico, a much weaker power.

And so the United States might reap a virtual victory over the British without engaging its troops and vastly superior navy.

An easily executed war against Mexico was also understood, in some quarters, as a tonic that would revive a country still struggling to shake off the torpor that had been the result of economic collapse. The war, said historian Justin Smith, "addressed a restlessness and a dissatisfaction resulting from energies that found no adequate outlet." In the western states especially, "times were hard. Every attempt at commercial or industrial enterprise had failed; farmers could not sell their crops at paying rates, with boundless force in heart and brain the young man could find nothing worthwhile to do." A Whig journal warned Americans on the eastern seaboard that the interior teemed with "great numbers of bold and restless spirits . . . ready for any movement that can minister to their reckless manner of life and love of danger and change."

The desire for action was not limited to the West. "The multitude cry aloud for war," the *New York Herald* said in August 1845. "We are restless, fidgety, discontented, anxious for excitement." "LET US GO TO WAR," agreed the *New York Journal of Commerce*. "The world has become stale and insipid, the ships ought to be all captured, and the cities battered down, and the world burned up, so that we can start again. There would be fun in that. Some interest—something to talk about."

◆ Redemption

> It had been a prevailing opinion in Europe, that the Americans were a nation of *traders*, not over scrupulous about the means of acquiring wealth, and consequently, that a high state of morality could not exist among us. The Mexican war, by illustrating the chivalrous gallantry of the citizen soldier, went far towards removing this prejudice. It was proved that a much higher degree of *patriotism* animated our people than Europe ever exhibited.
>
> —Lucien Chase, *History of the Polk Administration,* 1850

Once war was declared, much of the country was seized by a patriotic fervor. "People here are all in a state of delirium about the Mexican War," Herman Melville wrote from Lansingburgh, in upstate New York, two weeks after Congress' declaration. "A military ardor pervades all ranks. Militia Colonels wax red in their coat facings, and 'prentice boys are running off to the

war by scores. Nothing is talked of but the 'Halls of the Montezumas.'"
When the news reached the small town of Fulton, New York, "they had
the band out, and the boys paraded through the streets with their rifles."
War rallies in New York, Baltimore, and Philadelphia drew tens of thousands of people. The War Department called on Pennsylvania to produce
enough volunteers for six regiments, but

> The spirit was so strong and the number of adventurous persons so
> many, that General Bowman found, before the end of July, that he had
> a much greater force of volunteers than could be employed. . . . [O]n
> the 15th of July information was sent to the War Department that
> ninety companies—enough for nine regiments—had volunteered in
> the State. The responses from other portions of the Union came thick
> and fast, and the War Department was embarrassed.

Even Massachusetts, the hard core of anti-annexation sentiment, was not
immune to the war bug. The American Peace Society, holding its annual
meeting in Boston on May 25, found its proceedings disrupted by the arrival of news about American victories in early battles with the Mexicans near
the Rio Grande. "The war excitement could hardly be ignored. Newsboys
hawked accounts of the battles on the streets, and that night buildings were
grandly illuminated in celebration of the victories." Massachusetts met its
own target for volunteers within weeks of the declaration of war.

The War Department's call for recruits had an unintended but happy
consequence for the big cities of the northeast: a reduction in tensions between nativists and Irish immigrants. In the boom years before 1837, the
West had been imagined as a safety valve that would relieve "all the pent-up
passions and explosive or subversive tendencies" within northeastern cities.
During the depression, the West could not perform this role. To a degree,
the army took its place. Even before the Mexican War it was estimated that
Irish immigrants accounted for one-quarter of the regular army (and German immigrants another quarter). The war itself increased the army's capacity to absorb the cities' angry young men. A German immigrant from
Philadelphia described the battery which he joined in December 1846:
"Approximately a third were Germans; a third Irish, English, Scotch, Welsh,
and Canadians; and the final third Americans."

One Irish recruit from Philadelphia was William McMullen, a twenty-
two-year-old Irish Catholic who fought in the Kensington riot of 1844 and
joined the First Pennsylvania Infantry in 1846 to escape trial for assaulting a
policeman. McMullen's company included many other Irish gang members
and distinguished itself during the march from Veracruz to Mexico City,

winning a citation for the "extremest of bravery." McMullen returned to Philadelphia as a war hero. He became active in municipal politics and by 1856 he was an alderman and one of the overseers of Philadelphia's prison.

The participation of Irish Catholics in the Mexican War also complicated the nativists' attempts to challenge their patriotism. Nativists were certainly helped by the San Patricio Battalion, a force of deserters, some Irish Catholic, which fought for Mexico. But the San Patricios were widely understood to be anomalous. A speaker at a Democratic meeting in Philadelphia in early 1848 won loud applause for saying that the lists of killed and wounded proved the patriotism of Irish immigrants: "In truth, we are all Americans. . . . The terms Irishman, Frenchman, German, foreigner, should have no place for reproach in our political vocabulary; for we are all alike enobled by the proud title, *Citizen of the American Republic*." In New York City, the *United Service Journal* said that the phrase "Irish volunteers" ought to be banished entirely. "They are American citizen soldiers, that is what they are."

Enthusiasm for the war remained high for much of its first year. By early 1847, American forces had uncontested control of much of northeastern Mexico, New Mexico, and California. General Zachary Taylor's victory at Buena Vista in February 1847, the battle which ended the northern campaign, was a cause for national celebration. The lonely band of American pacifists lamented the flood of "glorious news from Mexico" peddled by the penny press, and a sprawling war literature that celebrated "the lives of victorious generals, the bloody feats of prowess, the histories of battles and sieges. . . . It is so cheap that all can buy it. It is so diffused, that it enters every nook and corner of the land. It is so stimulating to the curiosity and passions of half-educated minds, that they find it invested with all the charms of romance." But most Americans did not share the pacifists' gloom. In April 1847, Walt Whitman gave this appraisal of the war, with a telling eye to Europe's opinion of the United States:

> Such events as this victory at Buena Vista, and our former victories in Mexico must elevate the *true* self-respect of the American people to a far higher point than heretofore. Because, with all the charge of vainglory made against us by foreigners, our people do *not* hold that hightoned respect, becoming to such a great nation as ours really is. . . . It cannot be denied that unsurpassed brilliant successes in war—and continued ones, too—go far toward lifting up that desirable tone.

Later in 1847 the war seemed to bog down. The Mexican government would not sue for peace despite their defeat at Buena Vista, and the United

FIGURE 12. Richard Caton Woodville, *War News from Mexico,* 1848. Source: Crystal Bridges Museum of American Art.

States was compelled to begin another campaign led by General Winfield Scott, with troops landing at Veracruz and marching to Mexico City. And there were other troubles: conflict between Polk and his top commanders, Taylor and Scott, both Whigs with presidential aspirations; conflict among military commanders themselves; and conflict between soldiers of the regular Army and the larger mass of ill-trained and undisciplined volunteers. A lieutenant serving in northern Mexico complained in 1847 that the Army was "almost paralysed by the imbecility of its old officers," who faced no legal obligation to retire. Nine thousand American soldiers deserted, from a total force of about one hundred thousand. In May 1847, seven of Scott's volunteer regiments, reaching the end of their one year of service, insisted on returning home, leaving Scott exposed with a much reduced army fifty miles into the Mexican interior. Fortunately, the Mexican army was in no position to exploit the vulnerability.

"Well may we be grateful that we are at war with Mexico!" wrote George Meade, a lieutenant serving under Taylor. "Were it any other power, our gross follies would have been punished severely before now."

Such difficulties caused public support for the war to soften, but opposition to the war continued to be disorganized and confused. The war was not the dominant issue in either the 1846 or 1847 congressional elections. Abolitionists and pacifists in New England often struggled to fill the halls for their anti-war meetings. In Congress, many of Polk's critics, reluctant to appear as though they were undermining American troops on the battlefield, hesitated to make a full-throated challenge to the war. Senator Thomas Corwin, an Ohio Whig, was denounced as a traitor when he demanded the withdrawal of troops from Mexico in February 1847.

Most of Corwin's fellow legislators followed a more careful line, often questioning tactics or the expansion of war aims, but avoiding the fundamental question of whether the war should be fought at all. "When the country was engaged in war," North Carolina Senator William Magnum told other Whigs in 1847, "whatever the cause—whatever the blunder—whatever the want of foresight—whatever the lack of wisdom which had placed the country in that position—it was still the country's war and they must stand or fall by the country." In 1848, the Whigs inoculated themselves against charges of disloyalty by choosing General Taylor, hero of the northern Mexico campaign, as their presidential nominee.

The American forces under Winfield Scott finally occupied Mexico City and placed it under martial law in September 1847. (For Major General Robert Patterson, one of Scott's commanders, it was not the first experience in governing a city under martial law. He had done the same in Philadelphia three years earlier.) Five months of slow negotiation with the Mexican government, which had retreated to Querétaro, followed. Finally, in February 1848, Mexico surrendered. The Treaty of Guadalupe Hidalgo went into effect on July 4, 1848.

Coincidentally, this was the day on which the cornerstone of the Washington Monument was laid. Benjamin French, Grand Master of the Masonic Lodge of the District of Columbia, consecrated the cornerstone with a hope for happiness in every hamlet in the greatly extended nation, "from the Rio Bravo to the Bay of Fundy, from the Pacific to the Atlantic Oceans." The *Democratic Review* reported that the nation's birthday had never been "more generally or more joyfully commemorated. . . . The brilliant success of our brave and magnanimous army in Mexico was a great and unwonted stimulus to rejoicing."

In the glow of victory, the difficulties that confronted American forces during the Mexican campaigns were forgotten. Instead, the country resounded with tributes to the troops who had delivered such a decisive triumph. Even critics of the war conceded that the "willingness and ability of the citizen soldier to defend promptly and efficiently the country's flag [proved] to the world the inherent strength of our political system." The war, said editor Freeman Hunt in April 1848, "has shown . . . that a people, for the last thirty or forty years devoted to the arts of peace, possessing free political institutions, can vanquish a military people, governed by military despots."

These encomia to the country's troops were phrased in a distinctive way. The message was not simply that soldiers had performed honorably and well; it was also that they had *demonstrated to the world* their capacity to perform honorably and well. The war allowed the American people to give proof of the resilience and strength of the democratic form of government. For almost a decade, Americans had been taunted from Europe: that they were incapable of regulating themselves; that they were incapable of regulating their country; that they were incapable of honoring their commitments overseas. As Lord Ashburton, the British emissary to Washington, had said in 1842, the country appeared to be "a mass of ungovernable & unmanageable anarchy." The Mexican War allowed the American people to prove Europe wrong.

"This transformation of a plain working people, into a formidable, yes, an unconquered army, struck the tyrants of the old world with awe . . . England, that Carthage of Modern History, brutal in her revenge and Satanic in her lust for human flesh, beheld the American People, in arms, with trembling." This was a central theme of President Polk's address to Congress after the conclusion of the war. It had become commonplace, he said in December 1848, for writers interested in government "to impute to republics a want of that unity, concentration of purpose, and vigor of execution which are generally admitted to belong to the monarchical and aristocratic forms." However, the United States had, in the preceding two years, demonstrated all these qualities in its conduct of the war. The country had shown that a democratic government could act "with all the vigor usually attributed to a more arbitrary form of government. . . . [T]he war which we have just closed by an honorable peace evinces beyond all doubt that a popular representative government is equal to any emergency which is likely to arise in the affairs of a nation."

The importance of the war as a demonstration of the strengths of democratic government—and its usefulness in providing a retort to European critics—was widely acknowledged. John Frost, a popular historian and a Philadelphian Whig, wrote in 1848 that the gain in territory was actually the *least* important consequence of the war. More important was its effect on attitudes across the Atlantic: "Europe has long contemplated us as a mere commercial and business-loving nation, smothering our former military abilities, in inordinate love of wealth. . . . The war in Mexico has dissolved this vain dream, and taught astonished Europe a lesson, whose precepts will be remembered in every one of her belligerent assemblies for ages."

Another historian, Nathan Brooks, took nearly the same view. "The war with Mexico has been productive of the most beneficial consequences," Brooks wrote in 1850. "It has given our country a prominent rank among the nations of the earth. It has displayed to the eyes of doubting monarchists the existence of a majestic power and energy, a youthful freshness of spirit combined with a manly vigour, which are well calculated to insure prolonged peace. . . . The United States has not merely shown her ability for defensive war, but has successfully solved the problem of the capacity of a republic to engage in a foreign war."

War rejuvenated the nation. Whig historian William Hickling Prescott, a staunch opponent of the war, visited Philadelphia in the spring of 1847 and observed that

> The effects of the great shock it received [after 1839] were rapidly passing away. . . . There is a renovating power in the American character and institutions which readily repairs the ravages of a storm that would prostrate forever the communities of the older and worn out countries of Europe. Our years and hardy constitution soon throw off disease, and every day of our existence we are exhibiting stronger and stronger evidence of our elastic vigour and increasing resources. The spirit with which this present war has been conducted by our raw militia . . . is proof of the indomitable energy of our people, and their capacity for the highest and most difficult scenes of action.

The novelist James Fenimore Cooper agreed that "a great change has come over the country." The Mexican War had advanced the country "in a moral sense . . . by an age, in its progress toward real independence and high political influence. The guns that filled the valley of the Aztecs with their thunder, have been heard in echoes on the other side of the Atlantic."

There was another sense—less elevated, but more immediately important—in which the nation was redeemed by the war. Another unexpected consequence of the conflict was the definitive readmission of the United States into the world of international finance. The great irony was that it was a Democratic administration, proud of its Jacksonian roots, that accomplished this task. The accomplishment was completely unintended, and based in the Polk administration's management of war finances.

At first the Democratic leadership believed that the war would be short and inexpensive. In early 1846 the Democratic chair of the House Ways and Means Committee, James McKay, suggested that the entire cost of the war might be covered by the surplus of seven million dollars that remained in the Treasury from 1845, a product of the tariff increases adopted in 1842. The Polk administration was slightly less optimistic, estimating a total cost of twenty million dollars. Much of this—twelve million dollars—was the cost of raising a volunteer army of twenty-five thousand soldiers for one year's service. The rest went for expansion of the regular Army and, to a smaller degree, the Navy. Roughly, this implied a doubling of total government expenditures from 1845.

Public understanding of the true cost of the conflict came slowly. By early 1848, the Whig chairman of the House Ways and Means Committee, Samuel Vinton, was proclaiming his "utter want of confidence" in spending reports provided by Robert Walker, now serving as Polk's Treasury secretary. Many financiers shared this view. "Capitalists have no confidence in the statements of the government," the *New York Express* reported in December 1847. "They were told last year that no more money would be wanted until July 1848. Now they see the treasury is nearly empty, and new loans wanted."

With hindsight we can estimate that the total direct cost of military operations was probably over sixty million dollars by June 1848. Eventually there were other charges—such as a fifteen million dollar payment to Mexico under the Treaty of Guadalupe Hidalgo for land taken during the war, and at least sixty million dollars for veterans' pensions. The total cost of the war might well have been as much as two hundred million dollars—a bargain price for the territory acquired, but still vastly more than initial estimates.

While expenditures were rising, however, revenues were falling. Polk campaigned for the Democratic presidential nomination in 1844 on the promise that he would unwind the tariff law of 1842 by lowering duties to a level that provided just enough revenue for normal government operations. Protection against foreign competition would cease to be the primary aim of tariff policy. Polk softened his position to gain support in northern states during the 1844 election, but tariff reform was again restated as a priority in 1845. Congress adopted a law that substantially lowered tariffs in July 1846, two months after the declaration of war against Mexico. Treasury Secretary Walker predicted that the new tariff bill would spur trade and actually increase customs revenue in its first year.

Walker's estimate was wrong: revenue dropped by 10 percent between 1846 and 1847. This decline, combined with the increase in war spending, led to a deficit of thirty million dollars in 1847. In nominal terms, this was the largest deficit in the sixty years' history of the republic. Revenues were less than half of expenditures. This Democratic administration was showing a remarkable deal of flexibility in its application of Jacksonian principles about fiscal probity. The federal budget was in deficit again in 1848 and 1849. At first, the federal government attempted to finance these deficits by issuing short-term treasury notes, but the Polk administration quickly realized that the budget gap was too large to be covered in this way, and Congress began authorizing the sale of long-term government bonds. Between 1846 and 1849, the federal government issued forty-nine million dollars in long-term debt to finance the war.

The Polk administration's initial aim had been to place this debt mainly with American investors. Certainly Treasury Secretary Walker, the Mississippian, had no enthusiasm for engaging with foreign capitalists. "As a rule, I am opposed to foreign loans," Walker said much later, "and made none while Secretary of the Treasury, even to carry on our war with Mexico."

This was not true. By 1848 the American market was struggling to accommodate the federal government's demand for loans. Still, Walker was ambivalent about turning to foreign lenders. The Democratic press was already criticizing him for pandering to "the shylocks of Wall Street" in his attempt to place the war loans in the United States; he would be vulnerable to even sharper criticism for going overseas. Walker also wanted to avoid creating "an impression in Europe that we were greatly in want of money." But the demands of the war did not allow the Treasury to be so particular. Walker's attempts to lure American financiers with favorable terms had reached a limit. In April 1848, the Polk Cabinet agreed that it would be "proper to advertise & invite proposals" for a new sixteen million dollar loan "abroad as well as at home."

In August 1848 the Treasury took more dramatic action. William Corcoran, a Washington financier who played an important role in selling federal bonds, told Walker that he was still struggling to raise funds from a market comprised mainly of American investors. More aggressive measures were needed to engage European lenders. "If a portion of this Loan could be placed in London," Corcoran told Walker in August 1848, confidence in it would be bolstered: "You may rely upon it, there is no other mode to accomplish your wishes." Walker appointed Corcoran as an agent of the U.S. Treasury with a mandate to visit Europe and place five million dollars in U.S. bonds. As his travelling companion, Corcoran recruited John Davis, a former Whig governor of Massachusetts who helped negotiate the resumption of payments by the state of Illinois to British bondholders in 1846. Corcoran and Davis arrived in Liverpool on the packet *America* on August 30.

Hanging over their visit was the memory of the last attempt to sell U.S. bonds in Europe in 1842, when federal agents had gone "a-begging through all of the exchanges in Europe." In the fall of 1845, a New Orleans banker, Edmund Forstall, wrote to Walker reminding him of that earlier humiliation—that representatives of the United States had tried to "negotiate a pitiful loan of four to five millions of dollars, [and] had to return without finding a single taker." Success this time might well establish confidence, as Corcoran had promised, but another failure would be equally devastating.

Fortunately, circumstances were playing in favor of the United States. Bad weather in Europe in 1845 and 1846 caused two of the worst harvests in many years. By early 1847, prices for basic foodstuffs doubled across Europe, triggering riots and raising fears of famine. In June 1846, Britain's Conservative government abandoned its opposition to high tariffs on imported grains to avoid unrest among urban workers and placate the manufacturers who employed them. Europe's misfortune was a "streak of luck" for the United States, as demand for American grain and flour surged. The value of American exports of grain and flour averaged less than nine million dollars between 1838 and 1845, but rose to sixteen million dollars in 1846, and fifty-three million dollars in 1847. That year, the volume of freight carried on the Erie Canal, much of it grain and flour heading to European markets, was twice what it had been between 1837 and 1845. All of this was "unexpected good fortune," *Bankers' Magazine* reported in 1847. "The balance of trade is becoming so much in favor of this country that large amounts of coin are coming over by every steamer and packet ship."

European governments, seeing the rapid depletion of their reserves to pay for foreign grain, responded with restrictive monetary policies that induced recession at home. In 1848, Europe realized the political consequences that followed from two years of economic distress. The year began with a popular revolt in Sicily against King Ferdinand II. In February, protests in the streets of Paris led to the collapse of the French government. Radical movements also threatened regimes in the German states, Austria, Poland, and Denmark. In Hungary, mobs forced the resignation of Prince von Metternich, a pillar of the conservative European establishment. "What disorder the world has fallen into!" Metternich wrote in April. "Never before has there been such a greater, more deep-seated confusion."

The Rothschild family, closely tied to many of the continent's governments, were themselves assailed by radicals and threatened with violence. The family worried not just about their security but also about their securities, as the European bond market collapsed. By April 1848, French bonds were worth less than half their value in 1846, and even British long-term bonds had declined by almost a quarter. "We must hope for the best," Nathaniel de Rothschild wrote to his brothers. "In the meantime, I really recommend you most strongly to sell stocks & public securities of all sorts and descriptions." Other investors in Britain and the continent were doing the same.

The United States, by contrast, was seen by European investors to be at peace. The last American troops in Mexico had sailed from Veracruz at the start of August. Nor was there significant unrest within the United States itself. The season of widespread riot and rebellion was largely over, and law and order reestablished. The process of reforming state constitutions to impose restrictions on borrowing and spending was underway. American government bonds, the Rothschilds' U.S. agent advised, could "now be considered the safest of any government. . . . [I]t would be a very desirable thing for yourselves to invest a portion of your fortune in the securities of a country, which experience has shown not to be subject to the revolutions, the growing radicalism of Europe."

While Europe grappled with the unrest following from successive bad harvests, nature provided a second and more startling surprise for the United States. The *London Morning Chronicle* of August 21 delivered news to British investors of an emerging boom in California, triggered by the discovery of an array of minerals—mainly silver, zinc, and quicksilver (that is, mercury). Land prices were already spiraling upward. The *Chronicle*'s American correspondent marveled at how easily wealth could be extracted from the earth: "Almost the same expense and labour employed in Pennsylvania, in obtaining a ton of iron, will obtain a ton of quicksilver in California. Neither you nor your readers are expected to believe this most incredible story; yet, such is the fact. The quicksilver obtained at the Forbes mines, in one week, will pay for the machinery. When the expected works from Europe reach this country, the tons of quicksilver will show for itself." In the San Jose Valley, the *Chronicle* reported two weeks later, a prospector found a vein of silver that was estimated to be "three feet broad, having an uninterrupted run east for three miles. . . . With a few hours labour, several tons of ore were uncovered." North of San Francisco, explorers discovered "immense beds of copper ore, and caves of sulphur and saltpetre."

The market for Californian quicksilver was initially in Mexico, where it was used to extract gold and silver from ore. However, it soon became clear that California itself held vast reserves of gold as well. On October 2 the steamer *Hibernia* arrived in Liverpool with an extraordinary report about the new discoveries. "El Dorado is no longer a fabulous locality," said the *London Daily News*:

> On some branches of the Sacramento river . . . gold has been discovered in quantities scarcely credible. It is found in the sands of the shores of these rivers, in grains varying from the size of mustard-shot to that of nearly an ounce weight. So abundant is this gold, and so extensive are the districts where it is found, that the whole American population of California has repaired to the banks of these rivers. . . . Everything that will hold water, or, on the contrary, act as a sieve, is in demand, and the most extraordinary prices are paid for them by the gold washers. . . . [W]e hear of large ventures going out in the shape of machines to assist the operations of the gold washers, and food and clothing for those who have given up all their former occupations for the new one of which we speak.

The *Liverpool Mercury* reported that three-quarters of the houses in San Francisco were empty because their owners had gone to search for gold. Wages and prices were inflating rapidly. The editor of the *Californian* newspaper announced that he would cease publication until the gold madness was over and people were able to "resume the use of their reading faculties."

The news coming from California cheered businessmen in the United States. Still, nothing had been heard about the placement of the federal loan in Europe. On Wall Street, "the strongest anxiety was felt as to the result of Mr. Corcoran's mission to London." Finally, in October, the steamer *Cambria* brought good news. Corcoran had successfully placed several million dollars of U.S. bonds with investors in Britain and on the continent. The report "produced an immediate effect upon the price of our public securities," the *New York Courier and Enquirer* stated, "[and] induced a better feeling generally, which will grow."

On October 17, the newspaper reported that New York was waiting with anticipation for the arrival of the *Britannia,* the same ship that had brought Dickens to the new world six years earlier:

> This vessel has been eagerly looked for, especially in relation to the money market, and if Mr. Corcoran, who was to take passage in her, should arrive, and bring with him a million or so of dollars in coin, it will immediately operate to the advantage of business generally. Even his return without coin, but having accomplished the object of his mission in placing a considerable amount of United States Six per Cents abroad, will conduce to more ease and stability in the money market, which governs all the others.

The *Brittania's* news confirmed that the curse of 1842 was definitely broken. At that time, James de Rothschild had told the Americans that they "could not borrow a dollar, not a dollar." Now the House of Rothschild was the biggest single subscriber to the 1848 loan. The London Rothschilds also helped as middlemen in the payment of an American indemnity to Mexico that was part of the peace agreement. "We are glad to see the Messrs. Rothschilds again investing in American securities," said Baltimore's *Bankers' Magazine.* "It shows the confidence which the principal bankers of the European world place in American stocks."

Historian Mira Wilkins has observed that by 1849 it was clear that the United States had undergone a "dramatic turnaround" in European financial markets. "America's credit-worthiness was restored. Once more, in the 1850s, foreign individuals and firms would make sizable investments . . . in the United States. The lean years were over." Another boom in foreign investment in the United States was about to begin.

Conclusion
Freedom, Order, and Economic Crisis

> What, then, is the moral of the terrible crisis which has just convulsed the country? Of what national sin is it the consequence and punishment—of what departure from those true principles of political morals on which all national happiness must depend? . . . This question, then, becomes one of essential importance, which the American people ought to lay well to heart, and ponder earnestly.
>
> —*United States Democratic Review,* October 1837

In November 2010 the anti-secrecy group WikiLeaks released a vast trove of cable messages from the U.S. State Department that had been leaked to it by a government source. Buried within the cable traffic was a message that described a private meeting between Secretary of State Hillary Clinton and Australian Prime Minister Kevin Rudd in 2009. The subject of the meeting was the American and Australian relationship with China. "The Secretary affirmed the U.S. desire for a successful China," the cable said. At the same time, Clinton and Rudd recognized that China's increasing power would create diplomatic challenges. This was especially true for the United States, given the large amount of American debt held by the Chinese government. After all, Clinton asked: "How do you deal toughly with your banker?"

Clinton was not alone in posing this question. After the panics of 2007 and 2008, and the recession that followed, anxieties were frequently expressed about American dependence on Chinese creditors and the ensuing complications for American foreign policy. This was part of a larger preoccupation with the decline of American dominance in the era of economic globalization. The American economy, once thought to be "singularly self-sufficient," was now understood to be increasingly open and "hostage politically to the investment decisions of foreign governments." Some regard the coming era of interdependence and vulnerability as a completely unprecedented situation. We can see now that this is not the case at all. Indeed, it is the period of self-sufficiency—the thirty-five years from the end of the Second World War to the election of Ronald Reagan in 1980—that is historically anomalous. A much greater part of American history has been one in which interdependence and vulnerability have been foremost in the minds of the nation's leaders.

Clinton's question certainly preoccupied her predecessors in the Van Buren, Tyler, and Polk administrations. It was a central problem of American politics in the crisis years of 1836–1848: not only for diplomats, but also in Congress and state legislatures, in the popular press, and on the campaign trail. Of course, the banker at that time was Britain, not China. Britain was the primary source of foreign investment, and the major trading partner of the United States. But it was also a rival for territory and markets, and it had the advantage of a larger economy and more powerful armed forces. U.S. policy and its public institutions evolved to accommodate these economic and military realities. The architecture of government was adjusted to suit the prevailing conditions of interdependence and vulnerability. And if there could be said to be a central theme that colored debate over the reform of policy and institutions in that period, it was the need to strike a new balance between order and liberty within the American system. The ideals of individual freedom and self-rule had to be modified in a nation that was insufficiently powerful to dictate the terms on which the international economic order was run.

The United States in the nineteenth century was a world in which financial crises and depressions were a familiar phenomenon. Many contemporary economists tried to discern a pattern in the economy's progress. One saw a regular ten-year cycle: "Prosperity for five to seven years; Panic a few months to a few years; and Liquidation about a few years." Another saw a relationship between surges in sunspot activity and the onset of financial crises. (This is not so far-fetched as it may seem. Sunspots were thought to affect weather, which affected harvests, which affected the overall health of the economy.) However these efforts to identify predictable patterns usually failed. The truth was that the economic climate was highly volatile: Fair weather would suddenly be interrupted by an unexpected storm. Moreover, the storm could come from offshore: a panic in the United States could be triggered because of decisions taken across the Atlantic, by individuals or institutions for whom the welfare of Americans was a subordinate concern.

There is a tendency now to regard crises such as the First Great Depression as a purely economic phenomenon. From this perspective, the crisis began with the pressure in financial markets in the fall of 1836, and ended with signs of economic recovery around 1843–1844. However, it is a mistake to view this crisis—or any other—purely in economic terms. The story, as revealed here, was much more complicated, and therefore more prolonged, than that. The economic collapse quickly spawned other problems that were, on their own account, equally dire. In state capitals and in Washington, old animosities that were suppressed in years of prosperity were suddenly re-exposed. Legislative deadlock provoked questions about the capacity of newly formed democratic systems to act authoritatively in critical moments. Riots and rebellions in many parts of the country raised similar questions about the capacity to maintain social order. Even foreign policy was destabilized, as a humiliated and weakened nation chafed at its inability to make a firm stand against the expansion of British power.

In a sense, there was a parallel between the economic and non-economic aspects of the crisis. The key feature of a financial panic is the sudden dissolution of trust within the business community. With the collapse of trust, the vast and delicate web of commercial transactions collapses and economic activity grinds to a halt. As the economy declines, however, the breakdown of trust becomes more general. Legislators and political executives stop trusting one another. Politicians who are bound by partisan or legislative compacts stop trusting one another. Employers and workers, landlords and tenants, neighbors of different races and ethnicities—all stop trusting one another. Even among nations, trust declines and is displaced by rancor and antagonism. An initial problem of decaying commercial trust degenerates into a broader and more difficult problem of decaying societal and intersocietal trust.

By 1844, the crisis was so thorough and profound that it was understood to raise basic questions about the nation's political philosophy. The essential issue, as it was commonly recognized at the time, was whether U.S. political institutions could strike the right balance between liberty and order. In the decades before the crisis, the balance had been adjusted in favor of liberty. The emphasis had been on the capacity and right of the common man to govern himself—"the principle of the sovereignty of the people," as Alexis de Tocqueville called it in 1835. The extension of voting rights was the most obvious expression of faith in this principle. But the durability of a political system that placed such emphasis on liberty and popular sovereignty was understood to depend heavily on the capacity of citizens to regulate their own conduct; on their capacity, as Peleg Chandler put it in 1844, for "personal responsibility [and] manly self-denial." For many Americans, the crisis required a reappraisal of this assumption about human nature. For those Americans who settled on a more pessimistic view of human nature, it is also required a reappraisal of how public institutions should be organized so that order would be preserved.

The debate over state defaults was just one of the manifestations of this broader argument about the balancing of order and liberty. State legislatures were understood as mechanisms for the expression of the desires of a sovereign people. But the sovereign people had borrowed recklessly in the boom years to engage in ill-considered projects. Then they defaulted on their loans and destroyed their credit, and were humiliated in the eyes of foreign investors. This experience required a reappraisal of the quality of judgment exercised by legislators and voters. In moments of prosperity, they seemed liable to make imprudent decisions about borrowing. Then, in the initial moments of adversity, when faced with the consequences of those decisions, they made dishonorable choices about repayment. Some institutional check against the frailty of voter and legislator judgment, such as a constitutional restriction on borrowing, seemed necessary. As a speaker at Indiana's constitutional convention of 1850 said, "[We] bind and restrict ourselves . . . against the sudden and dangerous impulses of passion and prejudice."

Of course, there were other domains in which Americans were compelled to reconcile order and liberty. Economic distress encouraged social unrest. Sometimes this unrest could be regarded as the expression of a coherent political project, aimed at resolving grievances that had not weighed so heavily in better times. Many of the Americans who participated in these protests were the children of patriots who had fought in the Revolutionary War, and their own protests were framed in the rhetoric of that era. On the other hand, there were also instances, such as the rioting in major cities of the northeast, where the political content of the protests was less coherently expressed. In such cases, fears about the decline of individual self-discipline—about the irrationality of individual judgment, the surrender of individuals to a mob mentality, and the collapse of civic morality—were broadly aired. And the question, again, was what should be done to preserve order under such circumstances?

Initially, popularly elected governments tended to temporize about the use of force to preserve order, but when the threat became serious, force was invariably deployed. Dissent was tolerated only if it was channeled through established institutions. To preserve order, martial law was declared; the state militia and federal troops were rallied; mass arrests were made; and heavy sentences, including capital sentences, were levied. And if the capacity to suppress disorder did not exist, it was created, as it was in the cities of the northeast. Ironically, the idea of a police force—a civic army, as it was called—was itself imported from Britain. The champions of liberty borrowed an innovation from the champions of order.

The struggle to maintain order was not limited to state capitals or the streets of major cities. It was evident in Washington as well, as economic decline caused old political compacts to collapse and encouraged polarization and legislative stalemate. Here, too, the basic question—could a democratic polity regulate itself?—was presented with full force. By 1842, Congress appeared to be immobilized, "incompetent to legislate," as Navy Secretary Abel Upshur said. And once again the problem could be construed as one rooted in defects of character. Members of Congress seemed to have abandoned reason and decency; they had ceased to behave "in a manner befitting christians, gentlemen, or the representatives of a civilized people."

There was no institutional reform that provided a quick remedy to this difficulty. The problem of deadlock in Washington persisted throughout the crisis. But it might be argued that one of the effects of prolonged crisis was to enhance the power of the president relative to the legislative branch. John Tyler, often regarded as an ineffectual president, played an important role in this regard. For example, it is often argued that Andrew Jackson established a more assertive conception of executive power through the regular use of the presidential veto. Jackson, it has been argued, "legitimized the veto," exercising it twelve times during his eight years as president, more than all of the preceding six presidents combined. But if the frequent use of the veto is evidence of the consolidation of executive power, Tyler deserves credit as much as Jackson. He relied on it ten times in only four years.

There are other ways in which executive power was strengthened. The struggle by the White House and Treasury to control federal spending in the face of plummeting revenues led to the first tentative efforts to scrutinize and control spending by federal departments. The desire to avoid an escalation of conflict with the British led Tyler and Daniel Webster to use secret funds to manipulate public opinion about the settlement of the Maine border dispute. And, in response to the Anglo-American dispute over the Alexander McLeod case, Congress gave Tyler and succeeding presidents the power to remove from state courts cases that might affect the nation's international obligations.

Anglo-American relations were also destabilized by the economic collapse. Even in good times, a tension was present: although Great Britain and the United States were economically dependent on one another, they were also competing for territory and markets, and there were wounded sensibilities remaining from the War of 1812 and the revolutionary struggle. In times of prosperity, there was hope that these differences could be resolved amicably, but economic decline made reconciliation more difficult. In Britain, default and repudiation led to angry taunts about deficiencies in American character and institutions. In the United States, the sense of oppression and humiliation deepened. A crisis that began as a dry matter of banking was transformed into a question of national honor. In some quarters, this encouraged a restless and strident nationalism.

We should draw from this a caution about conclusions that have been drawn in the modern era about the pacific tendencies of economic globalization. It became commonplace in the 1990s to argue that economic interdependence leads inevitably to a reduction in armed conflicts between nations. It was argued that countries would realize that it was against their economic interests to provoke conflict, and also that economic engagement would foster mutual understanding. In 1996, Thomas Friedman reduced this argument to the proposition that no two countries that each have a McDonald's restaurant have ever fought a war.

Even in 1996 there was reason to doubt Friedman's argument. In 1910, British writer Norman Angell made a similar argument, that economic integration among European nations made war inconceivable. Events shortly proved otherwise. And we can see from the story of the First Great Depression more reasons why we should be skeptical about this benign view of interdependence. It is undoubtedly true that interdependence gives powerful constituencies a material incentive to avoid conflict wherever possible. Business interests on both sides of the Atlantic worked actively to preserve peace throughout the crisis of 1836–1848, and in fact the United States and Britain never engaged in direct conflict. However, mutual animosities did intensify during the crisis, and this happened precisely because the two nations were economically intertwined. Questions of national honor would not have arisen if the United States and Britain had not existed in the relationship of debtor and creditor. And there were points at which this entirely human preoccupation with national honor seemed likely to trump practical considerations about trade and finance. As the *Democratic Review* said, the conflict was no longer driven by a simple "opposition of interests." It was precisely the fact that the United States was wounded *and* dependent that made the situation so volatile.

Here was another domain in which the United States was compelled to wrestle with the problem of self-discipline. On the one hand, it was easy, and advantageous from the point of view of electioneering, to whip up popular anger over British predations. Politicians in New York and Maine were tempted to do it during the northern border disputes, Tyler and Secretary of State Abel Upshur were similarly tempted over Texas, and so were Polk and Mississippi Senator Robert Walker during the Oregon dispute. On the other hand, it was always clear that a straitened nation could not go to war against Britain. The burden of reconciling these two facts—of mediating between populist impulses and economic and military realities—fell heavily on the shoulders of presidents and their secretaries of state. And it was another way in which the power of the executive tended to increase as a result of the crisis. As questions of commerce blurred into questions of war and peace, they fell more naturally within the discretion of the executive branch.

Presidents managed this predicament in different ways. Sometimes they would attempt to tamp down nationalist irruptions, as Van Buren tried to do in 1837–1839. Sometimes they would bluster against the British publicly and conciliate with them privately, as Tyler and even Polk did. Finally, they could encourage the ventilation of domestic frustrations through less dangerous channels; for example, by allowing the Mexican War to serve as an outlet for anti-British sentiment. In a sense, the ideal of popular sovereignty was once again constrained. Popular antipathy against the British might be tamped, or frustrated, or redirected. But the one thing that presidents could not do was to allow popular anger to be translated into policy in the most obvious and direct way—in the form of open aggression against the British.

The changes to the American political community that resulted from the First Great Depression can be summarized in the following way. There was institutional change: new restrictions on the role of state governments, undertaken to reassure foreign investors and avoid a reprise of default; an expansion of police power, in response to domestic disorders caused by economic disruption; and an expansion of presidential power, partly as a consequence of legislative dysfunction, and partly because of the need to manage increasingly fragile relations with a more powerful nation, Britain. And, at the same time, there was ideational change: that is, a transformation in conventional wisdom about the role of government, which explained why institutional adaptations were necessary, and which emphasized the need to restore order in the midst of economic, political, and social crisis. Many of these institutional adaptations persist today, albeit with modifications demanded by later events. Still, it is remarkable to think that governmental structures existing today are to some degree the products of a time in which the United States was not a superpower, confident about its ability to shape its own destiny.

The process by which these institutional changes were made was long and painful. Politics was not an easy craft during the First Great Depression.

Politicians were not free to promote ambitious schemes for the development of their states, or the nation as a whole. Attention was seized by the more fundamental task of combating forces that were pulling political and social structures apart. There were wearying and sometimes fruitless negotiations to preserve party and sectional alliances, maintain good relations with creditors, and preserve civic order. Statesmen were occupied more than usual with the politics of denial: that is, explaining to powerful and angry constituencies why they had to be denied benefits or liberties, or why they were required to shoulder new burdens.

The United States in the 1830s was also a world in which domestic and international affairs were deeply intertwined. In an open economy, it was difficult to isolate a set of issues that did not have implications for overseas trade and finance. State policy on infrastructure and property taxation, municipal policy on policing, federal policy on distribution of revenue from land sales—these were but a few of the domestic matters which were also of great consequence to foreign investors. Decisions on how to resolve all of these issues had to be made with an eye to what overseas lenders might think of the result. Usually this was not hard to discern. In the depths of the crisis, agents of foreign lenders walked the halls of state and federal government, cajoling lawmakers and building coalitions to support their preferred policies. One man, Daniel Webster, might have been the personification of the American condition; an illustration of the extent to which domestic and foreign affairs were profoundly interconnected. An undoubted patriot, Webster served his country as congressman, senator, and secretary of state. But he also appealed to British investors to buy his land and bonds, owed money to British bankers, and served as a lobbyist for British financiers in the United States. He saw nothing unnatural in this combination of roles.

There was no neat way of disentangling Anglo-American affairs; but at the same time, there were strong domestic incentives to deny this reality. One of the implications of interdependence was that Americans were not fully in control of their economic and political affairs. For example, the Bank of England played an important role in determining the course of the U.S. economy, but was in no way accountable to American constituencies. However, this fact was not easily admitted; to do so would have been to concede a practical limitation on hard-won U.S. sovereignty. The back-and-forth of U.S. politics tended, on the contrary, to emphasize the significance of domestic factors, such as federal or state policy on finance, tariffs, or internal development. American politicians took credit for improvements and blamed their rivals for failures, and in the process created a misleadingly generous impression about the extent to which they, as a class, were in control of the country's economic and political development.

Of course, we must be cautious in drawing comparisons between the early nineteenth and twenty-first centuries. Obviously there are fundamental differences in the structure of the economy, and in the extent to which different regions of the country are distinguished in terms of the dominant form of economic activity. In addition, there is an important difference in the willingness of contemporary policymakers to intervene to stop panics, save tottering financial institutions, and avoid depressions. Few today would take the view held by many Democrats in the early 1840s that the government should look after its own revenues and let the moneyed interests fend for themselves. Moreover, modern policymakers have tools for intervention that were unavailable in the 1840s. The United States now has a sophisticated central bank, in the form of the Federal Reserve; an equally sophisticated Treasury Department; and mechanisms for taxing and spending that make it easier to provide stimuli in a tailored and timely way.

Furthermore, methods of international economic coordination are better developed today than they were in the nineteenth century. Central bankers and treasury officials in different countries now have well-developed routines for communicating with one another. There are also international coordinating organizations, like the International Monetary Fund and the Bank for International Settlements, which did not exist in the nineteenth century. And, of course, it is technically easier for policymakers and financiers to talk with one another. The recurrent problems of nineteenth-century communications—important news delayed in transit, handwritten letters whose meaning is difficult to discern, errors about important facts that lie uncorrected for weeks—no longer seem to exist. Today, global markets generate an ocean of instantaneously disseminated information.

We might think that all of these innovations make it easier to live in a world typified by interdependence and vulnerability. We identify looming problems sooner and take remedial action more quickly, so that the panics do not lead inexorably to full-scale economic collapse. Indeed, the economic crisis that began in 2007, and which continues to unfold, might seem to illustrate this point. Present conditions are very bad, but they might have been much worse. As Federal Reserve Chairman Ben Bernanke said in 2009, the system proved its resiliency and the United States avoided another great depression. There is something to this argument, although we should note that Martin Van Buren said much the same thing in December 1838.

In fact, the full consequences of the crisis that began in 2007–2008 have not yet been realized.

We might also overestimate the extent to which we have overcome old barriers to the flow of information. Contemporary financial markets are vastly more complicated today, and one of the lessons of the current crisis has been that we knew less about the true condition of those markets than we imagined. Moreover, we should not underestimate the significance of linguistic and cultural barriers in the today's globalized economy. Britain and the United States—countries with a common language, a shared political tradition, and relatively open legislative processes—enjoyed a kind of reciprocal transparency in the early nineteenth century that is not shared by China and the United States today.

We must also acknowledge that American political institutions are more highly developed, and better in responding to public discontent, than were those of the early nineteenth century. Parties and legislators can gauge public attitudes, and craft new policies that reflect shifting attitudes, more quickly. There is a close connection between the increased responsiveness of political institutions and the improved capacity of economic regulators to manage crises: one leads to the other, as politicians seek to avoid the political costs that follow from severe economic dislocation. At the same time, the likelihood of violent protest is diminished—either because of government programs that protect citizens from serious losses, or because of police powers that are effective in preventing violence.

Once again, though, we must be careful not to exaggerate the efficiency of contemporary public institutions in managing the discontent that follows from economic shocks. Even though today's economic conditions are much less grim than that of 1837–1848, we see similar patterns in political activity. Once again a panic in the financial sector has triggered a sequence of events that have resulted in broader political woes. Polarization in Washington and state capitals has increased. Political leaders find themselves preoccupied with the task of shoring up party and legislative coalitions that have been riven by disagreement about the allocation of losses as a consequence of economic decline. Meanwhile, public faith in the political process has tumbled. By 2011, the proportion of Americans who said they were optimistic about "our system of government and how well it works" had fallen to the lowest level recorded in forty years of surveying. A series of Gallup polls conducted in 2010–2011 found that four out of five Americans were "dissatisfied with the way things are going in the United States."

The sour mood of post-2008 American politics was illustrated by the debate over federal budget priorities in the summer of 2011. The immediate issue was whether Congress should approve an increase in the statutory limit on the amount of debt that may be issued by the U.S. Treasury. If the limit was not raised, the federal government would have been unable to raise the funds needed to honor maturing government debt. Treasury Secretary Timothy Geithner warned that a federal default was unprecedented and would have catastrophic consequences for the American economy. However, Republican leaders in Congress were determined to use the need for legislative approval as a device for negotiating concessions from the Obama administration and Democratic legislators on questions of taxing and spending.

The political difficulties were substantial. As a share of gross domestic product, the federal deficit increased after 2007 to levels not seen since the Second World War. This was attributable, in roughly equal measure, to a collapse in federal revenues and the increase in spending as a result of the financial crisis and the ensuing recession. Looming ahead were years of scheduled increases in spending on federal entitlement programs. Some long-term plan for reconciling spending and taxing was clearly necessary, but there was disagreement on how quickly budgetary balance should be achieved, and whether it should be attained primarily through spending reductions or tax hikes. The chances of agreement between the executive and legislative branches were diminished after the 2010 mid-term elections, which featured the second-highest turnover rate in the House of Representatives in the last half-century, and caused a Democratic majority in the House to be replaced by a Republican majority that was pledged to oppose new taxes. The capacity of the House leadership to compromise on that pledge was limited by the presence within the Republican caucus of a powerful new faction of Tea Party conservatives.

The dynamic that emerged in Washington in the summer of 2011 would not be unfamiliar to a legislator transported from 1842. The deadline for action on the debt ceiling grew closer, but agreement on a budget plan could not be reached. New York Mayor Michael Bloomberg complained that the country's "good name and credit" were being "held hostage to Washington gridlock." Federal Reserve Chairman Bernanke warned that even a short delay in raising the debt ceiling might "create fundamental doubts about the creditworthiness of the United States . . . [and shake] the confidence of investors in the ability and willingness of the U.S. government to pay its bills." Bond rating agencies said they might take more negative view of U.S. debt if the impasse was not resolved. (One agency also conceded that any sensible budget plan would "require fiscal adjustments that . . . will test social cohesion.") Many Tea Party conservatives used the debt ceiling controversy to advance their argument for a constitutional amendment that would force the federal government to maintain a balanced budget. This, said Republican Senator Ron Johnson, was the only effective way "to deliver real, true spending constraint."

The budget deadlock of 2011 is not strictly comparable to the dark days of 1842. There was no risk in 2011 that foreign investors would shun the United States entirely. Even if the creditworthiness of the United States was momentarily shaken, no one doubted that U.S. bonds would remain a good investment, and certainly safer than the sovereign debt of many other countries. Nor was there an immediate prospect that the United States would adopt a balanced budget amendment. (This would, in any case, be an unwise decision. Constitutional restrictions on the fiscal powers of a national government create more problems than do similar restrictions on state governments.)

Still, the 2011 deadlock was a portent of coming policy debates. Lawmakers knew that foreign investors now own a share of federal debt (roughly half) that is unprecedented in modern history. And they were conscious while making budgetary decisions that they would be watched closely by investors, who might choose to place their money elsewhere, thereby driving up the cost of servicing federal debt. Many chafed at this scrutiny: at the height of the debt limit debate, Ohio congressman Dennis Kucinich insisted that "No nation, agency or organization has the authority to dictate terms to the United States Government." Still, most understood that a credible agreement on long-term priorities would play an important role in reassuring financial markets. Today's legislators, like those of 1842, were learning that their freedom to do as they wished was checked by the "whims of foreign investors," and that the way to retain investors' support was through a demonstration of their own capacity to exercise budgetary discipline.

In many other countries, this predicament is a familiar one. Lacking the economic and political power of the United States, lawmakers in these other nations have been forced to reconcile their aspirations for self-determination with the demands of globalized markets. In many cases this has meant severe retrenchment in domestic policies and more modest expectations about the extension of influence abroad, through either military or diplomatic means. Today, Americans have an intimation of what politics will be like in a world in which it is no longer the hegemon. It is a difficult kind of politics, unfamiliar to those born in the era of dominance. But in the longer sweep of American history it is not unknown.

◆Note on Method and Acknowledgments

I have written this book so that it will be accessible to a broad readership. For this reason I have avoided discussion about the merits of previous scholarly works in the body of the text. Academic or technical terms are avoided when plain language is adequate. Quotations are drawn from original sources, rather than later scholarly works, wherever possible. Details about sources used in each chapter are provided at the end of the book.

However I should say a word about the approach that undergirds this study. For the last twenty years my main interest has been the study of government, and in particular the processes of government reform; in other words, how decisions are made about the tasks that governments should perform, and how governments should be organized to perform those tasks. The scholarly field in which I have worked primarily is known as public administration. It is dangerous to make generalizations about an entire field, but I think it may be said that in the United States, this field has had three traits. It has tended to prefer studies about discrete administrative or managerial innovations over broader surveys about the role of government. At the same time, it has tended to regard reform as a technical exercise rather than as a problem of political economy. And, finally, it has tended to avoid what are sometimes described as historical modes of inquiry.

Much valuable research has been undertaken within these constraints. But it is difficult, within these limits, to tell a convincing story about the overall evolution of governmental structures. There is a need for a complementary method of analysis that is capable of explaining how larger considerations—such as the character of the national and international economy, power relations between nations, technological innovations, domestic political conditions and culture, and institutional inheritances—influence the architecture of government over time. Elsewhere I have suggested that we might describe these larger forces as defining the macrodynamics of governmental reform. Without the systematic study of these larger forces, scholars in public administration are like the crew of a ship's engine room: we have a useful view of internal mechanisms, but no real sense of where the ship is heading, or why, or whether it is likely to reach its destination.

This is the third book in which I have attempted to apply this broader approach. In my 2008 book *The Collapse of Fortress Bush*, I sought to explain how broader forces influenced the Bush administration's response to the attacks of September 11, 2001; in *The Logic of Discipline* (2010), I considered how governments around the world have adapted to economic globalization over the last thirty years. The method in this book is the same: it is just applied to much older data. There are also strong thematic parallels between this book and the previous two. Readers who are interested in a more complete explanation of the approach taken in these three books may wish to read the following two articles: "The Path Not Taken: Leonard White and the Macrodynamics of Administrative Development," *Public Administration Review* 69, no. 4 (July 2009): 764–75; and "What's Wrong with the Intellectual History of Public Administration," *Public Voices* 11, no. 2 (December 2010): 10–15.

I would like to express my thanks for the generous advice given by my editor at Cornell University Press, Michael McGandy, and the two anonymous reviewers who evaluated early versions of the manuscript. I am also grateful for the support of my wife, Sandra, our children John and Constance, my parents James and Nancy Roberts, and my parents-in-law Guntis and Inta Sraders. Finally, I must thank Jerry and Phyllis Rappaport for their generosity in supporting the Jerome L. Rappaport Chair in Law and Public Policy at Suffolk University Law School, a position which I have been privileged to hold since 2008.

❧ Notes

Introduction

page 1. "as a huge and relatively self-sufficient country, in control of our own destiny": Paul Volcker, "The Time We Have Is Growing Short," *New York Review of Books* 57, no. 11 (2010).

page 1. "which supports a wide variety": Michael Mandelbaum, *The Case for Goliath: How America Acts as the World's Government in the 21st Century* (New York: Public Affairs, 2005), 10.

page 2. "It was a humbling and humiliating moment": Joseph Quinlan, *The Last Economic Superpower* (New York: McGraw-Hill, 2010), x.

page 2. "the indispensable leader": Jeffrey Sachs, "America Has Passed on the Baton," *Financial Times*, September 29, 2009, 9.

page 2. "the era of U.S.-led globalism": Yukio Hatoyama, "Japan Must Shake Off US-Style Globalization," *Voice*, August 19, 2009.

page 2. "have been forced to contend with the erosion of self-sufficiency": Matt Bai, "The Presidency, Chained to the World," *New York Times*, September 11, 2010.

page 3. "live up to our obligations": Henry M. Paulson Jr., *On the Brink* (New York: Business Plus, 2010), 18.

page 3. "be nice to the countries that lend you money": James Fallows, "Be Nice to the Countries That Lend You Money," *The Atlantic*, December 2008.

page 3. "the emerging superstate": Herman Kahn, *The Emerging Japanese Superstate* (Englewood Cliffs, NJ: Prentice-Hall, 1970).

page 3. "on a hegemonic scale": Koji Taira, "Japan, an Imminent Hegemon?" *Annals of the American Academy of Political and Social Science* 513 (1991): 151–163, 156.

page 7. "paralysis of credit": Jessica Lepler, "1837: Anatomy of a Panic" (PhD Dissertation, Brandeis University, 2007), 248.

page 7. "it would be difficult to describe": Henry Graff, *The Presidents: A Reference History* (New York: Simon and Schuster, 2002), 130.

page 7. "I doubt if, in the history of the world": *Times of London,* January 28, 1843, 11.

page 8. "was one of the most disastrous crises": Reginald McGrane, *The Panic of 1837* (Chicago: University of Chicago Press, 1924), 1.

page 8. "one of the most severe in our history": Douglass Cecil North, *The Economic Growth of the United States, 1790–1860* (Englewood Cliffs, NJ: Prentice-Hall, 1961), 190.

Chapter 1

page 14. "They certainly are not a humorous people" and other quotes from Dickens' travels: Charles Dickens, *American Notes* (New York: D. Appleton and Company, 1868).

page 15. "a great commercial and manufacturing mart and emporium": William H. Perrin, *History of Alexander, Union and Pulaski Counties* (Chicago: O.L. Baskin & Company, 1883), 28.

page 17. "I don't like the country": John Forster, *The Life of Charles Dickens* (New York: Baker and Taylor, 1911), 1.229.

page 17. "The Capitalist is the most easily frightened": Sidney George Fisher, "The Diaries of Sidney George Fisher," *Pennsylvania Magazine of History and Biography* 76, no. 2 (1952): 177–220, 215; Sidney George Fisher, "The Diaries of Sidney George Fisher 1841–1843," *Pennsylvania Magazine of History and Biography* 79, no. 2 (1955): 217–236, 230.

page 17. "next to nothing": *United States Magazine and Democratic Review* 9, no. 38 (August 1841): 206.

page 17. "The past season has been one of unusual prostration of business": *The Sailor's Magazine* 15, no. 5 (January 1843): 153

page 18. "a panic seized upon the whole people": Charles F. Briggs, *The Adventures of Harry Franco* (New York: F. Saunders, 1839), 2.212.

page 18. "those unlucky years": Charles F. Briggs, *Bankrupt Stories* (New York: John Allen, 1843), 298.

page 18. "It is intended to collect the import revenue": Philip Hone, *The Diary of Philip Hone, 1828–1851* (New York: Dodd Mead, 1889), 2.138.

page 19. "desolation, chaos, and ruin": Roy M. Robbins, *Our Landed Heritage: The Public Domain, 1776–1936* (Princeton, NJ: Princeton University Press, 1942), 71.

page 19. "Working men are becoming almost desperate": *Brooklyn Daily Eagle*, July 11, 1842, 2.

page 19. "almost without exception" and Paulding's tour of Illinois: Mentor Williams, "A Tour of Illinois in 1842," *Journal of the Illinois State Historical Society* 42, no. 3 (1949): 292–312.

page 19. "the hotels were emptied of guests": Eleanor Atkinson, *The Story of Chicago and National Development* (Chicago: The Little Chronicle Company, 1911), 58.

page 20. "like a tidal wave": James Buck, *Pioneer History of Milwaukee* (Milwaukee, WI: Milwaukee News Company, 1876).

page 20. "the sad, monotonous complaint": *Southern Cultivator* 1, no. 11 (May 24, 1843): 85.

page 20. "the pecuniary embarrassment": *The Journal of Banking* 1, no. 20 (March 30, 1842): 306.

pages 20–21. "that he thought it better to see his wife and children dead": *The American Masonic Register* 2, no. 39 (May 29, 1841): 467.

page 21. "presents a lamentable appearance": Ephraim Adams, ed., *British Diplomatic Correspondence Concerning the Republic of Texas, 1838–1846* (Austin: Texas State Historical Association, 1917), 52.

page 21. "All that is talked of nowadays": Ann Malone, *Sweet Chariot: Slave Family and Household Structure in Nineteenth Century Louisiana* (Chapel Hill: University of North Carolina Press, 1996), 309.

page 21. "I am distressed in mind": Rachel O'Connor, *Mistress of Evergreen Plantation: Rachel O'Connor's Legacy of Letters, 1823–1845* (Albany: State University of New York Press, 1983), 244.

page 21. "a good deal of emigration": *Niles' Register*, December 5, 1840, 219.

page 21. "all law, civil and criminal": James S. Buckingham, *The Slave States of America* (London: Fisher, Son & Co., 1842), 1.552.

page 21. "Never, we imagine": Quoted in ibid., 1.555–1.556.

page 22. "Our alms house is overrun": Quoted in *New Orleans Times Picayune*, January 21, 1840.

page 22. "to gauge the terrible havoc": Reginald McGrane, *The Panic of 1837* (Chicago: University of Chicago Press, 1924), 142.

page 22. "science of business": *Hunt's Merchants' Magazine* 35, no. 2 (August 1856): 265.

page 22. "vast comprehensiveness with a most minute grasp of details": Freeman Hunt, *Lives of American Merchants* (New York: Derby & Jackson, 1858), 1.3.

page 23. One of the longest and deepest recessions in U.S. history: Victor Zarnowitz, *Business Cycles: Theory, History, Indicators, and Forecasting* (Chicago: University of Chicago Press, 1992), 222.

page 24. "an economic crisis so extreme": James C. Curtis, *The Fox at Bay: Martin Van Buren and the Presidency, 1837–1841* (Lexington: University Press of Kentucky, 1970), 190.

page 24. "mass of ungovernable and unmanageable anarchy": Howard Jones and Donald A. Rakestraw, *Prologue to Manifest Destiny: Anglo-American Relations in the 1840s* (Wilmington, DE: SR Books, 1997), 114.

page 24. "It remains to be seen": *Times of London*, May 11, 1842, 6.

page 24. "The times are out of joint": Hone, *The Diary of Philip Hone, 1828–1851*, 1.340.

page 25. "should not be surprised to hear of popular outbreaks": Lyon G. Tyler, *Letters and Times of the Tylers* (Richmond, VA: Whittet & Shepperson, 1885), 2.157.

The following sources are particularly useful in understanding the boom and bust of 1835–1840: McGrane, *The Panic of 1837*; Robert Matthews, *A Study in Trade-Cycle History: Economic Fluctuations in Great Britain, 1833–1842* (Cambridge: Cambridge University Press, 1954); Douglass Cecil North, *The Economic Growth of the United States, 1790–1860* (Englewood Cliffs, NJ: Prentice-Hall, 1961); Peter Temin, *The Jacksonian Economy* (New York: Norton, 1969); Peter Rousseau, "Jacksonian Monetary Policy, Specie Flows, and the Panic of 1837," *Journal of Economic History* 62, no. 2 (2002): 457–488; Jessica Lepler, "1837: Anatomy of a Panic" (PhD Dissertation, Brandeis University, 2007).

page 25. "Everyone with whom I converse": Douglas H. Gordon and George S. May, "Michigan Journal, 1836, John M. Gordon," *Michigan History* 43 (1959): 257–293.

page 25. "perennial rebirth": Frederick Jackson Turner, *The Frontier in American History* (New York: Henry Holt and Company, 1920), 2.

page 26. "We are more like Europe": Frederick Jackson Turner, *The Significance of Sections in American History* (New York: H. Holt and Company, 1932), 32.

page 27. "connected . . . by the interchange": Anonymous, "Principles of Political Economy," *United States Literary Gazette* 3, no. 7 (1826): 261–266, 263.

page 27. "the wonder industry": Robert Allen, *The British Industrial Revolution in Global Perspective* (New York: Cambridge University Press, 2009), 182.

page 27. "the most striking example": Edward Baines, *History of the Cotton Manufacture in Great Britain* (London: H. Fisher, R. Fisher, and P. Jackson, 1835), 244.

page 27. "We see no ground for apprehending": Ibid., 505 and 512.

page 28. "It has thoroughly revolutionized this county": Frederick Engels, *The Condition of the Working-Class in England* (London: Swan Sonnenschein & Co., 1892), 8.

page 28. "greatest emporium of the British empire": J. R. M'Culloch, *M'Culloch's University Gazetter* (New York: Harper & Bros., 1844), 2.196.

page 28. "One person is able to perform": Levi Woodbury, *Letter on the Cultivation, Manufacture, and Foreign Trade of Cotton* (Washington, DC: Gales & Seaton, 1836), 23.

page 28. "made the raising of cotton": Lawton B. Evans, *A History of Georgia* (New York: American Book Company, 1898), 141.

page 29. "Every interest throughout the land": Israel Andrews, *The Cotton Crop of the United States* (Washington, DC: Department of the Treasury, 1853), 833–836.

page 30. "Buying a plantation": Frederick Law Olmsted, *Cotton Kingdom* (New York: Mason Brothers, 1861), 1.321.

page 31. "London is the centre of the credit system": *Extra Globe*, February 10, 1838, 5.

page 32. "On whatever side we turn our eyes": William Harlan Hale, *Horace Greeley, Voice of the People* (New York: Harper, 1950), 35.

page 32. "These extremely high prices are bad indeed": Quoted in *Hagerstown Mail*, March 11, 1836.

page 32. "The mania for obtaining land": *Ohio State Journal*, June 25, 1836.

page 33. "Speculators went to bed at night": *Magazine of Western History* 6, no. 3 (July 1887): 314.

page 33. "streets and avenues in beautiful and regular arrangement": Addison Fulwider, *History of Stephenson County, Illinois* (Chicago: S.J. Clarke Publishing Co., 1915), 401.

page 33. "Yet nobody perceived the illusion": Francis Wayland, *The Elements of Political Economy* (New York: George C. Rand & Avery, 1858), 401.

page 33. "A speculating mania is spreading like a contagion": *Gettysburg Republican Compiler*, May 10, 1836.

page 33. "It is nevertheless a cheap purchase": Quoted in *Niles' Register*, June 6, 1835, 233.

page 33. "We have heard of a good number of sales": *Niles' Register*, October 22, 1836.

page 33. "The speculators here . . . have a kind of *dare devil* feeling": *Niles' Register*, June 27, 1835, 291.

page 35. "All the evils": George S. Boutwell, *Reminiscences of Sixty Years in Public Affairs* (New York: McClure, Phillips & Co., 1902), 59, 63.

page 35. "contest between the cohorts": McGrane, *The Panic of 1837*, 2.

page 35. "removed a valuable brake on credit expansion": Arthur Schlesinger Jr., *The Age of Jackson* (Boston: Little, Brown and Company, 1945), 218.

page 36. "In the choice of investments": *Jackson's Oxford Journal*, August 20, 1836.

page 37. "prosperous condition of our beloved country": *Sixth Annual Message*, December 1, 1834, in James D. Richardson, ed., *A Compilation of the Messages and Papers of the Presidents* (New York: Bureau of National Literature, 1897), 3.1316

page 37. "began to believe that the sudden prosperity": David Salomons, *The Monetary Difficulties of America* (London: Pelham Richardson, 1837), 14.

page 37. "The direct and immediate effects": Albert Gallatin, *The Writings of Albert Gallatin* (Philadelphia: J.B. Lippincott & Co., 1879), 3.392.

page 37. "in a confused heap": Thomas Tooke, *A History of Prices and of the State of Circulation in 1838 and 1839* (London: Longman, Orme, Brown, Green, & Longmans, 1840), 2.

page 37. "There is a limit to speculating in land": *Milwaukee Advertiser*, September 8, 1836.

page 37. "Unless this mania is corrected": *Alton Observer*, March 16, 1836.

page 38. "When will the bubble burst?": William Cullen Bryant and Thomas G. Voss, *Letters of William Cullen Bryant* (New York: Fordham University Press, 1977), 69.

page 38. "It is evident": *Niles' Register*, April 23, 1836, 129.

page 38. "Speculations in public lands . . . have been entirely suspended": Quoted in Rousseau, "Jacksonian Monetary Policy," 479.

page 38. "The money pressure is . . . exceedingly severe": Quoted in *New York Commercial Advertiser*, October 22, 1836.

page 38. "Our citizens are in a perilous situation": *New York Spectator*, November 3, 1836.

page 38. "raging mania for wild speculations": *Niles' Register*, May 14, 1836, 186.

page 39. "system of fictitious credit": Henry MacLeod, *A Dictionary of Political Economy* (London: Longman, Green, Longman, Roberts and Green, 1853), 1.584.

page 39. "to be locked up in the coffers": Salomons, *The Monetary Difficulties of America*, 20.

page 39. "The whole trading and commercial interest": *Portsmouth Journal of Literature and Politics*, December 31, 1836. Emphasis in original.

page 39. "The monetary affairs of the whole country": *The New Yorker* (October 19, 1839): 75.

page 40. "the pin that pricked the bubble": David Kinley, *The History, Organization and Influence of the Independent Treasury of the United States* (New York: Thomas Y. Crowell & Co., 1893), 21.

page 40. "The pressure of 1836": James Gilbart, *An Inquiry into the Causes of the Pressure on the Money Market during the Year 1839* (London: Longman, Orme, Brown, Green & Longmans, 1840), 4.

page 40. "an inordinate amount of American paper": J. Horsley Palmer, *The Causes and Consequences of the Pressure upon the Money Market* (London: Pelham Richardson, 1837), 32.

page 41. "disarrangement": *London Dispatch*, September 17, 1836.

page 41. "from two sides at once": William G. Sumner, *A History of Banking in the United States* (New York: Journal of Commerce, 1896), 286.

page 41. "effectual check": Salomons, *The Monetary Difficulties of America*, 27–28.

page 42. "In all the attributes": *Inaugural Address*, March 4, 1837, in James D. Richardson, ed., *A Compilation of the Messages and Papers of the Presidents* (New York: Bureau of National Literature, 1897), 4.1531.

page 42. "Those who have been speculating in cotton": *New Orleans Times Picayune*, March 5, 1837.

page 42. "Failures are taking place daily": *New Orleans Times Picayune*, April 13, 1837.

page 42. "scene of melancholy transactions": *Baltimore Gazette*, May 11, 1837.

page 42. "unwilling to survive": Ibid.

page 43. "occasioned by strong mental excitement": Lepler, "1837: Anatomy of a Panic," 199.54; "a large body of troops under arms": *Niles' Register*, May 13, 1837.

page 43. "A dead calm has succeeded": Hone, *The Diary of Philip Hone, 1828–1851*, 258.

page 43. "The Americans have proved too cunning": *Times of London*, June 13, 1837.

page 44. "abundant and cheap": Gilbart, *An Inquiry into the Causes of the Pressure on the Money Market during the Year 1839*, 8.

pages 44–45. "Large sums of money": Ibid., 5.

page 45. "The general business of the community": *Annual Message to Congress*, December 3, 1838, in Richardson, ed., *A Compilation of the Messages and Papers of the Presidents*, 3.490.

page 45. "How long": *London Morning Chronicle*, August 2, 1839.

page 45. "A great alarm pervaded society": Walter Bagehot, *Lombard Street* (New York: Scribner, Armstrong & Co., 1877), 179.

page 46. "nearly as bad . . . as well they could be": *Times of London*, September 2, 1839.

page 46. "extraordinary pressure upon the money market": *New York Courier and Enquirer*, September 20, 1839, quoted in the *Ohio Statesman*, October 2, 1839.

page 46. "a concentrated money power": *London Era*, December 23, 1838.

page 47. "Life or death to the Bank": Bray Hammond, *Banks and Politics in America from the Revolution to the Civil War* (Princeton, NJ: Princeton University Press, 1991), 508.

page 47. "a feeling of hostility to the institution": Bank of the United States, *Report of the Committee of Investigation* (Philadelphia: Bank of the United States, 1841), 75.

page 47. "The distress in the country": *New Hampshire Gazette*, January 17, 1840.

page 47. "Business is at a stand": *Ohio State Journal*, March 11, 1840.

Chapter 2

For a more detailed discussion of state debts, generally, see Reginald McGrane, *Foreign Bondholders and American State Debts* (New York: Macmillan, 1935); and Benjamin Curtis, "Debts of the States," *North American Review*, no. 58 (1844): 109–157.

page 50. "We must repudiate all the bonds": John Bach McMaster, *A History of the People of the United States* (New York: D. Appleton and Company, 1910), 2.30.

page 51. "promote both the general welfare and economic growth": Howard Bodenhorn, *A History of Banking in Antebellum America: Financial Markets and Economic Development in an Era of Nation-Building, Studies in Macroeconomic History* (New York: Cambridge University Press, 2000), 44.

page 52. "The time will probably come": Alexander Trotter, *Observations on the Financial Position and Credit of Such of the States of the North American Union as Have Contracted Public Debts* (London: Longman, Orme, Brown, Green, and Longmans, 1839), 351–355.

page 52. "have a beneficial effect on the sale of stocks": McGrane, *Foreign Bondholders and American State Debts*, 21.

page 52. "A point of great centrality": C. H. Van Tyne, ed., *The Letters of Daniel Webster* (New York: McClure, Phillips, 1902), 725.

page 52. "would be an open violation of public faith": McGrane, *Foreign Bondholders and American State Debts*, 22.

page 52. "surprise and consternation": *Times of London*, March 10, 1840, 6.

page 53. "as soon as may be": Constitution of Michigan, 1835, Article XII, Sec. 3.

page 54. "a day which will be recollected": J. N. Ingersoll, "The Clinton and Kalamazoo Canal Celebration," *Michigan Pioneer and Historical Collections* 5 (1882): 469–471, 470.

page 54. "It became a question": Governor's Message, January 7, 1839, in *Journal of the Senate of the State of Michigan* (Detroit: John S. Bagg, 1839), 16.

page 55. "doctrine of repudiation. . . . against the treasury": *Journal of the House of Representatives of the State of Michigan* (Detroit: Bagg & Harmon, 1842), 163.

page 55. "What were the scenes enacted": H. Fowler, ed., *Report of the Debates and Proceedings of the Convention for the Revision of the Constitution of the State of Indiana* (Indianapolis: A.H. Brown, Printer, 1850), 675.

page 56. "Our citizens should be favored": Inaugural Address, December 9, 1840, in *Journal of the Senate of the State of Indiana* (Indianapolis: Douglass & Noel, 1840), 18.

page 56. "between the blameless inability to pay": Governor's Message, December 6, 1842, in *Journal of the House of Representative of the State of Indiana* (Indianapolis: Dowling and Cole, 1842), 19.

page 56. "the victim of preconcerted imposition": Governor's Message, December 7, 1841, in Gayle Thornbrough, *Messages and Papers Relating to the Administration of Samuel Bigger, Governor of Indiana* (Indianapolis: Indiana Historical Bureau, 1964), 329.

page 56. For Maryland state finances, generally, see Hugh Hanna, *A Financial History of Maryland, 1789–1848* (Baltimore: Johns Hopkins Press, 1907).

page 58. "in each county, in proportion to representation": William Worthen, *Early Banking in Arkansas* (Little Rock, AR: Democrat Printing and Litho. Co., 1906), 4.

page 58. "It has been the policy of other States": Statement of the committee reproduced in *Report of Accountants of the State Bank of Arkansas* (Little Rock, AR: Johnson & Yerkes, State Printers, 1858), 7.

page 58. "never be called upon to pay": McGrane, *Foreign Bondholders and American State Debts*, 248.

page 58. "the very best in the United States": Worthen, *Early Banking in Arkansas*, 24.

page 58. "The gentlemen who organized this bank": Ibid., 25.

page 58. "of a very high order": McGrane, *Foreign Bondholders and American State Debts*, 252.

page 59. "heartless tyranny": Worthen, *Early Banking in Arkansas*, 70.

page 59. "This doctrine of Yell's": *Times of London*, January 17, 1842, 4.

page 59. "So here ends, we hope forever": *Springfield State Register*, July 15, 1837.

page 60. "clearly convinced . . . of the utter failure": Evarts B. Greene and Charles M. Thompson, eds., *Governors' Letter-Books, 1840–1853* (Springfield: Illinois State Historical Library, 1911), 1.6.

page 60. "All the channels of trade are completely obstructed": Message of the Governor to the General Assembly, December 7, 1842, in *Journal of the Senate of the State of Illinois* (Springfield, IL: William Walters, 1842), 18.

page 60. "You want to know how it operates?": Ellen Call Long, *Florida Breezes* (Jacksonville, FL: Ashmead Bros., 1882), 84.

page 61. "as solid and desirable a security as any in the market": McGrane, *Foreign Bondholders and American State Debts*, 228.

page 61. "In every way the present bondholders are amply secured": *London Morning Chronicle*, February 19, 1839.

page 61. "To become suddenly rich": Kathryn Abbey, "The Union Bank of Tallahassee: An Experiment in Territorial Finance," *Florida Historical Quarterly* 15, no. 4 (1937): 207–231, 214.

page 61. "to act for and in the name of the People of Florida": Report of the House of Representatives' Committee on the Judiciary, February 25, 1840, 14.

page 62. "the multitudes were wild with a delirium of joy": Robert Lowry and William McCardle, *A History of Mississippi* (Jackson, MS: R.H. Henry and Company, 1891), 286–287.

page 62. "has hypothecated these bonds": Ivers J. Austin and Alexander McNutt, *An Account of the Origin of the Mississippi Doctrine of Repudiation* (Boston: Bradbury, Soden, 1842), 14.

page 63. "will never pay": Ibid., 5.

page 63. "necessitated the commencement of similar works . . . made defeat inevitable": Avard Bishop, "The State Works of Pennsylvania," *Transactions of the Connecticut Academy of Arts and Sciences* 13 (1907): 149–297, 153.

page 64. "the doctrine of repudiating state debts": Sidney George Fisher, "The Diaries of Sidney George Fisher," *Pennsylvania Magazine of History and Biography* 76, no. 2 (1952): 224.

page 64. "moral, legal or political obligation . . . so-called state debt": *Hazard's Commercial and Statistical Register* 6, no. 4 (January 26, 1842): 57–58.

page 64. "The substance of our State is swallowed up": *Smethport Settler and Pennon* (Smethport, PA), October 1, 1842.

page 64. "struggling on in the payment of their dividends": *Times of London*, November 18, 1842, 3.

page 64. "never have to repent their confidence": *Times of London*, January 19, 1842, 5.

page 65. "Louisiana will not shrink from the call": Charles Gayarré, *History of Louisiana* (New York: William J. Widdleton, 1866), 662.

page 65. "disastrous": *Times of London*, May 29, 1844, 3.

page 65. "Yankee Doodle borrows cash": *Literary Gazette*, January 18, 1845, 45.

page 65. "I was in England": *Niles' Register*, August 5, 1843, 358. Emphasis in original.

page 66. "Great bitterness of feeling is very naturally felt": McGrane, *Foreign Bondholders and American State Debts*, 267.

page 66. "[a]n American gentleman of the most unblemished character": *Times of London*, October 1844, 3.

page 66. "should in no degree affect the credit of the rest": *Annual Message to Congress*, December 7, 1841, in *Journal of the Senate of the United States of America* (Washington, DC: Thomas Allen, 1841), 16.

page 66. "in their anguish are crying out against *all* American stocks": Bates to Ward, December 3, 1841, Ward Papers, Massachusetts Historical Society.

page 66. "Let us get rid of that blasted country": Niall Ferguson, *The House of Rothschild: Money's Prophets, 1798–1848* (New York: Viking, 1998), 375.

page 67. "remonstrate and prevent the perpetration of such an act of injustice": *Leeds Mercury*, May 2, 1840.

page 67. It is quite in vain": *Times of London*, September 6, 1847.

page 67. "At a distance people do not see the local differences": Bates to Ward, October 17, 1841, Ward Papers, Massachusetts Historical Society.

page 67. "There is necessarily much ignorance": Van Tyne, ed., *The Letters of Daniel Webster*, 284.

page 67. "never make themselves acquainted": *Times of London*, January 3, 1842, 3.

page 67. "Until that scrip pass current in Europe": *London Morning Chronicle*, quoted in the *Smethport Settler & Pennon* (Smethport, PA), July 9, 1842, 1.

page 67. "a trifling loan": *Times of London*, April 3, 1843, 11.

page 67. "a–begging through all the exchanges of Europe": Curtis, "Debts of the States," 150.

page 67. "You may tell your government": Ferguson, *The House of Rothschild*, 374.

pages 67–68. "They cannot go to war": *Caledonian Mercury*, November 16, 1843.

page 68. "several of my most valued friends": Christopher Wordsworth, ed., *Memoirs of William Wordsworth* (Boston: Ticknor, Reed and Fields, 1851), 2.356–2.357.

page 68. "Men of the Western World!: *New York Review* 20 (April 1842): 416.

page 68. "The free utterance of a painful emotion": Ibid.

page 68. "The fame of Wordsworth": *The Dial* 1, no. 2 (October 1840): 150.

page 68. "If Pennsylvania refuse to pay": Park Benjamin, *Infatuation: A Poem* (Boston: William D. Ticknor and Company, 1844), 9.

page 69. "The personal interest which I attach to it": "Wordsworth's Strictures," *Times of London*, March 17, 1930, 8.

page 69. "Theirs is one of the richest countries in the world": William Knight, ed., *Letters of the Wordsworth Family* (Boston: Ginn and Company, 1907), 3.283.

page 69. "All who revere the memory of Penn": William Wordsworth, *Poems* (London, Edward Moxon, 1845), 387.

page 70. "The wittiest man in England": *United States Magazine and Democratic Review* (June 1844): 568.

page 70. "an act of bad faith which has no parallel, and no excuse": *The New World*, June 10, 1843, 688.

page 70. "swindling democrats": *The New World*, June 24, 1843, 751.

page 70. "There's Sydney Smith, poor foolish man": *Punch*, January 1844, 31.

page 71. "old protector of the country": *United States Magazine and Democratic Review* (June 1844): 567.

page 71. "a most severe, though just castigation": *Bankers' Magazine* (July 1844): 228.

page 71. "violent ebullitions of anger and spit": *Times of London*, August 8, 1843, 5.

page 71. "the income was greater because the security was less": *Quarterly Review* (December 1843): 136.

page 71. "I find myself involved, with the rest of the nation": Thomas G. Cary, *Letter to a Lady in France* (Boston: Benjamin H. Greene, 1844), 25.

page 71. "interfere with the states in any effectual way": *Times of London*, December 2, 1842, 3.

page 71. "[m]y bomb has fallen very successfully in America": George W. E. Russell, *Sydney Smith* (Norwood, MA: Norwood Press, 1905), 190.

page 72. "I never meet a Pennsylvanian at a London dinner": *Times of London*, November 4, 1843, 13.

page 72. "rough, coarse, red-faced": Leonard White, *The Jacksonians: A Study in Administrative History, 1829–1861* (New York: Macmillan, 1954), 263.

page 72. "It may be true that the Governments of Europe": *Times of London*, November 10, 1843, 3.

page 72. "What do I mean by war?": *London Examiner*, November 25, 1843.

page 73. "spiteful and malignant": *United States Magazine and Democratic Review* (October 1843): 348.

page 73. "A burnt child dreads the fire": H. Fowler, ed. *Report of the Debates and Proceedings of the Convention for the Revision of the Constitution of the State of Indiana* (Indianapolis: A.H. Brown, 1850), 661.

page 74. "sullen resentment": McGrane, *Foreign Bondholders and American State Debts*, 47.

page 74. "overwhelming prejudice against direct taxation": Hanna, *A Financial History of Maryland*, 45.

page 74. "had hardly known what a state tax was": *Niles' Register*, August 12, 1843, 371.

page 74. "a tax-free system of state finance": Peter Wallenstein, *From Slave South to New South: Public Policy in Nineteenth-Century Georgia* (Chapel Hill: University of North Carolina Press, 1987), 25.

page 74. "Both parties have found, when in power": Curtis, "Debts of the States," 151.

page 75. "oppress the people beyond their power of endurance": *Niles' Register*, June 17, 1843, 244.

page 75. "ruinous taxation": John Scharf, *History of Maryland* (Baltimore: John B. Piet, 1879), 3.213.

page 75. "in the construction of works of internal improvement": *Maryland Constitution of 1851*, Article III, Sec. 22.

page 76. "I wish to see State Government": *Report of the Debates and Proceedings of the Convention for the Revision of the Constitution of the State of Ohio, 1850–1851*, (Columbus, OH: S. Medary, 1851), 1.523.

page 76. "made *laissez-faire* the law of the land": James Henretta, "Rethinking the State Constitutional Tradition," *Rutgers Law Journal* 22 (1991): 819–839, 833.

page 76. "cannot be sued in its own courts": *Beers v. Arkansas*, 61 U.S. 527 (1857).

page 77. "notorious for his management of a concern": *Times of London*, August 26, 1843, 5.

page 77. "there was not much reason to fear": *Cohens v. Virginia* 19 U.S. 264 (1821).

page 77. "do so at their own risk and must abide the consequences": McGrane, *Foreign Bondholders and American State Debts*, 202.

page 77. "no concern with the securities in question": Ibid., 53.

page 78. "to abstain from taking up as international questions": *The Bankers' Magazine* 9 (July 1849): 412.

page 78. "By far the larger portion of us are persons in the middle ranks of life": *Niles' Register*, April 22, 1843, 12.

page 78. "The general government is not a party in the contracts of the separate states": *Niles' Register*, April 29, 1843, 134.

page 78. "received the deputation with the greatest politeness": *Niles' Register*, June 10, 1843, 226.

page 78. "in the most formal and explicit terms": Ibid., 243.

page 78. "The sole resort": Austin and McNutt, *An Account of the Origin of the Mississippi Doctrine of Repudiation*, 22.

page 79. "instinctive horror": Philip Ziegler, *The Sixth Great Power: A History of One of the Greatest of All Banking Families, the House of Barings, 1762–1929* (New York: Knopf, 1988), 154–155.

page 79. "humiliating fact": McGrane, *Foreign Bondholders and American State Debts*, 76.

page 79. "what might be termed a campaign of propaganda": Ralph Hidy, *The House of Baring in American Trade and Finance* (Cambridge, MA: Harvard University Press, 1949), 293.

page 79. "We wrote Maryland right": John E. Semmes, *John H.B. Latrobe and His Times, 1803–1891* (Baltimore: Norman, Remington, 1917), 461.

page 79. "a ruinous premium": Francis Wayland, *The Elements of Political Economy* (New York: George C. Rand & Avery), 323.

page 79. "stain of dishonesty": Francis Wayland, *Sermons Delivered in the Chapel of Brown University* (Boston: Gould, Kendall and Lincoln, 1849).

page 79. "Very, very busy days" and other Butler quotations: George Lewis Prentiss, *The Union Theological Seminary in the City of New York* (Asbury Park, NJ: M., W. and C. Pennypacker, 1899), 435–483.

page 80. "When a whole people": Henry Ward Beecher, *Lectures to Young Men on Various Important Subjects* (Boston: John P. Jewett, 1849), 58.

page 80. "an impulsive body": Prentiss, *The Union Theological Seminary in the City of New York*, 438, 454–456. Emphasis in original.

page 80. "You are little aware of the corrupt morals": McGrane, *Foreign Bond-holders and American State Debts*, 123–125.

page 80. "Among public men the great art": Ibid., 125.

page 81. "We have an abiding faith": *The United States Magazine and Democratic Review* 1, no. 1 (January 1838): 2.

Quotations from constitutional debates are drawn from: *Debates and Proceedings in the New York State Convention for the Revision of the Constitution* (Albany, NY: S. Croswell and R. Sutton, 1846); *Report of the Debates and Proceedings of the Convention for the Revision of the Constitution of the State of Kentucky* (Frankfort, KY: A.G. Hodges & Co., 1849); *Report of the Proceedings and Debates in the Convention to Revise the Constitution of the State of Michigan* (Lansing, MI: R.W. Ingals, 1850); *Report of the Debates and Proceedings of the Convention for the Revision of the Constitution of the State of Indiana* (Indianapolis: A.H. Brown, 1850); *Debates and Proceedings of the Maryland Reform Convention to Revise the State Constitution* (Annapolis, MD: William M'Neir, 1851); *Report of the Debates and Proceedings of the Convention for the Revision of the Constitution for the State of Ohio* (Columbus, OH: S. Medary, 1851); *Debates of the Constitutional Convention of the State of Iowa* (Davenport, IA: Luse, Lane & Co., 1857).

Chapter 3

page 85. "A general distrust": *The Examiner*, February 5, 1834, 214.

page 85. "a striking resemblance": Frederick Jackson Turner, "The Significance of the Section in American History," *Wisconsin Magazine of History* 8, no. 3 (1925): 255–280, 271.

On Van Buren's response to the crisis, see: James C. Curtis, *The Fox at Bay: Martin Van Buren and the Presidency, 1837–1841* (Lexington: University Press of Kentucky, 1970). On the 1840 election, see Robert Gray Gunderson, *The Log-Cabin Campaign* (Lexington: University of Kentucky Press, 1957). On the conflict between Tyler and congressional Whigs, see Oliver Perry Chitwood, *John Tyler, Champion of the Old South* (New York: Russell & Russell, 1964); Edward P. Crapol, *John Tyler: The Accidental President* (Chapel Hill: The University of North Carolina Press, 2006); David Stephen Heidler and Jeanne T. Heidler, *Henry Clay: The Essential American* (New York: Random House, 2010).

page 86. "We observe . . . a great nation": Daniel Mallory, *Life and Speeches of the Hon. Henry Clay* (New York: Robert P. Bixby and Co., 1843), 2.409.

page 87. "remarkably erratic and inconsistent": *New York Commercial Advertiser*, May 26, 1837.

page 87. "unshaken firmness": John B. Moore, ed., *The Works of James Buchanan* (Philadelphia: J.B. Lippincott Company, 1908), 253–255.

page 87. "has not a dollar of gold": Quoted in *Cincinnati Daily Gazette*, May 22, 1837.

page 88. "It is the duty of the government" and Gouge plan: William Gouge, *An Inquiry to the Expediency of Dispensing with Bank Agency and Bank Paper in the Fiscal Concerns of the United States* (Philadelphia: William Stavely, June 1837).

page 88. "Our opponents charge the difficulties": Curtis, *The Fox at Bay*, 79.

page 88. "warfare against the banking institutions": *Congressional Globe* [appendix] (September 1837), 232.

page 89. "an opportunity of making a political movement": Reginald McGrane, ed., *The Correspondence of Nicholas Biddle Dealing with National Affairs, 1807–1844* (Boston: Houghton Mifflin, 1919), 308.

page 89. "The present prospect may thus be briefly summed up": *London Morning Chronicle*, October 10, 1837.

page 89. "Our trade is lamentably dull": *Derby Mercury*, November 8, 1837.

page 89. "It is obviously important": *Annual Message to Congress*, December 5, 1837, in James D. Richardson, ed., *A Compilation of the Messages and Papers of the Presidents* (New York: Bureau of National Literature, 1897), 4.1599.

page 89. "The effect of this bill": *Times of London*, March 1, 1838.

page 90. "The breaking up of Congress": Quoted in *Northern Star and Leeds General Advertiser*, August 11, 1838.

page 90. "the uncertainty and discouragement": *Times of London*, June 21, 1838.

page 90. "I beg you in the most emphatic terms": Charles H. Ambler, *Thomas Ritchie: A Study in Virginia Politics* (Richmond, VA: Bell Book & Stationery Co., 1913), 204.

page 90. "abandon[ed] all idea of proceeding": *The Era*, December 16, 1838.

page 90. "[t]he gloom which had spread over our country": George H. Baker, ed., *Works of William H. Seward* (New York: Redfield, 1853), 2.183.

page 91. "very doubtful": *London Examiner*, July 19, 1840.

page 91. "a second Declaration of Independence": *New Hampshire Patriot*, September 9, 1840.

page 91. "the money power, the aristocracy of the rich against the poor": *Times of London*, August 22, 1840.

page 91. "The scene was highly exhilarating": *New York Weekly Herald*, August 1, 1840.

page 91. "great meeting of merchants": *Ohio Statesman*, October 2, 1840.

page 91. "hoard their funds": *Times of London*, August 18, 1840.

page 91. "Everything on this side of the Atlantic": *Newcastle Courant*, September 11, 1840.

page 92. "They have at last learned": *United States Magazine and Democratic Review* 7, no. 30 (June 1840): 486.

page 92. "the degradation . . . which still oppresses": *Albany Evening Journal*, September 14, 1840.

page 92. "almost perish for lack of bread": John Bach McMaster, *A History of the People of the United States* (New York: D. Appleton and Company, 1910), 6.584.

page 92. "The greatest excitement prevails": Philip Hone, *The Diary of Philip Hone, 1828–1851* (New York: Dodd Mead, 1889), 2.48–49.

page 92. "bricks flew like hail": *Baltimore Sun*, November 4, 1840.

page 93. "a row of such a serious nature": *New Orleans Times-Picayune*, November 22, 1840.

page 93. "We have many recruits": Gunderson, *The Log-Cabin Campaign*, 12.

page 93. "a mighty democratic uprising": Frederic A. Ogg, *The Reign of Andrew Jackson* (New Haven, CT: Yale University Press, 1919), 114.

page 93. "General Harrison will be our next President": *Hudson River Chronicle*, November 10, 1840.

page 93. "However the question be settled": Quoted in *Times of London*, December 1, 1840.

page 94. "The Independent Treasury Bill has now passed": Quoted in *Times of London*, June 18, 1841.

page 94. "mayor of the palace": Lyon G. Tyler, *Letters and Times of the Tylers* (Richmond, VA: Whittet & Shepperson 1885), 2.11.

page 94. "What is now to be regarded": *Special Session Message to Congress*, June 1, 1841, in Richardson, ed., *A Compilation of the Messages and Papers of the Presidents*, 4.1899.

page 94. "long catalogue of crime": Alexander G. Abell, *Life of John Tyler* (New York: Harper and Brothers, 1843).

page 95. "anxious suspense": *Times of London*, August 30, 1841.

page 95. "Huzza for Clay!" Chitwood, *John Tyler, Champion of the Old South*, 330.

page 95. "The President and his friends": Tyler, *Letters and Times of the Tylers*, 2.113.

page 95. "We are not yet sure what system": *Farmers' Register*, August 31, 1841.

page 95. "Tyler the Traitor": *Charleston Southern Patriot*, September 23, 1841.

page 95. "They possess an overwhelming majority": *Plattsburgh Republican*, September 11, 1841.

page 95. "There is no longer the shadow of a hope": *Times of London*, January 17, 1842.

page 96. "confusion and tumult": *Alexandria Gazette*, August 3, 1842.

page 96. "can really possess American hearts": *Baltimore Clipper*, March 15, 1842.

page 96. "unlegalized system": David Kinley, *The History, Organization and Influence of the Independent Treasury of the United States* (New York: Thomas Y. Crowell & Co., 1893), 35.

page 96. "As long as these folks are sitting": Charles Sellers, *James K. Polk: Continentalist, 1843–1846* (Princeton, NJ: Princeton University Press, 1966), 469.

page 97. "[The Polk Administration] rode into power": *Daily National Intelligencer*, October 13, 1846.

page 97. "Had a very favorable effect": *Leeds Mercury*, May 16, 1846.

page 97. "loosening the screws a little": *Milwaukee Sentinel*, October 9, 1848.

page 97. "Mr. Walker has become what Mr. Nicholas Biddle": Quoted in *Portsmouth Journal*, October 10, 1848.

page 98. "The union of the country is factitious": Sidney George Fisher, "The Diaries of Sidney George Fisher 1841–1843, *Pennsylvania Magazine of History and Biography* 79, no. 2 (1955): 490.

page 99. "*hated* debt": James Parton, *Life of Andrew Jackson* (Boston: Houghton, Osgood and Company, 1879), 1.243.

page 99. "incompatible with real independence": *Inaugural Address*, March 4, 1829, in Richardson, ed., *A Compilation of the Messages and Papers of the Presidents*, 2.437.

page 99. "We shall then exhibit": *State of the Union Address*, December 6, 1831, in ibid., 2.556.

page 99. "a burthen upon the American people": *Journal of the United States Senate*, Twentieth Congress, Second Session, 1828, 48.

page 99. "total emancipation of the nation": *Niles' Register*, June 2, 1832, 248.

page 100. "earned a distinction": *Financial Register of the United States*, December 19, 1838, 392.

page 100. "Our public debt is cancelled": *Tait's Edinburgh Magazine* (August 1836): 541.

page 100. "stand the shock of war": John C. Calhoun, *The Works of John C. Calhoun* (New York: D. Appleton and Company, 1874), 2.164.

page 100. "We shall ere long be compelled to calculate the value of our union": *Niles' Register*, September 8, 1827, 32.

page 101. "would form a crisis in which the political destiny": Charles C. Johnston, "Letter from Charles C. Johnston to John B. Floyd," *William and Mary Quarterly* 2nd Series, 1, no. 3 (1921): 201–206, 202.

page 101. "they must relieve the South or fight them": Merrill D. Peterson, *Olive Branch and Sword: The Compromise of 1833* (Baton Rouge: Louisiana State University Press, 1982), 25.

page 101. "a gloom, foreboding & uncertainty": Samuel E. Morison, *Life and Letters of Harrison Gray Otis* (Boston: Houghton Mifflin, 1913), 2.291.

page 101. "when the money is not required": *State of the Union Address*, December 4, 1832, in Richardson, ed., *A Compilation of the Messages and Papers of the Presidents*, 2.598.

page 101. "the oppression of drawing money out of the pockets": *Gales and Seaton's Register*, February 27, 1832, 484.

page 101. "the present state of the Treasury": Johnston, "Letter from Charles C. Johnston to John B. Floyd," 203.

page 102. "a sort of temporary annex to the Constitution, and consequently sacred": Edward G. Bourne, *The History of the Surplus Revenue of 1837* (New York: G.P. Putnam's Sons, 1885), 18.

page 102. "It is evident": Message of the Governor, in *Journal of the Senate of the Commonwealth of Kentucky* (December 4, 1838): 11.

page 103. "It is not easy to see how the government can carry on its affairs": *Financial Register* 1, no. 3 (August 2, 1837): 47.

page 103. "justified by any want": *Journal of the Senate of the State of Ohio* (Columbus, OH: Samuel Medary, 1838), 285.

page 103. "serious embarrassment. . . . The United States are in immediate danger": *Financial Register* 1, no. 23 (May 9, 1838): 382.

page 103. "We had our dream of inexhaustible surpluses": *Register of Debates Congress*, Twenty–Fifth Congress, First Session, September 18, 1837, 70.

page 104. "There is not one single act": *Niles' Register*, June 23, 1838, 261.

page 104. "Here now, is another emergency—another unexpected crisis": Ibid., 262.

page 104. "It was the more manly course": Rafael Bayley, *The National Loans of the United States, from July 4, 1776, to June 30, 1880* (Washington, DC: Government Printing Office, 1882), 69.

page 105. "The brilliant prospect that had been held out": Frederick Jackson Turner and Avery Craven, *The United States, 1830–1850* (New York: Norton, 1965), 464–465.

page 105. "a relief measure to the indebted states": *United States Magazine and Democratic Review* 9, no. 38 (August 1841): 207.

page 105. "unparalleled pecuniary pressure": John Nicolay and John Hay, eds., *Abraham Lincoln: Complet Works* (New York: The Century Company, 1894), 75.

page 105. "Thousands of mechanics and labouring men cannot obtain employment": William Handey, *Political Equilibrium* (Hagerstown, MD: Schnebly and Weis, 1842), 139.

page 105. "selfish and sectional": Ibid., 90.

page 106. "the under-fed and over-worked": Joseph Blunt, *Speeches, Reviews, and Reports* (New York: James Van Norden & Co., 1843), 236.

page 106. "Our manufacturers and laboring artisans": *Niles' Register,* April 23, 1842, 118.

page 107. "That body is *incompetent* to legislate": Tyler, *Letters and Times of the Tylers*, 2.165.

page 107. "a spirit of mutual harmony and concession": President Tyler's *Message to Congress*, March 25, 1842, in Richardson, ed., *A Compilation of the Messages and Papers of the Presidents*, 3.1960.

page 107. "arbitrary, despotic and corrupt use": Lonnie Maness and Richard Chesteen, "The First Attempt at Presidential Impeachment," *Presidential Studies Quarterly* 10, no. 1 (1980): 51–62, 58.

page 107. "The unsettled state of the tariff question": *Preston Chronicle*, August 6, 1842, 1.

page 107. "The condition of the county is most appalling": *London Morning Chronicle*, August 25, 1842, 1.

page 107. "The Tariff of 1842 is doing wonders for us": Calvin Colton, *The Junius Tracts* (New York: Greeley & McElrath, 1844), 122.

page 108. "with no ordinary feelings of satisfaction": Blunt, *Speeches, Reviews, and Reports*, 241.

page 108. "and now, when the time has arrived": Douglas Irwin, "Antebellum Tariff Politics: Regional Coalitions and Shifting Economic Interests," *Journal of Law and Economics* 51 (2008): 715–741, 733.

page 108. "was in fact a treaty, made between belligerent parties": David Houston, *A Critical Study of Nullification in South Carolina* (New York: Longmans, Green and Co., 1896), 155.

page 108. "If the states were relieved from their present difficulties": Census Office, *Report on Valuation, Taxation, and Public Indebtedness in the United States* (Washington, DC: Government Printing Office, 1884), 528.

page 109. "of interest merely, a paper bond": Sidney George Fisher, "The Diaries of Sidney George Fisher." *Pennsylvania Magazine of History and Biography* 76, no. 2 (1952): 177–220, 490.

For the best overview of the development of the administrative apparatus of the federal government in this era, see Leonard White, *The Jacksonians: A Study in Admin-*

istrative History, 1829–1861 (New York: Macmillan, 1954). A succinct description of the predicament of the Post Office is provided in George L. Priest, "History of the Postal Monopoly in the United States," *Journal of Law and Economics* 18, no. 1 (1975): 33–80; see also Richard R. John, *Spreading the News: The American Postal System from Franklin to Morse* (Cambridge, MA: Harvard University Press, 1995). Useful surveys of the development of the Army and Navy are provided by Russell Frank Weigley, *History of the United States Army* (New York: Macmillan, 1967); and Stephen Howarth, *To Shining Sea: A History of the United States Navy, 1775–1998* (Norman: University of Oklahoma Press, 1999).

page 109. "What worse than senseless babbling": *Niles' Register*, November 12, 1842, 173.

page 110. "make them larger than is necessary": White, *The Jacksonians*, 81.

page 110. "judge which will best bear any reduction": Ibid., 79.

page 110. "Retrenchment fever ran high": John Quincy Adams, *Memoirs of John Quincy Adams* (Philadelphia: J.B. Lippincott & Co., 1876), 11.95.

page 110. "manifested a very warm disposition": Adams, *Memoirs of John Quincy Adams*, 11.111.

page 110. "the response was a general request": White, *The Jacksonians*, 151.

page 110. "excited debate": *The Monthly Chronicle*, August 1842, 379.

page 110. "There is no more striking illustration": Quoted in *Niles' Register*, October 6, 1832, 83.

page 111. "enjoyed the advantages": *Congressional Globe* [appendix] (December 1840), 16.

page 111. "destroying the post-office": *Hunt's Merchants' Magazine* 11, no. 6 (December 1844): 529. Emphasis in original.

page 111. "the subject of more public discussion": *Hunt's Merchants' Magazine* 10, no. 1 (January 1844): 27.

page 112. "put an end to all interference": *Senate Documents*, Twenty-eighth Congress, First Session, Vol. III, Doc. 137, 2.

page 112. "the unblushing violation": Ibid., 10.

page 112. "a mere fragment": *North American Review* 34, no. 74 (January 1832): 257.

page 112. "most conducive to the evolution": Thomas Lawson, *Statistical Report on the Sickness and Mortality in the Army of the United States* (Washington, DC: Jacob Gideon, Jr., 1840), 219–228.

page 113. "dangerous to the safety": *Army and Navy Chronicle*, December 12, 1839, 392.

page 113. "the bulwark of our defense": *Inaugural Address*, March 4, 1829, in Richardson, ed., *A Compilation of the Messages and Papers of the Presidents*, 3.1001.

page 113. "3,000 good troops (not volunteers)": Emory Upton, *The Military Policy of the United States* (Washington, DC: Government Printing Office, 1912), 167–168.

page 113. "causes beyond the control of the government": *Annual Message to Congress*, December 5, 1840, in Richardson, ed., *A Compilation of the Messages and Papers of the Presidents*, 3.1834.

page 113. "This Florida war ought to be a lesson": Frederick Marryat, *Second Series of a Diary in America* (Philadelphia: T.K. & P.G. Collins, 1840), 273–274.

page 114. "declining fast": *Army and Navy Chronicle* 13, no. 18 (May 21, 1842): 273.

page 114. "a vast sum of money": Senate, *Public Documents*, Twenty-eighth Congress, First Session, 5.

page 114. "plan for the gradual reduction": *Congressional Globe*, February 7, 1843, 225.

page 115. "A considerable addition to our force": *Army and Navy Chronicle*, December 28, 1837, 401.

page 115. "all of the west coast of America": Kenneth J. Hagan, *This People's Navy: The Making of American Sea Power* (New York: Free Press, 1991), 112.

page 115. "The sentiment in the mind": *Inaugural Address*, March 4, 1817, in Richardson, ed., *A Compilation of the Messages and Papers of the Presidents*, 2.7.

page 115. "I was filled with astonishment": Frederick F. de Roos, *Personal Narrative of Travels in the United States and Canada in 1826* (London: William Harrison Ainsworth, 1827), 62–63.

page 116. "a little puffed up": Sir John Barrow, *Life of Sir George Anson* (London: John Murray, 1839), 445.

page 116. "partial injuries and occasional mortifications": *Inaugural Address*, March 4, 1829, in Richardson, ed., *A Compilation of the Messages and Papers of the Presidents*, 2.438.

page 116. "the most dangerous moment": Bernard Steiner, *Life of Roger Brooke Taney* (Baltimore: Williams & Wilkins Company, 1922), 160.

page 116. "Suppose for one moment": *Army and Navy Chronicle* 3, no. 14 (October 6, 1836): 220.

page 117. "give to defense its greatest efficiency": *Farewell Address*, March 4, 1837, in Richardson, ed., *A Compilation of the Messages and Papers of the Presidents*, 4.1526.

page 117. "mortified at his own weakness": *Southern Literary Messenger* 6, no. 4 (April 1840): 233–240.

page 117. "Times were never more propitious": *Southern Literary Messenger* 8, no. 1 (January 1842): 92.

page 118. "It is now the settled policy": *Niles' Register*, December 25, 1841, 266.

page 118. "The wheels of Government": Donald MacLeod, *Biography of Hon. Fernando Wood* (New York: O.F. Parsons, 1856), 118. Emphasis in original.

page 118. "To all their enquiries": *Army and Navy Chronicle*, May 21, 1842, 273.

page 118. "*many millions* from waste": Colton, *The Junius Tracts*, 11. Emphasis in original.

page 118. "ships of a small class": *Annual Message to Congress*, December 7, 1842, in Richardson, ed., *A Compilation of the Messages and Papers of the Presidents*, 3.2056.

page 119. "altogether too expensive": *Congressional Globe*, Twenty-seventh Congress, Third Session, Appendix, 38.

page 119. "an effect terrible and almost incredible": Howarth, *To Shining Sea,* 155.

page 119. "a receptacle of death": A Washington newspaper quoted in *Times of London*, March 27, 1844.

pages 119–120. "Never had the United States possessed": Walter A. Roberts, *The U.S. Navy Fights* (New York: Bobbs-Merrill, 1942), 94.

For more on the size of fleets: Francis Bowen, *American Almanac for the Year 1847* (Boston: James Munroe and Co., 1846), 127–131.

page 121. "Here are two nations in the worst possible humor": Nicholas Biddle, "The Debt of Pennsylvania," *Niles' Register* 64 (1843): 381–382, 381.

page 121. "a rising nation": Thomas Jefferson, *First Inaugural Address*, March 4, 1801, in Richardson, ed., *A Compilation of the Messages and Papers of the Presidents*, 1.309.

page 121. "extension of our Empire": John Tyler, *Special Session Message*, June 1, 1841, in Richardson, ed., *A Compilation of the Messages and Papers of the Presidents*, 3.1895.

page 121. "We are the nation of human progress": *United States Magazine and Democratic Review* 6, no. 23 (November 1839): 426.

page 121. "John Bull scatters his garrisons": *The New World,* May 13, 1843, 563.

page 122. "Your cause is popular here": Catharina Bonney, *A Legacy of Historical Gleanings* (Albany, NY: J. Munsell, 1875), 2.68.

page 122. "settled determination of vengeance": Howard Jones and United States, *To the Webster-Ashburton Treaty: A Study in Anglo-American Relations, 1783–1843* (Chapel Hill: University of North Carolina Press, 1977), 26.

page 122. "the civil authorities have no adequate force to control these men": Curtis, *The Fox at Bay*, 172.

page 123. "much popular favor": Thomas Hart Benton, *Thirty Years' View* (New York: D. Appleton and Company, 1873), 208.

page 123. "WITH DEEP, DEEP MORTIFICATION": in William L. Mackenzie, *The Life and Times of Martin Van Buren* (Boston: Cooke & Co., 1846), 289.

page 123. "sincerely striving, as far as so weak and feeble": Curtis, *The Fox at Bay,* 179, 181.

page 124. "Should you go *against* us upon this occasion": Ibid., 185.

page 124. "the peace of the country when I reached Washington": Tyler, *Letters and Times of the Tylers*, 2.228.

page 124. "This country will not be quiet much longer": Bates to Ward, September 17, 1841, Thomas Ward Papers, Massachusetts Historical Society.

page 125. "a matter of deep anxiety to all engaged in commercial transactions": Jay Sexton, *Debtor Diplomacy: Finance and American Foreign Relations in the Civil War Era, 1837–1873* (Oxford: Clarendon, 2005), 31.

page 125. "consequences of the most disastrous nature": Arthur Benson, *The Letters of Queen Victoria* (London: J. Murray, 1907), 1.368.

page 125. "the prince of British merchants": *Plymouth and Cornish Advertiser,* January 6, 1842, 1.

page 125. "the material interests of the two countries": Sexton, *Debtor Diplomacy*, 35.

page 125. "I rather think this has been bro't about by Webster's letters to me": Bates to Ward, January 3, 1842, Thomas Ward Papers, Massachusetts Historical Society.

page 125. "in the pay of the great English bankers": Carol K. R. Bleser, *Secret and Sacred: The Diaries of James Henry Hammond* (Columbia: University of South Carolina Press, 1997), 89.

pages 125–126. "I should like to have it in my power": Ward to Bates, April 22, 1842; Ward to Bates, June 1, 1842; Bates to Ward, July 4, 1842; Thomas Ward Papers, Massachusetts Historical Society.

page 126. "No public man possesses a more correct knowledge": *Times of London*, February 17, 1842, 6

page 126. "the result of Lord Ashburton's mission is known to be favourable": Bates to Webster, April 15, 1842, Thomas Ward Papers, Massachusetts Historical Society.

page 126. "new mode of approaching the subject": *Niles' Register*, May 16, 1846, 172.

page 126. "for the contingent expenses of intercourse": Jones and United States, *To the Webster-Ashburton Treaty*, 94.

page 126. "adjust the tone and direction of the party presses": Richard Current, "Webster's Propaganda and the Ashburton Treaty," *Mississippi Valley Historical Review* 34, no. 2 (1947): 187–200, 189.

page 126. "the administration had no press in Maine": Frederick Merk and Robert J. Walker, *Fruits of Propaganda in the Tyler Administration* (Cambridge, MA: Harvard University Press, 1971), 193.

page 127. "Great Britain [should] consider that we cannot legislate as a unit": Ward to Bates, July 2, 1842, Thomas Ward Papers, Massachusetts Historical Society.

page 127. "Peace is the first of our wants": Calhoun, *The Works of John C. Calhoun*, 236.

page 127. "The Treaty with Great Britain": *Niles' Register*, August 27, 1841, 1.

page 128. "impossible to overrate the importance of the Hawaiian group": Senate Committee on Foreign Relations, *Papers Relating to the Annexation of the Hawaiian Islands* (Washington, DC: Government Printing Office, 1893), 109.

page 128. "placed so as to give its possessor": *Times of London*, August 29, 1843.

page 128. "content with [the] independent existence": Ibid., 35.

page 128. "as dangerous to our peace and safety": Albert B. Hart, *The Monroe Doctrine* (Boston: Little, Brown and Company, 1920), 90.

page 129. "according to the custom of nations, an exclusive claim": *Times of London*, August 29, 1843, 3.

page 129. "have no port that is defensible": Charles Wilkes, *Voyages around the World* (Philadelphia: George W. Gorton, 1849), 584.

page 129. "from want of right": *Times of London*, August 26, 1843, 4.

page 129. "it was best not to do too much at once": Ralph Kuykendall, *The Hawaiian Kingdom* (Honolulu: 1976), 1.194.

page 129. "if the offer were made it was certainly declined": Senate Committee on Foreign Relations, *Papers Relating to the Annexation of the Hawaiian Islands*, 108.

page 129. "saw that England would not permit": Alexander Simpson, *The Sandwich Islands* (London: Smith, Elder and Company, 1843), 90.

page 130. "an act of sheer, simple, downright and outright spoliation": *United States Magazine and Democratic Review* 13, no. 61 (July 1843): 14.

page 130. "a settled and determination hatred to all that is American": *Hunt's Merchants' Magazine* 9, no. 2 (August 1843): 126.

page 130. "It remains to be seen": *Niles' Register*, June 10, 1843, 239.

page 130. "might even feel justified . . . in interfering by force": Senate Committee on Foreign Relations, *Papers Relating to the Annexation of the Hawaiian Islands*, 110.

page 131. "as the overwhelming numbers of Americans": Leslie Scott, "Report of Lieutenant Peel on Oregon in 1845–46," *Oregon Historical Quarterly* 29, no. 1 (1928): 51–76, 53.

page 131. "really willing to agree": Joseph Schafer, "The British Attitude toward the Oregon Question, 1815–1846," *American Historical Review* 16, no. 2 (1911): 273–299, 295.

page 132. "concurred entirely": Charles Carey, *History of Oregon* (Chicago: Pioneer Historical Publishing Company, 1922), 488.

page 132. "I wish to avoid . . . any action": Merk and Walker, *Fruits of Propaganda in the Tyler Administration*, 18.

page 132. "formal and immediate possession": Edwin Miles, "Fifty-Four Forty or Fight—An American Political Legend," *Mississippi Valley Historical Review* 44, no. 2 (1957): 291–309, 294.

page 132. "clear and unquestionable": Carey, *History of Oregon*, 490.

page 132. "hold dominion over any portion": Miles, "Fifty-Four Forty or Fight," 294.

page 132. "The subject has given rise to so much excitement": Robert Clark, "Aberdeen and Peel on Oregon, 1844," *Oregon Historical Quarterly* 34, no. 3 (1933): 236–240, 239.

page 132. "The only way to treat John Bull": Bernard Augustine De Voto, *The Year of Decision, 1846, The American Heritage Library* (Boston: Houghton Mifflin, 1989), 26.

page 133. "The territory of the Oregon will never be wrested": *Times of London*, March 28, 1845, 4.

page 133. "to gain a general knowledge": Joseph Schafer, "Documents Relative to Warre and Vavasour's Military Reconnaissance in Oregon, 1845–6," *Quarterly of the Oregon Historical Society* 10, no. 1 (1909): 1–99, 6.

page 133. "to let the Americans see clearly": Sellers, *James K. Polk*, 235.

page 133. "resolved and prepared": *Times of London*, April 5, 1845, 6.

page 133. "the distinct and emphatic declaration of the British government": Ibid.

page 133. "the time has come when we must endeavour": Wilbur Jones and J. Chal Vinson, "British Preparedness and the Oregon Settlement," *Pacific Historical Review* 22, no. 4 (1953): 353–364, 357.

page 133. "were almost mad": James K. Polk, *Diary of James K. Polk during His Presidency* (Chicago: A.C. McClurg, 1910), 140.

page 133. "I am for the whole": *Niles' Register*, August 9, 1845, 364. Emphasis in original.

page 133. "the whole of Oregon, or none": Miles, "Fifty-Four Forty or Fight," 302.

page 134. "It is very clear that if a rupture with the United States": *Niles' Register*, February 11, 1846, 179.

page 134. "stares everyone in the face": *Niles' Register*, November 8, 1845, 145.

page 134. "paralyzed by the uncertainty": *A Compilation of All the Acts, Resolutions, Reports and Other Documents in Relation to the Bank of the State of South Carolina* (Columbia, SC: A.S. Johnston and A.G. Summer, 1848), 640.

page 134. "my political friend": Polk, *Diary of James K. Polk during His Presidency*, 1.73.

page 134. "a very general anxiety": *Niles' Register*, January 3, 1846, 285

page 134. "the war feeling springing up among the people": George Lewis Prentiss, *The Union Theological Seminary in the City of New York* (Asbury Park, NJ: M. W. and C. Pennypacker, 1899), 476.

page 134. "The credit of the Union has been injured": Albert Gallatin, *The Oregon Question* (New York: Bartlett & Welford, 1846), 66.

page 134. "How is our government to obtain": Robert Hare Jr., *Oregon: The Cost, and the Consequences* (Philadelphia: John C. Clark, 1846), 9.

page 135. "They have no cotton crops": George Ticknor Curtis, *Life of Daniel Webster* (New York: D. Appleton and Company, 1870), 2.260.

page 135. "the abstract question of title": Polk, *Diary of James K. Polk during His Presidency*, 372.

page 135. "greatest danger": Ibid., 107.

page 135. "Britain is fully committed on that point": Gallatin, *The Oregon Question*, 48.

page 135. "could not possibly have considered this offer as made in earnest": Hermann von Holst, *Constitutional and Political History of the United States, 1846–1850* (Chicago: Callaghan and Company, 1881), 160.

page 135. "offensive operations": Jones and Vinson, "British Preparedness and the Oregon Settlement," 361.

page 136. "that the door was not closed": Polk, *Diary of James K. Polk during His Presidency*, 244.

page 136. "despoiled . . . by a traitorous alliance" Miles, "Fifty-Four Forty or Fight," 307.

page 136. "take the stump and denounce": Sellers, *James K. Polk: Continentalist, 1843–1846*, 413.

Chapter 4

page 138. "It was a state of war": *Luther v. Borden*, 48 U.S. 1 (1849).

page 138. "lost in the flesh": Thomas W. Bicknell, *History of the State of Rhode Island* (New York: American Historical Society, 1920), 783.

page 139. "regular, and if necessary, repeated": *People's Democratic Guide* 1, no. 8 (June 1842): 241.

page 139. "never seemed to arise from any strong feeling": William Goodell, *The Rights and Wrongs of Rhode Island* (Oneida, NY: Oneida Institute, 1842), 34.

pages 139–140. "Before 1840, [t]here was no definite": Arthur Mowry, *The Dorr War* (Providence, RI: Preston & Rounds, 1901), 43.

page 140. "a few men without wealth": Jacob Frieze, *Concise History of the Efforts to Obtain an Extension of Suffrage in Rhode Island* (Providence, RI: Thomas S. Hammond, 1842), 28, 29.

page 140. "the time has gone by": Bicknell, *History of the State of Rhode Island*, 790.

page 140. "There were vital questions abroad": Frances Whipple Green, *Might and Right* (Providence, RI: A.H. Stillwell, 1844), 74.

page 140. "So much for equality": Seth Luther, *Address to the Working Men of New England* (New York: George H. Evans, 1833), 19.

page 140. "Peaceably if we can": Louis Hartz, "The Story of a Working-Class Rebel," *The New England Quarterly* 13, no. 3 (1940): 401–418, 407.

page 141. "It may be said that these views": Green, *Might and Right*, 86. Emphasis in original.

page 142. "and almost nightly paraded the streets": Frieze, *Concise History of the Efforts to Obtain an Extension of Suffrage in Rhode Island*, 54.

page 142. "The controversy": William G. Goddard, *Political Writings* (Providence, RI: Sidney S. Rider and Brother, 1870), 73.

page 142. "affecting the very existence of society": Francis Wayland, *The Affairs of Rhode Island* (Providence, RI: William D. Ticknor, 1842), 6.

page 142. "should any crisis occur to demand our aid": Goddard, *Political Writings*, 153.

page 143. "without law": John Lawson, ed., *American State Trials* (St. Louis, MO: Thomas Law Book Co., 1914), II.8.

page 143. "The first duty of government": Green, *Might and Right*, 195.

page 143. "agitated by revolutionary movements": Mowry, *The Dorr War*, 142.

page 143. "manifested by lawless assemblages": *Hazard's United States and Commercial Register*, April 1842, 255.

page 143. "was a virtual declaration of war": Green, *Might and Right*, 225.

page 145. "will stand ready to succor": *Niles' Register*, May 21, 1842, 179.

page 145. "carrying the Constitution into effect": *Providence Daily Journal*, May 19, 1842.

page 145. "the time may not be far distant": Mowry, *The Dorr War*, 173.

page 145. "The contest will then become national": Ibid., 174.

page 146. "several large boxes of muskets": James D. Richardson, ed., *Compilation of the Messages and Papers of the Presidents* (New York: Bureau of National Literature, 1897), 5.2155.

page 146. "ready to join in any mischief": Ibid.

page 146. "the traitor Thomas Wilson Dorr": Mowry, *The Dorr War*, 226.

page 147. "Dorr was politically dead": Bicknell, *History of the State of Rhode Island*, 801.

page 147. "wickedly and traitorously devising": Lawson, ed., *American State Trials*, 20.

page 148. "of the most dangerous character": *Journal of the House of Representatives*, April 10, 1844, 766.

page 148. "the only -*ism* about which I feel": Bernard Steiner, *Life of Roger Brooke Taney* (Baltimore: Williams & Wilkens Company, 1922), 85.

page 148. "to meet the peril": *Luther v. Borden*, 48 U.S. 1 (1849).

The main contemporary works on the anti-rent war are Henry Christman, *Tin Horns and Calico: A Decisive Episode in the Emergence of Democracy* (Cornwallville, NY:

Hope Farm Press, 1975); Reeve Huston, *Land and Freedom: Rural Society, Popular Protest, and Party Politics in Antebellum New York* (New York: Oxford University Press, 2000); and Charles W. McCurdy, *The Anti-Rent Era in New York Law and Politics, 1839–1865* (Chapel Hill: University of North Carolina Press, 2001).

page 149. "[Anti-Renters are] the most violent faction": Walt Whitman, *Collected Works* (New York: Peter Lang, 2003), 2.100. Emphasis in original.

page 150. "a scholarly man with intellectual tastes": Cuyler Reynolds, *Genealogical and Family History of Southern New York and Hudson River Valley* (New York: Lewis Historical Publishing Company, 1914), 3.1167.

pages 150–151. "We will take up the ball of the Revolution": Christman, *Tin Horns and Calico*, 40.

page 151. "They took [him] to Lawrence's tavern": *Message of the Governor in Relation to the Difficulties in the Manor of Rensselaerwyck*, March 14, 1840, in George E. Baker, ed., *Works of William H. Seward* (New York: Redfield, 1853), 2.357.

page 151. "When we got to the Helderbergs": Albert C. Mayham, *The Anti-Rent War on Blenheim Hill* (Jefferson, NY: F.L. Frazee, 1906), 23.

page 152. "The Governor has ordered": Philip Hone, *The Diary of Philip Hone, 1828–1851* (New York: Dodd Mead, 1889), 1.396.

page 152. "For the ignorant big-breeched Dutchmen": Christman, *Tin Horns and Calico*, 56.

page 152. "pacific offers": George H. Baker, ed., *Works of William H. Seward* (New York: Redfield, 1853), 2.366.

page 153. "more accordant with the principles": *Annual Message of the Governor*, January 7, 1840.

page 153. "was injurious and unjust": *Bronson v. Kinzie*, 42 U.S. 311 (1843).

pages 153–154. For New York legislative turnover, see generally L. Ray Gunn, "The New York State Legislature: A Developmental Perspective, 1777–1846," *Social Science History* 4, no. 3 (1980): 267–294.

page 154. "cannot legislate backwards": *Quackenbush v. Danks*, 1 Denio 128 (1845).

page 155. "a number of brave and resolute men": George Hewes, *Traits of the Tea Party* (New York: Harper & Brothers, 1835), 174.

page 155. "cell structure": Christman, *Tin Horns and Calico*, 92.

page 155. "compelled to run around the town pump": Ibid., 104.

page 155. "He was carried to the ground": *The Rover* 4 (1845): 10.

page 155. "carry on a *guerrilla warfare*": McCurdy, *The Anti-Rent Era in New York Law and Politics*, 173. Emphasis in original.

page 155. "The Anti-Rent organization is so powerful": quoted in *The Northern Star and Leeds Advertiser*, October 12, 1844.

page 156. "A patrol for each night of twenty citizens": Stephen Miller, *Historical Sketches of Hudson* (Hudson, NY: Bryan & Webb, 1862), 57.

page 156. "presented the appearance of a military encampment": Ibid., 60.

page 156. "But no alternative is left": Ibid., 58.

page 156. "Power comes from God": Christman, *Tin Horns and Calico*, 135.

page 157. "constituted authorities . . . to carry the laws into execution": Ibid.

page 157. "the boldest acts of violence are perpetrated": Daniel Dewey Barnard, "The Anti-Rent Movement," *The American Review* 2, no. 6 (1845): 577–598, 596.

page 157. "[a]rson, anti-rentism, attempts at murder": James Fenimore Cooper, *The Redskins* (New York: Burgess & Stringer, 1846), 112.

page 157. "CONCERTED, PRACTICAL REPUDIATION": Barnard, "The Anti-Rent Movement," 580.

page 157. "a shock": *Annual Message of the Governor*, January 7, 1845.

page 157. "scouring the infected districts": Jay Gould, *History of Delaware County* (Philadelphia: Robb, Pile & McElroy, 1856), 283.

page 158. "The convictions were in a measure political ones": Mayham, *The Anti-Rent War on Blenheim Hill*, 71.

page 158. "open rebellion": Gould, *History of Delaware County*, 283.

page 158. "has done more by this one act": Christman, *Tin Horns and Calico*, 243.

page 158. "the base and guilty": *Niles' Register,* September 20, 1845, 39.

page 158. "Your [Broughton's] offence, though in form": *Niles' Register*, October 12, 1845, 88.

page 159. "This Association disapprove[s]": McCurdy, *The Anti-Rent Era in New York Law and Politics*, 171.

page 159. "mad spirit of insubordination": *Annual Message of the Governor*, January 6, 1846.

page 159. Generally, on the number of manorial contracts in force in Albany County, see McCurdy, *The Anti-Rent Era in New York Law and Politics*, 315.

page 159. King's settlement with tenants: Ibid., 272–273.

page 160. Agricultural production and population trends: Huston, *Land and Freedom*, 229.

A useful overview of the Philadelphia riots is provided by Michael Feldberg, *The Philadelphia Riots of 1844: A Study of Ethnic Conflict, Contributions in American History* (Westport, CT: Greenwood Press, 1975).

page 160. "Order must be restored": Ibid., 115.

page 161. Growth of the General Trades Union and number of strikes, generally, see William Sullivan, *The Industrial Worker of Pennsylvania: 1800 to 1840* (PhD Dissertation, Columbia University, 1951), 151, Appendix B.

page 161. Proportion of Philadelphians in organized labor: John R. Commons, "Labor Organization and Labor Politics, 1827–37," *Quarterly Journal of Economics* 21, no. 323–329 (1907): 324.

page 161. "We preach no religion": John R. Commons, et al., *A Documentary History of American Industrial Society* (Cleveland, OH: Arthur H. Clark Company, 1910), 5.391.

page 162. "With the first descent": John R. Commons, et al., *History of Labour in the United States* (New York: Macmillan Company, 1918), 1.456.

page 162. "The bankruptcy of that great institution": *De Bow's Review*, May 1853, 477.

page 162. "God knows": Norman Ware, *The Industrial Worker, 1840–1860* (Chicago: Quadrangle Books, 1964), 63.

page 162. "generally more occupied": H. C. Carey, *Principles of Political Economy* (Philadelphia: Carey, Lea & Blanchford, 1837), 108.

page 163. "A boundary street": Howard Sprogle, *The Philadelphia Police* (Philadelphia: Howard O. Sprogle, 1887), 85.

page 163. "took for the time the appearance": John Scharf and Thompson West-cott, *History of Philadelphia* (Philadelphia: L. H. Everts & Company, 1884), 1.661.

page 164. "social and economic competition": W.E.B. Du Bois, *The Philadelphia Negro* (Philadelphia: University of Pennsylvania, 1899), 31.

page 164. "Philadelphia . . . is now in a state": Noel Ignatiev, *How the Irish Became White* (New York: Routledge, 2009), 159.

page 165. "The great mass": *Brownson's Quarterly Review* (January 1845): 82–83.

page 165. "What northern man": John H. Lee, *Origin and Progress of the American Party in Politics* (Philadelphia: Elliott & Gihon, 1855), 222.

page 165. "The foreign population": Hector Orr, *The Native American* (Philadelphia: Hector Orr, 1845), 141, 159.

page 167. "Is it safe to go to Philadelphia?": *Philadelphia Enquirer*, May 16, 1844.

page 167. "The alarming occurrences in Pennsylvania": *London Morning Chronicle*, May 29, 1844.

page 167. "[A] more outrageous and bloody disturbance": *Times of London*, May 30, 1844, 4.

page 167. "*whatever force is necessary*": Feldberg, *The Philadelphia Riots of 1844*, 114. Emphasis in original.

page 168. "unquestionably be taken": *Western Law Journal* 9, no. 1 (June, 1844): 420–421.

page 168. "men who array themselves": *Pennsylvania Law Journal*, 3 (1844): 397.

page 168. "whiff of grapeshot": Quoted in Feldberg, *The Philadelphia Riots of 1844*, 5.

page 168. "Four barouches": John H. Lee, *Origin and Progress of the American Party in Politics* (Philadelphia: Elliott & Gihon, 1855), 139–140.

page 169. "a continued discharge": Feldberg, *The Philadelphia Riots of 1844*, 155.

page 169. "presented a truly warlike appearance": Anonymous, *A Full and Complete Account of the Late Awful Riots in Philadelphia* (Philadelphia: John B. Perry, 1844), 18.

page 169. "We are in the midst of a civil war!": Elizabeth Geffen, "Violence in Philadelphia in the 1840's and 1850's," *Pennsylvania History* 36, no. 4 (1969): 381–410, 403.

page 170. "This is worse": Ibid.

page 170. "dreadful massacre": *London Morning Chronicle*, July 30, 1844.

page 170. "deeply injurious": *Bristol Mercury*, August 3, 1844.

page 170. "What are the effects": *Philadelphia Public Ledger*, November 13, 1844.

page 170. "The great problem in politics": *Spectator*, quoted in *The Living Age*, September 14, 1844, 338.

pages 170–171. "from an impaired sense of the obligations": *Philadelphia Public Ledger*, November 30, 1839.

page 171. "a full regiment of Infantry": Anonymous, *Street Talk about an Ordinance of Councils Passed the 11th July, 1844, Organizing a Military Force for the Government of Philadelphia* (Philadelphia: n.p., 1844), 4.

page 171. "saddled and bridled": Ibid., 7.

page 171. "the conservators of the peace": Ibid., 3. Emphasis in original.

page 171. "The great object": Selden Bacon, *The Early Development of American Municipal Police* (New Haven, CT: Yale University, 1939), 555.

page 172. "the disastrous and destructive mobs of 1844": Eli Price, *The History of the Consolidation of the City of Philadelphia* (Philadelphia: J.B. Lippincott and Company, 1873), 16.

page 172. "inquire into the cause of the prevailing distress": Augustine Costello, *Our Police Protectors* (Montclair, NJ: Police Department of the City of New York, 1887), 80.

page 172. "rich and powerful": Quoted in Edward K. Spann, *New Metropolis: New York City, 1840–1857* (New York: Columbia University Press, 1981), 317.

page 172. "some more prompt means": City of Boston, *Inaugural Addresses of the Mayors of Boston* (Boston: Rockwell and Churchill, 1894), 1.226.

page 172. "internal police. . . . personal responsibility [and] manly self-denial": Peleg W. Chandler, *The Morals of Freedom* (Boston: John H. Eastburn, 1844).

page 173. "even if concentrated upon one point": Bacon, *The Early Development of American Municipal Police*, 486.

Chapter 5

An overview of the military and political aspects of the Mexican War is provided by K. Jack Bauer, *The Mexican War 1846–1848* (Lincoln: University of Nebraska Press, 1974), although it is affected by the controversy over the Vietnam war that was ongoing at the time of its writing. A helpful corrective is provided by Robert Johannsen, *To the Halls of the Montezumas* (New York: Oxford University Press, 1988). See also Daniel Walker Howe, *What Hath God Wrought: The Transformation of America, 1815–1848*, *The Oxford History of the United States* (New York: Oxford University Press, 2007), 731–791. An acerbic view of the pro-annexation campaign is provided by Frederick Merk, *Slavery and the Annexation of Texas* (New York: Alfred E. Knopf, 1972). On opposition to the war, see John Schroeder, *Mr. Polk's War* (Madison: University of Wisconsin Press, 1973). The financial aspects of the war are discussed by James Cummings, *Towards Modern Public Finance: The American War with Mexico, 1846–1848* (Brookfield, VT: Pickering & Chatto, 2009).

page 176. "For now we've crossed the Rio Grande": William M'Carty, *National Songs, Ballads, and Other Patriotic Poetry, Chiefly Relating to the War of 1846* (Philadelphia, PA: William M'Carty, 1846), 77.

page 177. "give new violence and passion": William E. Channing, *Letter to the Hon. Henry Clay on the Annexation of Texas* (Boston, MA: James Munroe and Company, 1837), 51–53.

page 177. "raise[d] up as a barrier": Frederick Marryat, *A Diary in America* (Philadelphia: Carey & Hart, 1839), 117.

page 178. "just balance of power": Ephraim Adams, ed., *British Diplomatic Correspondence Concerning the Republic of Texas, 1838–1846* (Austin: Texas State Historical Association, 1917), 144.

page 178. "If this [trade agreement with Texas] can be done": Ephraim Adams, *British Interests and Activities in Texas, 1838–1846* (Baltimore: Johns Hopkins University Press, 1910), 71–72.

pages 178 and 179. "We do not conceive"/"the vast amount of British Capital": Adams, ed., *British Diplomatic Correspondence Concerning the Republic of Texas*, 509.

page 179. "coldness, reserve, or palpable discouragement": *Houston Democratic Telegraph*, September 30, 1847.

page 179. "slave-breeding conspiracy": John Quincy Adams, *Address to Constituents of the Twelfth Congressional District* (Boston: J.H. Eastburn, 1842), 16.

page 179. "touching both the welfare and honor": *Madisonian*, November 15, 1843, quoted in Merk, *Slavery and the Annexation of Texas*, 249.

page 179. "Her object is to attack": Ibid.

page 180. "ruin and havoc": James Parton, *Life of Andrew Jackson* (Boston: Houghton, Osgood and Company, 1879), 3.659.

page 180. "preventing Texas falling into the hands": Merk, *Slavery and the Annexation of Texas*, 221–223.

page 181. "exciting the prevalent distrust": Justin H. Smith, *The Annexation of Texas* (New York: Baker and Taylor, 1911), 115.

page 181. "jealousy of English power": *United States Magazine and Democratic Review* 14, no. 70 (April 1844): 423.

page 181. "Texas must either be annexed": George P. Garrison, "Diplomatic Correspondence of the Republic of Texas," in American Historical Association, ed., *Annual Report of the American Historical Association for the Year 1908* (Washington, DC: Government Printing Office, 1911), 4–807, 240.

page 182. "impudence": Merk, *Slavery and the Annexation of Texas*, 31.

page 182. "Hostilities between nations": *United States Magazine and Democratic Review* 14, no. 70 (April 1844): 335.

page 183. "purely commercial" and other excerpts from Aberdeen letter: *Southern Literary Messenger* 10, no. 10 (October 1844): 584.

page 183. "a light gauze": John Tibbatts, *Speech on the Reannexation of Texas* (Washington, DC: Washington Globe, 1844), 11.

page 183. "avowal of a policy"/"forced on the Government": Richard K. Crallé, *Reports and Public Letters of John C. Calhoun* (New York: D. Appleton and Company, 1888), 345–348.

page 184. "national pride . . . and hatred of British power": Chauncey Boucher and Robert Brooks, "Correspondence Addressed to John C. Calhoun, 1837–1849," in American Historical Association, ed., *Annual Report of the American Historical Association for the Year 1929* (Washington, DC: Government Printing Office, 1929), 125–533, 231.

page 184. "dangerous sentiments . . . decorated with rose leaves": Clyde N. Wilson, *Papers of John C. Calhoun* (Columbia: University of South Carolina Press, 1988), 583–584.

page 184. "an open advocate of Mississippi Repudiation": *Niles' Register,* July 26, 1845, 330.

page 184. "text-book of the Democratic Party": *United States Democratic Review* 16, no. 80 (February 1845): 162.

page 184. "Look at her press" and Walker letter excerpts: Frederick Merk and Robert J. Walker, *Fruits of Propaganda in the Tyler Administration* (Cambridge, MA: Harvard University Press, 1971), 221–246.

page 185. "equivalent to a declaration of war": United States Senate, *Public Documents* (Washington, DC: Gales and Seaton, 1843).

page 186. "as a direct aggression": Charles Francis Adams, *The Complaint of Mexico and the Conspiracy against Liberty* (Boston: J.W. Alden, 1843), 24.

page 186. "Annexation and war with Mexico": *National Intelligencer*, April 17, 1844.

page 186. "The Administration . . . have been mixing": Truman Smith, *Speech on the Oregon Question* (Washington, DC: J. & G.S. Gideon, 1846), 11.

page 187. "count upon succour"/"whatever disposition"/"do not conceive"/"to avoid war": Adams, *British Interests and Activities in Texas,* 104, 202, 204, 192.

page 187. "Because Great Britain is powerful": Thomas Hart Benton, *Three Speeches on the Annexation of Texas to the United States* (New York: n.p., 1844), 22.

page 187. "Only one bold, swift dash": Justin H. Smith, *The War with Mexico* (New York: Macmillan, 1919), 1.125.

page 187. "a deplorable condition": *Times of London*, October 6, 1845, 5.

page 188. "Mexico . . . is unable to carry on a war": M.A.D. Howe, ed., *Home Letters of General Sherman* (New York: Charles Scribner's Sons, 1909), 23.

page 188. "The more we see of the Mexicans": John Y. Simon, ed., *The Papers of Ulysses S. Grant* (Carbondale: Southern Illinois University Press, 1967), 1.56.

page 188. "We will have no fight": Robert H. Ferrell, *Monterrey Is Ours! The Mexican War Letters of Lieutenant Dana 1845–1847* (Lexington: University Press of Kentucky, 1990), 12.

page 188. "The annexation is not, of course, palatable": *Richmond Enquirer*, September 2, 1845.

page 188. "We're on our way to the Rio Grande": M'Carty, *National Songs, Ballads, and Other Patriotic Poetry*, 37.

page 189. "addressed a restlessness": Smith, *The War with Mexico*, 1.124.

page 189. "great numbers of bold and restless": *The American Review* 2, no. 3 (September 1845): 227.

page 189. "The multitude cry aloud"/"LET US GO": Quoted in Ibid.

page 189. "It has been a prevailing opinion in Europe": Lucien Chase, *History of the Polk Administration* (New York: George P. Putnam, 1850), 467.

page 189. "People here are all in a state of delirium": Hershel Parker, *Herman Melville: A Biography, 1819–1851* (Baltimore: Johns Hopkins University Press, 1996), 1.421.

page 190. "they had the band out": "Friend of Lincoln Sees War in Mexico," *New York Times*, March 23, 1916.

page 190. "The spirit was so strong": John Scharf and Thompson Westcott, *History of Philadelphia* (Philadelphia: Howard O. Sprogle, 1887), 1.679.

page 190. "The war excitement could hardly be ignored": Johannsen, *To the Halls of the Montezumas*, 270.

page 190. "all the pent-up passions": Essex Agricultural Society, *Transactions of the Essex Agricultural Society* (Salem, MA: Salem Gazette, 1850), 16.

page 190. "Approximately a third": Frederick Zeh, *An Immigrant Soldier in the Mexican War* (College Station: Texas A&M Press, 1995), 7.

page 191. "extremest of bravery": Harry Silcox, *Philadelphia Politics from the Bottom up: The Life of Irishman William McMullen* (Philadelphia: Balch Institute Press, 1989), 42.

page 191. "In truth, we are all Americans": *United States Catholic Magazine*, February 1848, 98.

page 191. "They are American citizen soldiers": *United Service Journal*, July 12, 1851, 231.

page 191. "glorious news from Mexico": Abiel A. Livermore, *War with Mexico* (Boston: American Peace Society, 1850), 227–230.

page 191. "Such events as this victory": Walt Whitman, *The Gathering of the Forces* (New York: Knickerbocker Press, 1920), 82.

page 192. "almost paralysed by the imbecility": Charles H. Ambler, "Correspondence of Robert M.T. Hunter," in American Historical Association, ed., *Annual Report of the American Historical Association for the Year 1916* (Washington, DC: American Historical Association, 1918), 2.86.

page 193. "Well may we be grateful": George Meade, *The Life and Letters of George Gordon Meade* (New York: Charles Scribner's Sons, 1913), 1.152.

page 193. "When the country was engaged in war": Cummings, *Towards Modern Public Finance*, 74–75.

page 193. "from the Rio Bravo to the Bay of Fundy": Robert Winthrop, *Oration on the Laying of the Cornerstone of the National Monument to the Memory of Washington* (Washington, DC: J. & G.S. Gideon, 1848), 49.

pages 193–194. "more generally or more joyfully": *United States Magazine and Democratic Review* 23, no. 62 (August 1848): 187.

page 194. "willingness and ability": A. R. McIlvaine, *Speech on the Mexican War* (Washington, DC: Blair and Rives, 1847), 8.

page 194. "has shown . . . that a people": *Hunt's Merchants' Magazine* 18, no. 4 (April 1848): 463.

page 194. "a mass of ungovernable & unmanageable anarchy": Howard Jones and Donald A. Rakestraw, *Prologue to Manifest Destiny: Anglo-American Relations in the 1840s* (Wilmington, DE: SR Books, 1997), 114.

page 194. "This transformation of a plain working people": George Lippard, *Legends of Mexico* (Philadelphia: T. B. Peterson, 1847), 13.

page 194. "to impute to republics": *State of the Union Address*, December 5, 1848, in James D. Richardson, ed., *A Compilation of the Messages and Papers of the Presidents* (New York: Bureau of National Literature, 1897), 4.248.

page 195. "Europe has long contemplated": John Frost, *The Mexican War and Its Warriors* (Philadelphia: H. Mansfield, 1848), 331–332.

page 195. "The war with Mexico has been productive": Nathan C. Brooks, *A Complete History of the Mexican War* (Philadelphia: Grigg, Elliot & Company, 1851), 539.

page 195. "The effects of the great shock": W. H. Prescott and R. Wolcott, *The Correspondence of William Hickling Prescott, 1833–1847* (New York: Houghton Mifflin Company, 1925), 657–658.

page 195. "a great change": *Southern Literary Messenger* 15, no. 5 (May 1849): 311.

page 196. "utter want of confidence": Rafael Bayley, *The National Loans of the United States, from July 4, 1776, to June 30, 1880* (Washington, DC: Government Printing Office, 1882), 73.

page 196. "Capitalists have no confidence": quoted in *Niles' Register*, December 11, 1847, 240.

page 197. "As a rule": Robert J. Walker, *Our National Finances* (Washington, DC: Chronicle Print, 1867), 4.

page 197. "the shylocks of Wall Street": Cummings, *Towards Modern Public Finance*, 56.

page 197. "an impression in Europe": James P. Shenton, *Robert John Walker* (New York: Columbia University Press, 1961), 116.

page 197. "proper to advertise": James K. Polk, *Diary of James K. Polk during His Presidency* (Chicago: A.C. McClurg, 1910), 3.420.

page 198. "If a portion of this Loan": Jay Sexton, *Debtor Diplomacy: Finance and American Foreign Relations in the Civil War Era, 1837–1873* (Oxford: Clarendon, 2005), 54.

page 198. "a-begging through": Benjamin Curtis, "Debts of the States," *North American Review* 58 (1844): 109–157, 150.

page 198. "negotiate a pitiful loan": United States Treasury, *Reports of the Secretary of the Treasury of the United States* (Washington, DC: John C. Rives, 1851), 452.

page 198. "streak of luck": Thomas Martin, "Cotton and Wheat in Anglo-American Trade and Politics, 1846–1852," *Journal of Southern History* 1, no. 3 (1935): 293–319, 301.

page 198. Tonnage of freight carried on the Erie Canal: Peter L. Bernstein, *Wedding of the Waters: The Erie Canal and the Making of a Great Nation* (New York: W.W. Norton, 2005), 377.

page 198. "unexpected good fortune": *The Bankers' Magazine* 1, no. 9 (March 1847): 513.

page 199. "What disorder the world has fallen into!": Niall Ferguson, *The House of Rothschild: Money's Prophets, 1798–1848* (New York: Viking, 1998), 458.

page 199. "We must hope for the best": Ibid., 451.

page 199. "now be considered the safest": Sexton, *Debtor Diplomacy*, 56.

page 199. "Almost the same expense and labour": *London Morning Chronicle*, August 21, 1848.

page 200. "three feet broad": *London Morning Chronicle*, September 7, 1848.

page 200. "El Dorado is no longer a fabulous locality": *London Daily News*, October 3, 1848.

page 200. "resume the use of their reading faculties": *Liverpool Mercury*, October 10, 1848.

page 200. "the strongest anxiety": *Times of London*, October 11, 1848, 6.

page 200. "produced an immediate effect": *New York Courier & Enquirer*, quoted in *The Manchester Times*, October 28, 1848.

page 201. "This vessel has been eagerly looked for": Quoted in *Times of London*, November 2, 1848, 6.

page 201. "We are glad to see": *The Bankers' Magazine* 2, no. 11 (May 1848): 638.

page 201. "dramatic turnaround": Mira Wilkins, *The History of Foreign Investment in the United States to 1914* (Cambridge: Harvard University Press, 1989), 75–76.

Conclusion

Citations for quotations already used earlier in the book are not provided.

page 203. "What, then, is the moral": *United States Magazine and Democratic Review* 1, no. 1 (October 1837): 108.

page 203. "How do you deal toughly with your banker?": "US Embassy Cables: Hillary Clinton Ponders US Relationship with Its Chinese 'Banker,'" *Guardian. co.uk*, December 4, 2010.

page 203. "singularly self-sufficient"/"hostage politically": Robert J. Shapiro, *Futurecast: How Superpowers, Populations, and Globalization Will Change the Way You Live and Work* (New York: St. Martin's Press, 2008), 148.

page 204. "Prosperity for five to seven years": W. Thom DeCourcy, *A Brief History of Panics and Their Periodical Occurrence in the United States* (New York: G.P. Putnam's Sons, 1893), 22.

page 205. "the principle of the sovereignty of the people": Alexis De Tocqueville, *Democracy in America*, trans. Henry Reeve (New York: D. Appleton and Company, 1904), 64.

page 205. "personal responsibility [and] manly self-denial": Peleg W. Chandler, *The Morals of Freedom* (Boston: John H. Eastburn, 1844).

page 206. "[We] bind and restrict ourselves": *Report of the Debates and Proceedings of the Convention for the Revision of the Constitution of the State of Indiana* (Indianapolis: A.H. Brown, 1850), 1.660.

page 207. "in a manner befitting christians": *Alexandria Gazette*, March 12, 1842.

page 207." legitimized the veto": Leonard White, *The Jacksonians: A Study in Administrative History, 1829–1861* (New York: Macmillan, 1954), 29.

page 208. "opposition of interests": *United States Magazine and Democratic Review* 14, no. 70 (April 1844): 335.

page 213. "good name and credit": "Michael Bloomberg Calls for Debt Deal," *Politico*, July 12, 2011.

page 213. "create fundamental doubts": Speech by Chairman Bernanke to the Annual Conference of the Committee for a Responsible Federal Budget, Washington, DC, June 14, 2011.

page 213. "require fiscal adjustments": "Moody's Says U.S. Debt Could Test Triple-A Rating," *New York Times*, March 15, 2010.

page 214. "to deliver real, true spending constraint": "Tea Party-backed Senators Take U.S. Debt Deal into Their Own Hands," *Dow Jones Newswires*, July 12, 2011.

page 214. "No nation, agency or organization": Press release, Office of Congressman Dennis J. Kucinich, July 13, 2011.

page 214. "whims of foreign investors": House of Representatives Report 111–060, March 27, 2009.

☞INDEX